# Knowing and Being

*Essays by Michael Polanyi*

Edited by Marjorie Grene

The University of Chicago Press

International Standard Book Number: 0–226–67284–0 (clothbound);
0–226–67285–9 (paperback)

Library of Congress Catalog Card Number: 76–77151

The University of Chicago Press, Chicago 60637
Routledge & Kegan Paul Ltd., London E.C.4

85   84   83                          87654

# Contents

# Acknowledgements

Acknowledgement is gratefully made to the following publishers and periodicals for permission to reprint the essays in this collection:

1. To the Cambridge University Press for permission to reprint *Beyond Nihilism* (1960).
2. To the *American Scholar* for 'The Message of the Hungarian Revolution', *35* (1966), 261–276.
3. To *Encounter* for 'Two Cultures', *13* (1959), 61–64.
4. To *Minerva* for 'The Republic of Science', *1* (1962), 54–73, and for 'The Growth of Science in Society', *5* (1967), 533–545.
5. To *Science* for 'The Potential Theory of Adsorption', *141* (1963), 1010–1013, copyright 1963 by the American Association for the Advancement of Science, and for 'Life's Irreducible Structure', *160* (1968), *1308–1312*, copyright 1968 by the American Association for the Advancement of Science.
6. To the International Union of Crystallography for 'My Time with X-rays and Crystals', reprinted from *Fifty Years of X-ray Diffraction*, P. P. Ewald, ed., 1962, published for the International Union of Crystallography by A. Oosthoek, Utrecht.
7. To *Philosophy* for 'The Unaccountable Element in Science', *37* (1962), 1–14; for 'The Logic of Tacit Inference', *41* (1966), 1–18; and for 'Sense-Giving and Sense-Reading', *42* (1967), 301–325.
8. To *Mind* for 'Knowing and Being', *70* N.S. (1961), 458–470.
9. To *Reviews of Modern Physics* for 'Tacit Knowing: Its Bearing on Some Problems of Philosophy', *34* (1962), 601–616.
10. To *Brain* for 'The Structure of Consciousness', *88* (1965), 799–810.

# Introduction

It is one of the paradoxes of modern epistemology that we take science as the paradigm case of knowledge, yet insist upon a conception of wholly *explicit* truth. For science lives by discovery and ever further discovery; without the itch to solve problems, to follow hunches, to try out new and imprecise ideas, science would cease to exist. Yet discovery cannot be explained in terms of wholly formalizable, wholly explicit knowledge. The problem inherent in this contrast—between truth and the search for truth—was put for us by Plato when he made Meno ask:

> Why, on what lines will you look, Socrates, for a thing of whose nature you know nothing at all? Pray, what sort of thing, amongst those that you know not, will you treat us to as the object of your search? Or even supposing, at the best, that you hit upon it, how will you know it is the thing you did not know?

In other words, as Michael Polanyi has argued on a number of occasions, this single question asked by Plato at the very start of inquiry into the nature of knowledge already puts paid to the centuries of effort in which men have sought to formulate canons of wholly explicit truth. Instead, he insists, we must alter radically the foundation of our epistemology, and admit as essential to the very nature of mind the kind of groping that constitutes the recognition of a problem.

How, positively, can we do this? Polanyi's solution to the problem of *Meno* rests on the distinction, which he introduces in Chapter Four of *Personal Knowledge*, between two kinds of awareness: *focal* and *subsidiary*. The types of knowledge grounded in these two kinds of awareness he has later called 'knowledge by attending to' and 'knowledge by relying on'. His central thesis is that no knowledge is, or can be, *wholly* focal. And in the case of a problem, the subsidiary aspect looms large. We do not know, in the focal sense, what we are looking for, and yet we can look for it, because we rely, in looking for it, on clues to its nature, clues through which we somehow anticipate what we have not yet plainly understood. Such clues we hold in *subsidiary* rather than *focal* awareness.

The class of examples through which Polanyi introduces this distinction is that of tool-using; reading is another paradigm case. I follow the marks on a page, relying on them in order to attend to the meaning, to attend, in fact, indirectly, to the person who wrote them. The same structure holds for a problem. Focally, at the centre of attention, we are aware, so far, of the problem only as a puzzle, a discomfort, a conflict. If, however, it is a good problem, and if we are on the track of a solution, the clues on which we are relying do have a bearing on the solution: they are in fact aspects of the entity we are seeking to comprehend.

At the same time, such clues are also aspects of ourselves: they are points in our own attitudes, skills, memories, or crypto-memories, hunches. To put it in existentialist language, they are aspects of our transcendence, and at the same time of our facticity. So we live in the tension between what we are and what we seek: between the world whose facticity we share and ourselves whose shaping makes the world a world. Our explicit awareness, the focal core of consciousness, is always founded in and carried by the tacit acceptance of something not explicit, which binds, heavily and concretely, ourselves to and within our world. This means that knowledge is always personal. The impersonal aspect of knowledge arises from and returns to personal participation in the search for and acceptance of the object to be known. For only the explicit, formulable core of knowledge can be transferred, neutrally, from person to person. Its implicit base (since it is not verbalized and cannot be formulated and so impersonalized) must be the groping *of someone*.

But while personal, the subsidiary, or tacit, root of knowing is primarily directed away *from* the inner core of my being *to* the focal centre of my attention. All knowledge consists in a *from–to* relation. Of course, subsidiary knowledge is mine: indeed, it is what, relevantly to the present focal point of my attention, I have assimilated to my very self; it is what, out of my being-in-the-world, I have interiorized to the point where I can rely on it to guide me towards a distally located goal. All knowing—whether tacit, as in perception or in skills, or explicit (though never totally so), as in the mastery of an intellectual discipline—displays this dual structure. I attend *from* a proximal pole, which is an aspect of my being, *to* a distal pole, which, by attending *to* it, I place at a distance from myself. All knowing, we could say, in other words, is orientation. The organism's placing of itself in its environment, the dinoflagellate in the plankton, the salmon in its stream or the fox in its lair, prefigures the process by which we both shape and are shaped by our world, reaching out from what we have assimilated to what we seek.

Unlike the traditional ideal of a wholly explicit, self-guaranteeing truth, from–to knowledge cannot be instantaneous; it is a stretch, not only of attention, but of effort, effort must be lived, and living takes time. Knowledge, therefore, is imbedded both in living process (as Piaget, too, has argued in *Biologie et Connaissance*, and as Suzanne Langer is arguing in her study of *Mind*) and in the uniquely human form of living process: in history.

Yet, be it noted, the emphasis on the personal participation of the knower, and on knowing as a form of living process, does *not* entail, in Polanyi's theory, a retreat to an irrational subjectivity. We are dealing, again, with a from–to structure, not with 'pure inwardness'. Polanyi is *not* suggesting, as Kierkegaard or Sartre would do, that I seek in some isolated, empty centre the utter self-sufficiency of my original choice of myself. It is, indeed, quite true, as Polanyi and others have convincingly argued, that pure objectivity, pure exteriority, is impotent to account for the existence of conscious life, or, indeed, of any life at all. Laplacean science contains no concepts which could by the wildest stretch of the imagination make intelligible the existence of an *I*. The atomic topography of my central nervous system is not myself; it is a set of objectified conditions of my existence, and only self-delusion can equate my existence with its conditions, however complex and however necessary. But that is another story: see the essays of Part Four below. The point here is that pure activity, like pure potency, is equally an illusion. The assimilation of the world into total inwardness would be as self-contradictory, as annihilating, as the collapse of the active centre into the pure exteriority of atomism. But that is not our situation. In the from–to stretch by which we grope our way forward out of and into and within a world, we both make and are made, possess and are possessed, in tension, indeed, and even paradox, but not in contradiction. For what we have here is not an all-or-none affirmation or denial, but a *polarity*.

We may even call it, following the lead of that Goethean concept, a tension between Faustean energy and *Hingabe*, 'das ewig Weibliche'. The action through which we appropriate is also the passion through which we give ourselves to being. Our self-integration is also self-surrender, our self-surrender is also the process through which we find ourselves.

As the emphasis on the personal does indicate, however, the conception of from–to knowledge puts *responsibility* squarely at the centre of epistemology. Responsibility appears as the human way of being an active centre: total, indeed, in that only *I* can surrender myself to being, to the sheer factual contingencies, the social lore, the practical and intellectual disciplines, to which, however, I must pledge myself in order both to affirm my being and at the same time to submit, through these manifold *nexus*, to the goals of my further search. Let me again compare Polanyi's view here briefly with Sartre's. It is *I* who make my values values; on this they both agree. But I do so, Polanyi argues, by acknowledging these values responsibly, as standards, as principles which I assert, and accept, *with universal intent*. For Sartre, of course, since such an acceptance takes me beyond myself, it is inevitably in bad faith. For Polanyi, it may be so, as it is, for instance, in his epistemological example of pseudo-substitution. But it need not be so. The risk of forfeiture, like the risk of error, is always with us; living is the hope of achievement and the risk of failure. But this risk, this tension, need not be, except for the mistaken dream of utter self-containment and pellucidity, a stretching on the rack. It evokes, rather, in the perspective of tacit knowing, a sense of calling. Within the limitations of my facticity, and relying on the limited powers it gives me, I ought to strive for an integration, a comprehension, which I could not, indeed, acquire by my own unaided efforts, by which I may, with grace, in part achieve.

This theory of knowledge, first adumbrated in *Science, Faith, and Society* (Oxford, 1945), and systematically developed in *Personal Knowledge* (Routledge, 1958), has since been consolidated and expanded in a number of directions. In the present volume I have collected a group of papers which exemplify this development.

*Personal Knowledge*, starting with the critique of the positivist claim for total objectivity in scientific knowledge, exhibited the culture of science as a subculture in our society, given existence and authority by our fundamental evaluations. Indeed, it is a subculture which claims for itself—and for which the layman claims—an overriding authority, over against all other evaluations or appraisals, which are conceived as merely 'emotional' or 'subjective'. The dilemma of the modern mind, Polanyi argues, arises from the peculiar relation between this scientistic claim and the unprecedented moral dynamism that has increasingly characterized the social and political aspirations of the last century or more. This interpretation, presented in outline in the 'Conviviality' chapter of *Personal Knowledge*, was elaborated in Polanyi's Eddington lecture, *Beyond Nihilism*, which here represents the broadest social and political framework of his analysis of science and scientific knowledge. This lecture was delivered in 1959; its optimism sounds alien, in 1969, to American ears, but its diagnosis of our situation is clearly pertinent, even though we may question the prognosis.

Seeing our general intellectual situation in this light, moreover, we can both understand, and seek to alter, the refusal of social scientists to acknowledge the normative nature of their disciplines; this theme Polanyi develops in the second essay of this collection, 'The Message of the Hungarian Revolution'. To remedy fundamentally the claims of scientism, however, we must consider explicitly the structure of scientific discovery itself. A transition to this problematic is provided by the note on Snow's 'Two Cultures' which concludes Part One.

It was, indeed, the problem of the organization of science which moved Polanyi, in the first instance, to embark on philosophical reflection. Twenty years ago, when there was a vigorous movement for scientific planning, he was concerned to justify to himself and others his belief that centralization is incompatible with the life of science, a view represented here, in Part Two, in the essay 'The Republic of Science'. Fundamentally, what makes such a libertarian form of organization, operating indirectly through consensus rather than directly through planning, necessary to science is the unspecifiability inherent in the processes of discovery, of understanding and even of verification (or falsification). For what is essentially unspecifiable must either resist or be stifled by the specifiability of a master plan. The thesis of unspecifiability as an essential ingredient of any knowledge held by any one or any group as knowledge formed, of course, a central theme of *Personal Knowledge*; it is reaffirmed and consolidated in the first essay of this section. But on the other hand, if science so understood demands a free and consensual administration, any administration, including the institution of science, also demands authority. The role of tradition and authority in science, in its balance with that of originality or novelty—which is often treated as if it could flourish somehow in vacuo, outside *any* traditional context: this role is discussed and exemplified in Essay 8 in reference to the Velikovsky case, and in Essays 6 and 7 in terms of incidents from Polanyi's own scientific career.

The essays on tacit knowing included in Part Three proceed directly, as Polanyi's epistemology has always done, out of his preoccupation with the nature of scientific discovery: of scientific life, as distinct from a pristine but unreal scientific 'logic'. In this way they too carry forward themes already stated in *Personal Knowledge*, but in a form refined and elaborated in his later writing. *Personal Knowledge* was directed not so much to tacit knowing as to the problem of intellectual commitment, the question how I can justify the holding of dubitable beliefs. The theory of tacit knowing is indeed the foundation of the doctrine of commitment, but while the latter probes deeper into the foundation of human personality, the former is more far-ranging. It reveals a pervasive substructure of all intelligent behaviour.

The theory of tacit knowing has been worked out most plainly in Chapter One of *The Tacit Dimension*, and it may be of assistance to the reader if I summarize its argument briefly here. Polanyi starts with the fact that we know more than we can tell, witness the import of experiments in subception (see Essays 11 and 12 of the present volume). He could also take, as he has done in other essays, including those that follow here, the case of seeing with inverting spectacles, the recognition of a physiognomy, stereoscopic seeing, the feat of medical diagnosis: the instances are endless. Take the second case: the achievement of normal vision with inverting lenses. After a period of disorientation I come to rely on the clues available within my body in order to attend to, to see effectively, the things out there. The function of my subsidiary knowledge is to direct me to the coherent sight of my surroundings. This is the *functional* import of tacit knowing: it guides me from proximal, interiorized particulars to the integration of a coherent, distal whole. This is the familiar lesson of gestalt psychology. The bearing of particulars on a total pattern produces the phenomenon of pattern. And this is, secondly, the *phenomenal* aspect of tacit knowing. The particulars, therefore, thirdly, bear on what they mean. Reading, indeed, is, once more, a paradigm case of tacit knowing. All *explicit* knowledge, however crystallized in the formalisms of words, pictures, formulae, or other articulate devices, relies on the grasp of meaning *through* its articulate forms: on the comprehension that is its tacit root. And wholly tacit knowing, as in skills, is still a grasp of significance, though without the mediation of articulate utterance. Thus tacit knowing directs us from particulars to the whole which they signify: that is its *semantic* aspect. But in so guiding us, finally, subsidiaries, which are aspects of our being, draw us beyond ourselves to their distal referent. They guide us toward the comprehension of something *real*, in many cases, at least, to the comprehension of a reality having the same structure as our knowing of it: that is, to a whole of parts, whose significance ranges in ways perhaps unguessed by us beyond its specifiable particulars or even beyond the presently visible outline of the whole. This is the *ontological* import of tacit knowing.

All four aspects of tacit knowing are dealt with in Part Three. 'Knowing and Being' stresses the ontological theme: the claim of tacit knowing to bring the knower into contact with reality, a claim which, though never wholly indefeasible, is nevertheless not arbitrary or irrational: it constitutes, indeed, the only rationality in our power. 'Tacit Knowing: Its Bearing . . .', although its philosophical implications are far-ranging, may be read as taking off from the phenomenal aspect, from a reinstatement of 'secondary' qualities as germane to the veridical import of perception. 'The Logic of Tacit Inference', a paper presented at the international meeting on philosophy of science in Jerusalem, effectively resolves the traditional problem of induction by displaying the structure of the non-explicit inference on which scientific discovery depends; thus it develops the functional or integrative dimension of tacit knowing. And finally, 'Sense-Giving and Sense-Reading' elaborates the semantic aspect of tacit knowing, suggesting a context within which the discoveries of contemporary linguists might be acknowledged and understood without recourse to a revival of 'innate ideas'.

Again, as in *Personal Knowledge*, so in Polanyi's more recent work, the veridical claims of tacit knowing, from perception through the most sophisticated theory building of the sciences, suggest, through their ontological import, the development of an ontology, in particular an ontology of life and mind. All knowing, I suggested earlier, is a kind of orientation: in which we rely on clues within our bodies to reach beyond ourselves, to attend to what is out there. To render such an achievement intelligible we must develop, as the chief, Cartesian-Kantian, tradition of modern thought has forbidden us to do, a theory of the nature of living things in general, and within that theory an account of that aspect of ourselves as living things which we call 'mind'. Polanyi has treated both these cognate themes in a number of recent papers, which are here represented by the pair of essays in Part Four. In the earlier essay, 'The Structure of Consciousness', living beings are characterized as comprehensive entities subject to *dual control*: where the boundary conditions left open by a lower principle, e.g., chemistry or physiology respectively, are prescribed by a higher principle, e.g., physiology or consciousness respectively. In the terminology of the later essay the use of the concept of 'boundary conditions' has changed so as to contrast the boundary conditions characteristic of physics and chemistry with the role of boundary conditions in the sciences of life. We meet here, therefore, a distinction of two types of boundary condition: the test-tube type, where we are interested in the laws exhibited *within* the test-tube, not in it—the boundary condition—itself, and the machine type, where it is the boundary conditions themselves that interest us, and where these constitute the structure or the function in whose interest the lower level laws have been harnessed. Instead of saying, therefore, that in the case of comprehensive entities higher principles govern the boundary conditions defining the system within which lower-level laws are at work, Polanyi now identifies these higher principles with boundary conditions of a special type. It is, however, the same hierarchical ontology of life and mind with which, in both cases, he is concerned.

The elaboration of a coherent philosophy entails the reworking of its *leitmotif* and its application in a variety of contexts. If the themes exemplified in this volume have all been stated, in one way or another, in *Personal Knowledge* and anticipated, even earlier, in *Science, Faith and Society*, Polanyi's fundamental conception of knowledge, and of man as knower, receives a sharper and more powerful formulation in a number of the essays collected here. And above all, the relevance of his major discovery—that is, of the structure of tacit knowing—to the problems of social philosophy, to the interpretation of science, both its history and its methods, to traditional philosophic problems like those of perception, of universals, of induction and of meaning, to the mind–body problem and to the task of understanding living nature: its relevance in all these areas both strengthens the theory of tacit knowing itself and opens for further reflection roads which more conservative methods find blocked. Of course such restatement of a basic theme, especially through the vehicle of occasional pieces like those collected here, entails some repetition; yet each makes a unique contribution to the whole enterprise. On the other hand, papers of equal interest have been omitted, when they seemed to repeat in very large part the arguments of those included, and even those included have been edited in order to minimize repetitions. If the selection or revision has been faulty, the responsibility is entirely mine.

MARJORIE GRENE
*University of California, Davis*

# PART ONE

# Society and the Understanding of Society

# *I*
# Beyond Nihilism
## 1960

The Statutes of the Eddington Lectures show that their founders were preoccupied with the tardiness of moral improvement as compared with the swift advances of science, and that they desired that this disparity be clarified by these lectures. Since none of my predecessors has taken up this question, I propose to do so and should like to state in advance the gist of my answer. I shall argue that the assumptions underlying the question are false, or at least profoundly misleading. For I believe that never in the history of mankind has the hunger for brotherhood and righteousness exercised such power over the minds of men as today. The past two centuries have not been an age of moral weakness, but have, on the contrary, seen the outbreak of a moral fervour which has achieved numberless humanitarian reforms and has improved modern society beyond the boldest thoughts of earlier centuries. And I believe that it is this fervour which, in our own lifetime, has outreached itself by its inordinate aspirations and thus heaped on mankind the disasters that have befallen us. I admit that these disasters were accompanied by moral depravation. But I deny that this justifies us in speaking of moral retardation. What sluggish river has ever broken the dams which contained it, or smashed the wheels which harnessed it? We have yet to discover the proper terms for describing this event. Ethics must catch up with the pathological forms of morals due to the modern intensification of morality. We must learn to recognize moral excesses.

I shall suggest that modern nihilism is a moral excess from which we are suffering today, and I shall try to look past this stage and see whether there is in fact anything beyond it. For our passion for nihilistic self-doubt may be incurable, and it may come to an end only when it has finally destroyed our civilization.

To speak of moral passions is something new. Writers on ethics, both ancient and modern, have defined morality as a composed state of mind. The great spiritual elevation of the fifth century B.C. established throughout its immense area—in China, India, and Greece—a picture of moral man achieving serenity by curbing his passions. It is true that Greek thought has already discussed to what extent moral happiness may be flavoured by a calm enjoyment of the senses. The union of pleasure and morality has been a recurrent theme of ethical speculations down to modern times. But modern nihilism is not a form of moral laxity, and it can be understood, on the contrary, only as part of a comprehensive moral protest that is without precedent in history. So novel is the present state of morality that it has been overlooked by all writers on ethics. The idea that morality consists in imposing on ourselves the curb of moral commands is so ingrained in us that we simply cannot see that the moral need of our time is, on the contrary, to curb our inordinate moral demands, which precipitate us into moral degradation, and threaten us with bodily destruction.

There is, admittedly, one ancient record of more admonitions which were outbreaks of moral passion: the sermons of the Hebrew prophets. I might have disregarded these since their fulminations were fired by religious zeal, and the religious zeal of Judeo-Christianity is not primarily moral. But these prophetic utterances are relevant here because their Messianism, reinforced by the apocalyptic messages of the New Testament, gave rise in the Middle Ages and after to a series of chiliastic outbursts in which the inversion of moral passions into nihilism made its first appearance.

This has been followed up recently by Norman Cohn in *The Pursuit of the Millennium*. He shows that the initial impetus to the repeated Messianic rebellions which occurred in Central Europe from the eleventh to the sixteenth centuries was given by the great moral reforms of Gregory VII. His violent resolve to purge the Church of simony, to prohibit the marriage of the clergy and enforce their chastity retrieved the Church from imminent decay, but it did so at the cost of inciting the populace to rebellion against the clergy. These rebellions were both religious and moral. Their master ideas could be conceived only in a Christian society, for they assailed the spiritual rulers of society for offending against their own teachings. Rulers who did not preach Christian ideals could not be attacked in these terms.[1]

Since no society can live up to Christian precepts, any society professing Christian precepts must be afflicted by an internal contradiction, and when the tension is released by rebellion its agents must tend to establish a nihilist Messianic rule. For a victorious rising will create a new centre of power, and as the rising had been motivated by Christian morality, the new centre will be beset by the same contradictions against which its supporters had risen in rebellion. It will, indeed, be in a worse position, for its internal balance will not be protected by any customary compromise. It can then hold on only by proclaiming itself to be the absolute good: a Second Coming greater than the first and placed therefore beyond good and evil. We see arising then the 'amoral superman', whom Norman Cohn compares with the 'armed bohemians' of our days, the followers of Bakunin and Nietzsche. For the first time the excesses of Christian morality turned here into fierce immoralism.

*

But these events were but scattered prodromal signs. The full power of the disturbance which had caused them became manifest only after the secularization of Europe in the eighteenth century. This change was neither sudden nor complete: but secularization was broadly completed in half a century. It was decisively advanced by the new scientific outlook; the victory of Voltaire over Bossuet was the triumph of Newton, even though Newton might not have wanted it. The scientific revolution supplied the supreme axiom of eighteenth-century rationalism, the rejection of all authority; '*Nullius in Verba*' had been the motto of the Royal Society at its foundation in 1660. Science served also as a major example for emancipating knowledge from religious dogma.

The new world view was expected to set man free to follow the natural light of reason, and thus to put an end to religious fanaticism and bigotry, which were deemed the worst misfortunes of mankind. Humanity would then advance peacefully towards ever higher intellectual, moral, political, and economic perfection. But already quite early in the development of this perspective—almost forty years before universal progress was first envisaged by Condorcet—Rousseau had challenged its hopes in his *Discourses on the*

*Arts and Sciences* (1750) and *On Inequality* (1754). He declared that civilized man was morally degenerate, for he lived only outside himself, by the good opinion of others. He was a 'hollow man', an 'other-directed person', to use terms which were given currency two centuries later. Rousseau actually attributed this degeneration 'to the progress of the human mind', which had produced inequalities and consolidated them by the establishment of property. Man's original virtue had thus been corrupted and his person enslaved. Here is moral fury attacking all that is of good repute: all accepted manners, custom, and law, exalting instead a golden age which was before good and evil.

Admittedly, his fervent dedication of the *Discourse on Inequality* to the city of Geneva shows that Rousseau's text was vastly hyperbolic. Yet by his argument and rhetoric he poured into the channels of rationalism a fierce passion for humanity. His thought so widened these channels that they could be fraught eventually with all the supreme hopes of Christianity, the hopes which rationalism had released from their dogmatic framework. But for this infusion of Christian fervour, Voltaire's vision of mankind purged of its follies and settling down to cultivate its garden might have come true, and Gibbon's nostalgia for a civilization restored to its antique dispassion might have been satisfied. However, the legacy of Christ blighted these complacent hopes; it had other tasks in store for humanity. So it came that the *philosophes* not only failed to establish an age of quiet enjoyment, but induced instead a violent tide of secular dynamism. And while this tide was to spread many benefits on humanity, nobler than any that the *philosophes* had ever aimed at, it also degenerated in many places into a fanaticism fiercer than the religious furies which their teachings had appeased. So even before the principles of scientific rationalism had been fully formulated, Rousseau had conjured up the extrapolation of these principles to the kind of secular fanaticism which was actually to result from them.

And he went further. Having anticipated the passions of the European revolution without himself intending any revolution, he anticipated even its sequel which was never intended—and indeed abhorred—by most of those who were to become its actual agents. He realized that an aggregate of unbridled individuals could form only a totally collectivized political body. For such individuals could be governed only by their own wills, and any governmental will formed and justified by them would itself necessarily be unbridled. Such a government could not submit to a superior jurisdiction any conflict arising between itself and its citizens.[2] This argument is the same which led Hobbes to justify an absolutist government on the grounds of an unbridled individualism, and the procedure Rousseau suggested for establishing this absolutism was also the same as postulated by Hobbes. It was construed as a free gift of all individual wills to the will of the sovereign, under the seal of a Social Contract, the sovereign being established in both cases as the sole arbiter of the contract between the citizens and itself.

The congruence between the conclusions derived from an absolute individualism, both by Hobbes, who had set out to justify absolutism, and Rousseau, who hoped to vindicate liberty, testifies to the logical cogency of their argument. It suggests that when revolutions demanding total individual liberty were eventually to lead to the establishment of a collectivist absolutism, these logical implications were actually at work in the process.

*

Meanwhile this logic was still only on paper, and even on paper the tyrannical consequences of his position were sometimes vigorously denied by Rousseau himself. The predominant opinion of the Enlightenment certainly opposed both the premises and the conclusions of Rousseau and continued confidently to pursue the prospect of free and reasonable men in search of individual happiness, under a government to which they would grant only enough power to protect the citizens from encroachments by their fellow citizens or by foreign enemies. The logic of Hobbes and Rousseau was suspended by disregarding the question as to who would arbitrate between the government and the citizens. Fascinated by the examples of British parliamentary government, political philosophy was ready to accept the current maxims of British success. It was not Rousseau but Locke, therefore, whose teachings triumphed in the first revolution, which was to be American and not French. And it was still Locke whose diction prevailed in the *Declaration of the Rights of Man* at the beginning of the French Revolution.

By that time, however, the secularization of the most active minds of Europe and America had advanced nearly to completion, and the rising stream of Christian aspirations, emerging from its shattered dogmatic precincts, was effectively entering the field of public life. The French Revolution and the collateral movements of reform in all the countries of Europe brought to an end a political state common to mankind for a hundred thousand years, from the beginnings of human society. All during these immemorial ages—throughout their myriad tribes and numerous civilizations—men had accepted existing custom and law as the foundation of society. There had been great reforms, but never before had the deliberate contriving of unlimited social improvement been elevated to a dominant principle. The French Revolution marks the dividing line between the immense expanse of essentially static societies and the narrow strip of time over which our modern experience of social dynamism has so far extended.

Little indeed did the great rationalists realize the transformation they were engendering. Voltaire wrote that not all the works of philosophers would cause even as much strife as the quarrel about the length of sleeves to be worn by Franciscan friars. He did not suspect that the spirit of St Francis himself would enter into the teachings of the philosophers and set the world ablaze with their arguments. And even more remote from his horizon lay the fact that rationalism, thus inflamed, would transform the emotional personality of man. Yet this is what followed. Man's consciousness of himself as a sovereign individual evoked that comprehensive movement of thought and feeling now known as romanticism. Of this great and fruitful germination I pick out only the strand which leads on from Rousseau's exaltation of uncivilized man who, like Adam and Eve before the Fall, has yet no knowledge of good and evil. The scorn which Rousseau had poured on all existing society presently found vent in his defiant assertion of his own individuality. His *Confessions* were to show a man in the starkness of nature, and that man would be himself, whom no other man resembles. His lowest vices would be exposed and thrown as a gauntlet in the face of the world. The reader shall judge, wrote he, 'whether nature was right in smashing the mould into which she had cast me'.

This is modern immoralism. Rascals had written their lives before and had shamelessly told of their exploits. The wrongdoings which a Benvenuto Cellini or a Boswell related exceed those of Rousseau, and their authors showed no compunction. Yet they were not immoralists. For they did not proclaim their vices to the world in order to denounce the world's hypocrisy—but merely told a good story.

True, sceptical rationalism had already spread a philosophy of pleasure. Mme de Châtelet wrote that men set free from prejudices should seek no other purpose in life than to enjoy agreeable sensations, and she acted on this principle. But enlightened libertinism envisaged men pursuing pleasure peacefully within the limits of natural morality. Rousseau's prophetic temper transmuted this hedonism into an angry protest against society and flaunted an immoral individuality in contemptuous defiance of society.

\*

There had been periods of moral scepticism in antiquity. The angry young men of Greece had said that the law is but 'the will of the stronger'. And in Greece too, secularism and critical analysis may have stimulated this view and have contributed also to the immoralism of Alcibiades and his like-minded contemporaries. But this immoralism was not romantic, for it was not proclaimed in protest against the moral shallowness of society.

Likewise, when Thucydides acknowledged that national interests overrule moral standards in dealings between city states, he declared this as a bitter truth. Machiavelli reasserted this teaching and expanded it by authorizing the prince to override all moral constraints in consolidating his own power. And later, Machiavellism was to develop into the doctrine of *Staatsraison*, exercising a steady influence on modern rulers and contributing greatly to the formation of modern states. This *Realpolitik* culminated in the writings, actions, and achievements of Frederick the Great, but still lacked romantic colour. For it still justified itself as a regrettable necessity.

But romantic dynamism transformed this tight-lipped immorality of princes into the exaltation of nationhood as a law unto itself. The uniqueness of great nations gave them now the right to unlimited development at the expense of their weaker neighbours. Such national immoralism developed furthest in Germany and was upheld there with a strong feeling of its own moral superiority over the moralizing statesmen of other countries. This

German attitude duplicated on the national scale Rousseau's flaunting of his uniquely vicious nature against a hypocritical society.

Meanwhile, let me make it clear that I am not concerned with the effect of Rousseau's writings on the course of history. Their effect was considerable, but even had his works been overlooked, the fact would remain that a great thinker anticipated in three respects the inherent instability of the rationalist ideal of a secular society. He saw that it implied an unrestrained individualism, demanding absolute freedom and equality far beyond the limits imposed by any existing society. He saw, next, that such absolute sovereignty of individual citizens is conceivable within society only under a popular government, exercising absolute power. And thirdly, he anticipated the ideal of an amoral individualism, asserting the rights of a unique creative personality against the morality of a discredited society. And though the transposition of romantic immoralism onto the national scale was admittedly strange to Rousseau's cosmopolitan outlook, yet this too was largely prefigured by his thought.

Now that these implications have proved to be paths of history, the fact that they were discerned at a time when no one had yet thought of them as lines of action strongly suggests that they were in fact the logical consequences of their antecedents: i.e., of a sceptical rationalism combined with the secularized fervour of Christianity. I do not say that these logical consequences were bound to take effect, and I shall show that they have in fact remained unfulfilled in some important areas. But I do suggest that wherever they did come to light during the two centuries after Rousseau, they may be regarded as a manifestation of a logical process which first ran its course in Rousseau's mind.

*

I have set the scene and introduced the ideas which were to move the past five generations up to the stage which is our own responsibility today. I see the course of these hundred and fifty years as the rise of moral passions which, though mostly beneficent, sometimes assumed terrible forms, culminating in the revolutions of the twentieth century. I see the present generation still reeling under the blows of these moral excesses, groping its way back to the original ideals of the eighteenth century. But since

these have once collapsed under the weight of their logical implications, can they possibly be restored to guide us once more? This
is now the question.

I have said that the situation in which the modern mind finds
itself today has emerged in two stages from the mentality of a
static society. The first stage was the process of intellectual
secularization, spreading the new scientific outlook of the universe and yet evoking no profound emotions and calling for no
vast political actions; the second was the dynamic process which
released these emotions and actions. At this point the thoughts of
philosophers were transformed into ideologies. Ideologies are
fighting creeds. They fought against the defenders of the static
age, and they also fought against each other, as rivals. Those who
speak today of 'the end of ideologies' mean that dynamism has
abated and can therefore move men today without commitment to
a theoretical fighting creed.

The effectiveness of dynamic political action, carried on with
little ideological guidance, is illustrated by the development of
Britain in the first half of the nineteenth century. The abolition of
slavery, the factory laws, the emancipation of non-Conformists
and Catholics, the reform of Parliament, the Lunacy Laws,
criminal and penal reform and the many other humanitarian
improvements for which this period was named the 'Age of
Reform' were promoted by people of widely different persuasions.
The reforms had their early roots in the sustained struggle against
oppression and social injustice which had already found influential advocates in politics for centuries before the Enlightenment. They were not achieved by a secularized anti-clerical movement, but by ancient political forces, quickened by a new zeal for
social improvement. With his theory of British political practice,
Montesquieu gave an ideology to France; yet in Britain this
theory was never an ideology, but a commentary on established
forms of life. No one objected, for example, to the fact that Britain's chief executive was responsible to Parliament and that
British judges continued to make case-law, although these proceedings infringed on the theoretical division of powers. Such
was indeed the fate of all political theory in England: it never
became more than a set of maxims, subject to interpretation by
customary practice. The genius of Hobbes was disregarded, for
his teachings were not consonant with practice. Locke was

exalted and the gaps in his theory ignored; since practice readily filled these gaps. The views of Bentham, whose paramount influence should in strict logic have resulted in the establishment of Aldous Huxley's *Brave New World*, were reduced in practice to a corrective against rigid traditionalism; while Burke's inordinate traditionalism was quietly assimilated as a mere corrective to the predominance of utilitarianism. Later, J. S. Mill achieved lasting influence with his theories of liberty and representative government which ignored all the questions raised by Hobbes and Rousseau and also by German Idealism; and finally, at the turn of the century, even Hegel was domesticated in T. H. Green's adaptation of his philosophy to British constitutional practice.

Yet dynamism did take deep hold on England. Only it did so piecemeal, by arousing those people whom the established order had wronged and by appealing to the conscience of those responsible for maintaining these injustices. As a result, today, after a hundred and fifty years of reform that have transformed every particle of her life, Britain's institutions still form a single harmonized system, upheld without serious dissent by the entire nation. The 'end of ideologies' will signify no more in this case than the termination of a brief period of doctrinaire Socialism.

Thus Britain avoided the self-destructive implications of the Enlightenment of which she was one chief author. Remember David Hume's game of backgammon, to which he turned in disgust over the consequences of his scepticism—it has remained the paradigm of British national life. It has preserved down to this day the movement of eighteenth-century humanism. In America the same result was achieved through a passionate veneration of the Constitution. Hence Britain, whose pioneering scepticism was feared by French conservatives in the eighteenth century, came to be looked upon in the nineteenth century as old-fashioned by the dynamic intelligentsia of the Continent. I have mentioned already how the German romantics, who denied the relevance of moral standards to the external actions of states, indignantly rejected the moralizing talk of English and American statesmen as stupid or dishonest or both. But German socialists were equally nonplussed by the religious and moral exhortations of British labour leaders. Continental Marxists kept on discussing the curious 'backwardness' of English and American politics—even as Communists in Albania today are probably wondering how countries like Germany, France, and England could fall so far behind the enlightened example of Albania.

*

There was a similar relationship between England and the Continent also in respect to romantic individualism. Byron had spread the image of the noble romantic immoralist through European literature as far as the Russian steppes. The poet Lenski in Pushkin's *Onegin* (1833) has a portrait of Byron in his remote country house. But England itself got rid of Byron without a trace. The problem of evil, the possibility that evil may be morally superior to good, which affected all nineteenth-century thought on the Continent, was never raised in England. Morley, in his book *On Compromise*, deplores the fact that England's civic genius had restrained the adventures of speculative thought so as to keep them politically innocuous. Had he lived to see our own day, Morley might have felt that England had remained backward only on the road to disaster. Or, perhaps more positively, he would have seen that England—like America—had effectively relaxed the internal contradictions inherent in any Christian or post-Christian society, by gradually humanizing society, while strengthening the affection between fellow citizens for the sake of which they may forgive mutual injustices. For it was this achievement that has preserved the eighteenth-century framework of thought almost intact in these countries up to this day.

However, in 1789 France broke away and led the world towards a revolutionary consummation of the contradiction inherent in a post-Christian rationalism. The ideology of total revolution is a variant of the derivation of absolutism from absolute individualism. Its argument is simple and has yet to be answered. If society is not a divine institution, it is made by man, and man is free to do with society what he likes. There is then no excuse for having a bad society, and we must make a good one without delay. For this purpose you must take power and you can take power over a bad society only by a revolution; so you must go ahead and make a revolution. Moreover, to achieve a comprehensive improvement of society you need comprehensive powers; so you must regard all resistance to yourself as high treason and must put it down mercilessly.

This logic is, alas, familiar to us, and we can readily identify its more or less complete fulfilment from Robespierre and St Just to Lenin, Bela Kun, Hitler, and Mao Tse-tung. But there is a progression from Robespierre to his successors *which transforms Messianic violence from a means to an end into an aim in itself.* Such is the final position reached by moral passions in their modern embodiments, whether in personal nihilism or in totalitarian violence. I call this transformation a process of *moral inversion.*

J. L. Talmon's richly documented account of the ideas which moved the French Revolution and filled the revolutionary movements up to about 1848 makes us realize the depth of this transformation and supplies already some signs of its beginnings.[3] Here is the language in which Robespierre addressed his followers:

> But it exists, I assure you, pure and sensitive souls; it exists, that passion, so tender, imperious, irresistible, the torment and joy of generous hearts, that deep horror of tyranny, that compassionate zeal for the oppressed, that sacred love of the fatherland, that sublime and sacred love of humanity, without which a great revolution is but a manifest crime that destroys another crime; it exists, that generous ambition to found on this earth the first Republic of the world; that selfishness of men not degraded, which finds its celestial delight in the calm of a pure conscience and the charming spectacle of the public good. You feel it burning at this very moment in your souls. I feel it in my own.

Yes, it existed, this passion of pure and sensitive souls, this sublime and sacred love of humanity—and it still exists today, only it no longer speaks of itself in these terms. Robespierre's text contains some seeds of the more modern terms, when he speaks of that selfishness (*egoisme*) which delights in the public good. This phrase echoes Helvetius' utilitarianism, which would establish the ideals of humanity scientifically, by rooting them in man's desire for pleasure. The next step was to reject humanitarian ideals as such; Bentham contemptuously spoke of natural rights and laws of nature as senseless jargon. 'Utility is the supreme object,' he wrote, 'which comprehends in itself law, virtue, truth and justice.'

We have seen that the logic of Bentham's scientific morality was mercifully suspended and its teachings interpreted in support of liberal reforms in England, but on the Continent we see henceforth the scientific formulation of dynamism entering into ever more effective competition with its original emotional manifestations. Both were revolutionary in scope, and the Utopian phantasies of both bordered on insanity; but as time went on all these inordinate hopes became increasingly assimilated to teachings claiming the authority of science. And the new scientific utopianism declared that the future society must submit absolutely to its scientific rulers; once politics has been elevated to the rank of a natural science, liberty of conscience would disappear.[4] The infallibility of Rousseau's general will was transposed into the unassailable conclusions of a scientific sociology.

\*

About the same time, the personal immoralism that had issued from Rousseau underwent a similar scientific incrustation. It resulted in the character first described by Turgenev as a *nihilist*. The line of romantic immoralists which Pushkin had started in Russia with the Byronian figure of Onegin and of Herman (the Napoleon-struck hero of *The Queen of Spades*) was not discontinued. Raskolnikov develops their problems further, by committing a murder only to test the powers of his immorality. The figure of Raskolnikov was independently recreated by Nietzsche in his tragic apologia of the Pale Criminal in *Zarathustra*, and this figure, with others akin to it, gained popular influence in Germany and France. But not in Russia. The popular ideal of the Russian enlightened youth from about 1860 onwards was the hard, impersonal scientific nihilist, first embodied in Turgenev's hero, the medical student Bazarov.

Men of this type were called 'realists', 'progressives', or simply 'new men'. They were strict materialists, who combined their total denial of genuinely moral ideals with a frenzied hatred of society on account of its immorality .Thus they were morally dedicated to commit any act of treachery, blackmail, or cruelty in the service of a programme of universal destruction. On November 21, 1869, the nihilist leader Nechaev had his follower, the student Ivanov, assassinated in order to strengthen party discipline. This is the story which Dostoievsky has told in *The Possessed*, representing Ivanov by Shatov and Nechaev by Piotr Stepanovitch Werchovenski.

The structure of this crime prefigured the murder by Stalin of his own followers; but there was yet some theoretical support needed. It was supplied by a new scientific sociology claiming to have proved three things: namely (1) that the total destruction of the existing society was the only method for achieving an essential

c

improvement of society; (2) that nothing beyond this act of violence was required, or even to be considered, since it was unscientific to make any plans for the new society; and (3) that no moral restraints must be observed in the revolutionary seizure of power, since (a) this process was historically inevitable, and so beyond human control, and (b) morality, truth, etc., were mere epiphenomena of class-interests so that the only scientific meaning of morality, truth, justice, etc., consisted in advancing those class-interests which science had proved to be ascendant.

This scientific sociology was supplied by Marxism–Leninism. Though said to transform Socialism 'from Utopia into a science', its convincing power was due to the satisfaction it gave to the Utopian dreams which it purported to replace. And this proved sufficient. Any factual objection to the theory was repelled as a reactionary attack against socialism, while Socialism itself was safe from criticism, since any discussion of it had been condemned as unscientific speculation by Marx. Marxism provides a perfect ideology for a moral dynamism which could express itself only in a naturalistic conception of man; this is its historic function.

The generous passions of our age could now covertly explode inside the engines of a pitiless machinery of violence. The pure and sensitive souls to whom Robespierre had appealed still existed, and were indeed more numerous than ever, and his sublime and sacred love of humanity was still burning as intensely as ever. But these sentiments had become *immanent* in policies of *manifest* immorality. Their accents had become scientifically didactic. Here is Lenin's language in the programmatic statement made in June 1917:

> The dictatorship of the proletariat is a scientific term stating the class in question and the particular form of state authority, called dictatorship, namely, authority based not on law, not on elections, but directly on the armed force of some portion of the population.

Robespierre's terror had justified itself by its noble aspirations; Marx refused such justification and left violence alone as the path of a scientific Socialism. This is moral inversion: a condition in which high moral purpose operates only as the hidden force of an openly declared inhumanity.

\*

In *The Possessed*, the earlier type of *personal* inversion is embodied in Stavrogin, whom the modern *political* immoralist Wercho-

vensky is vainly trying to draw into his conspiratorial organization. But by the twentieth century the two types become con-
vertible into each other throughout Europe. The personal immoralist bohemian converts his anti-bourgeois protest readily into
social action by becoming an 'armed bohemian' and thus supporting absolute violence as the only honest mode of political action.

The two lines of antinomianism meet and mingle in French
existentialism. Mme de Beauvoir hails the Marquis de Sade as a
great moralist when Sade declares through one of his characters:
'. . . I have destroyed everything in my heart that might have
interfered with my pleasures.'⁵ And this triumph over conscience,
as she calls it, is interpreted in terms of her own Marxism:
'. . . Sade passionately exposes the bourgeois hoax which consists
in erecting class-interests into universal (moral) principles.'⁶

I have said before that romanticism recognized the extension of
national power as a nation's supreme right and duty. This political
immoralism is also a moral inversion, akin to the personal immoralism of the romantic school. Meinecke has shown that German *Realpolitik*, the identification of Might and Right in international relations, was the ultimate outcome of the Hegelian
teaching of 'immanent reason'. The strength of immanent morality
is proved by the violence of manifest immorality. This, Meinecke
thinks, is the grim truth blandly overlooked or hypocritically
papered over by moralizing statesmen and English-speaking
people in general. He admitted that the knowledge of this truth
tended to brutalize its holders, but thought that the English-
speaking people had avoided this depravation only by turning a
blind eye on the disparity between their teachings and their actions.

A great wave of anti-bourgeois immoralism sweeping through
the minds of German youth in the inter-war period formed the
reservoir from which the SA and SS were recruited. They were
inspired by the same truculent honesty and passion for moral
sacrifice which turned the nihilists of Russia, whether romantic or
scientistic, into the *apparatchiks* of Stalinism.

People often speak of Communism or Nazism as a 'secular religion'. But not all fanaticism is religious. The passions of the total
revolutions and total wars which have devastated our age were not
religious but moral. Their morality was inverted and became immanent in brute force because a naturalistic view of man forced
them into this manifestation. Once they are immanent, moral

motives no longer speak in their own voice and are no longer accessible to moral arguments; such is the structure of modern nihilistic fanaticism.

*

Here, then, is my diagnosis of the pathological morality of our time. What chance is there of remedying this condition?

The healer's art must rely ultimately on the patient's natural powers for recovery. We have unmistakable evidence of these powers in our case. From its origins in the French Revolution the great tide of dynamism had been mounting steadily, both spreading its benefits and causing its pathological perversions, during roughly a hundred and fifty years; and then—at the very centre of revolutionary dynamism—the tide turned. Pasternak dates the change in Russia around 1943. It arose in an upsurge of national feeling. Hatred of Stalin gave way to the resolve of conquering Hitler in spite of Stalin. Victory was in sight, and with this prospect came the growing realization that the existing system of fanatical hatreds, lies, and cruelties was in fact pointless. Intimations of freedom began to spread. These thoughts repudiated the core of Messianic immoralism and for a moment broke its magic. A process of sobering had set in. In 1948 Tito defected from Stalin, invoking truth and national dignity as principles superior to party discipline.

The decline of ideological dynamism set in also on this side of the Iron Curtain. In England, in Germany, and in Austria, the change of heart was noticeable from the early 1950s. Socialists who, even in notoriously reformist countries like Britain, had demanded a complete transformation of society, began to re-interpret their principles everywhere in terms of piecemeal progress.

Finally, the events following the death of Stalin (1953) clearly revealed that a system based on a total inversion of morality was intrinsically unstable. The first act of Stalin's successors was to release the thirteen doctors of the Kremlin, who had quite recently been sentenced to death on their own confession of murderous attempts against the life of Stalin and other members of the government. This action had a shattering effect on the Party. A young man who at that time was a fervent supporter of Stalinism in Hungary described to me how he felt when the news came through on the wireless. It seemed as if the motion picture of his whole political development had started running off backwards. If party-truth was now to be refuted by mere bourgeois objectivity, then Stalin's whole fictitious universe would presently dissolve, and so the loyalty which sustained this fiction—and was in its turn sustained by it—would be destroyed as well.

The alarm was justified. For it is clear by now that the new masters of the Kremlin had acted as they did because they believed their position would be safer if they had more of the truth on their side and less against them. So deciding, they had acknowledged the power of the truth over the Party and the existence of an independent ground for opposition against the Party. And this independent ground—this new Mount Ararat laid bare by the receding flood of dynamism—was bound to expand rapidly. For if truth was no longer defined as that which serves the interests of the Party, neither would art, morality, or justice continue to be so defined, since all these hang closely together—as it has eventually become clearly apparent.

*

So it came to pass that the whole system of moral inversion broke down in the Hungarian and Polish risings of 1956. These movements were originally not rebellions against the Communists, but a change of mind of leading Communists. The Hungarian rising not only started, but went a long way towards victory, as a mere revulsion of Communist intellectuals from their earlier convictions. The first revolutionary event was the meeting of a literary circle, the Petöfi Society, on June 27, 1956. An audience of about six thousand, overflowing into the streets to which the proceedings were transmitted by loudspeakers, met for nine hours. Speaker after speaker demanded freedom to write the truth; to write about real people, real streets and fields, real sentiments and problems; to report truthfully on current events and on matters of history. In making these demands many speakers were reverting to beliefs they had previously abhorred and even violently suppressed.

In the months that followed these reborn principles worked their way rapidly further, frequently bursting out in self-accusations by Communist intellectuals who repented their previous connivance in reducing truth, justice, and morality, to mere instruments of the Party.

Miklos Gimes, a leading Communist who was hanged by Kadar for his part in the Hungarian Revolution, wrote in this sense in *Béke és Szabadság* on October 3, 1956. He asked how it could have happened that he himself had become unable to see the difference between truth and falsehood:

> Slowly we had come to believe, at least with the greater, the dominant part of our consciousness, that there are two kinds of truth, that the truth of the Party and the people can be different and can be more important than the objective truth and that truth and political expediency are in fact identical. This is a terrible thought, yet its significance must be faced squarely. If there is a truth of a higher order than objective truth, if the criterion of truth is political expediency, then even a lie can be 'true', for even a lie can be momentarily expedient; even a trumped-up political trial can be 'true' in this sense for even such a trial can yield important political advantage. And so we arrive at the outlook which infected not only those who thought up the faked political trials but often affected even the victims; the outlook which poisoned our whole public life, penetrated the remotest corners of our thinking, obscured our vision, paralysed our critical faculties, and finally rendered many of us incapable of simply sensing or apprehending truth. This is how it was, it is no use denying it.

Thus had the decision matured which Gyula Hay, since then imprisoned by Kadar, declared on September 22 in *Irodalmi Ujság*:

> The best Communist writers have resolved—after many difficulties, serious errors, and bitter mental struggles—that in no circumstances will they ever write lies again.

Hay realized that on these grounds all writers, both inside and outside the Party, were now reunited. In a speech made on September 17 he declared:

> We Hungarian writers, irrespective of party allegiance or philosophic convictions, form hereby a firm alliance for the dissemination of the truth.

It was this alliance which lent its voice to the hitherto mute and powerless dissatisfaction of the workers. When the students marched into the streets to hold their forbidden demonstration, tens of thousands streamed from the factories to join them. Within hours the army had changed camp, the secret police was dissolved. The heavily armed and severely disciplined organization of a totalitarian state evaporated overnight, because its convictions had been consumed by its own newly-awakened conscience.

This upsurge of truth resembled up to a point the Enlightenment of the eighteenth century, but it differed from it profoundly. For the Encyclopaedists were not repudiating a string of lies which they had deliberately swallowed in order to strengthen their own political convictions. There was no occasion for them to restore a belief in truth and morality, which had never been questioned by the orthodoxy they were attacking, nor ever been scorned by themselves.

By contrast, the process of the Communist revulsion has been dramatically told by the Polish poet Adam Waczek, himself a Party stalwart, in his *Poem for Adults*, written a year before the events in Hungary started. Fourier had promised that Socialism would turn the seas into lemonade, and so the Party members had eagerly swallowed sea water as if it were lemonade. But eventually their stomachs turned, and from time to time they had to retire and vomit. The word 'vomiting' has since become a technical term for describing the recoil of morally inverted man: the act by which he violently turns himself right way up. A new term was needed, because nothing of this kind had ever happened before.

\*

The Hungarian Revolution is the paradigm of an intellectual movement which, in less dramatic forms, has spread all through the area of receding dynamism, almost everywhere outside Communist China. The Soviet Government has condemned its manifestation within its own domain as revisionism, and I think the name 'revisionism' may be applied to the different forms of this movement everywhere.

Revisionism recoils from a negation. The negation took place when the Enlightenment, having secularized Christian hopes, destroyed itself by moral inversion; and the recoil from this negation occurred when moral inversion proved unstable in its turn. This recoil is the source of all revisionism.

But, unfortunately, to recognize these antecedents is to call in question all the ideas which have hitherto guided revisionist movements. A re-awakened national feeling has been one of these ideas. Pasternak tells us how it humanized the Soviet regime during the war; it then served the restoration of humane ideals in

Poland, Hungary, and Yugoslavia; and it has formed new bonds of civility in France under de Gaulle. And perhaps above all, it has rejuvenated the ancient societies of Asia and Africa, creating, along with much wasteful strife, new popular communities which transcend the ideological conflicts of European dynamism.

Another revisionist idea lay in the new-found alliance between liberalism and religious beliefs. The churches seemed to recall modern man from a state beyond nihilism to his condition before the secular enlightenment. And finally, the sceptical mood of the Enlightenment itself has been given a new lease of life. The more sober, pragmatist attitude towards public affairs which has spread since 1950 through England and America, Germany, and Austria, reproduces in its repudiation of ideological strife the attitude of Voltaire and the Encyclopaedists towards religious bigotry.

But revision cannot succeed by merely returning to ideas which have already proved unstable. The rule of a dogmatic authority is no more acceptable today than it was in the days of Voltaire. We shall not go back on the scientific revolution which has secularized extensive domains of knowledge. We shall not go back either on the hopes of Christianity and become as calmly indifferent to social wrongs as secularized antiquity had been. And national feeling has proved in the past no safeguard against the descent of dynamism into moral inversion. In fact, *all the logical antecedents of inversion are present today just as they were before*. Can the very channels which had previously led into moral inversion now offer a retreat from it?

All the same, we *have* arrived beyond nihilism today, even though the place at which we have arrived is similar to that where we stood before it and even though we cannot foresee the creative possibilities by which men may discover an avenue which will not lead back to nihilism. But one possibility should be mentioned. Perhaps the present recoil may be stabilized by the upsurge of a more clear-sighted political conscience. We might conceivably achieve a kind of suspended logic, like that which kept England and America so happily backward on the road to disaster, and indeed this might come about the way it had in England. The religious wars of Europe reached this country in mid-seventeenth century and strife tore England for many years. One king was beheaded, another deposed. But the settlement of 1688, the Petition of Rights, the doctrine of John Locke, have put an end to this conflict and established, for the first time since the rise of Christianity, the foundations of a secular society. Civility prevailed over religious strife, and a society was founded which was dynamic and yet united. May not Europe repeat this feat? May we not learn from the disasters of the past forty years to establish a civic partnership, united in its resolve on continuous reforms— our dynamism restrained by the knowledge that radicalism will throw us back into disaster the moment we try to act out its principles literally?

It may happen. But this is hardly a legitimate field for speculation; for from here onwards, thought must take on the form of action.

[1] I am concerned here only with risings proclaiming moral principles which the existing rulers profess, and are accused of failing to observe. This does not apply generally to outbursts of millenarism among primitive people. Even so, such movements are most frequently induced by the teachings of Christian missionaries. See PETER WORSLEY, *The Trumpet Shall Sound*, London: MacGibbon and Kee, 1957, p. 245.

[2] ROUSSEAU, *Le Contrat Social* (I, Chapter VI).

[3] J. L. TALMON, *The Origin of Totalitarian Democracy*, London: Secker & Warburg, 1952.

[4] See F. A. HAYEK, *The Counter-Revolution of Science*, Glencoe, Illinois: Free Press, 1952, particularly his study of Comte.

[5] SIMONE DE BEAUVOIR, *The Marquis de Sade*, London: Evergreen, 1954 and New York: Grove Press, 1953, p. 54. 'Owing to his headstrong sincerity . . . he deserves to be hailed as a great moralist' (p. 55).

[6] *Ibid.*, p. 63.

# 2
# The Message of
# the Hungarian Revolution
## 1966

In February, 1956, Krushchev denounced the insane regime of
Stalin at the Twentieth Party Congress. Four months later, in
June 1956, the repercussions of this act led to an open rebellion
of the Hungarian writers at the meetings of the Petöfi circle in
Budapest. This was the actual beginning of the Hungarian Revolution, which broke out violently in October of the same
year.

It has often been mentioned, but never realized in its full importance, that the rebellion of the Petöfi Circle was an uprising of
Communist Party members. There were many among them who
had won high honours and great financial benefits from the government. They had been, until shortly before, its genuine and
passionate supporters.

The Petöfi Circle, where this first rebellion broke out, was an
official organ of the Party, presided over by trusted representatives
of the ruling clique. But in June 1956 other Party members,
forming the bulk of the audience, overcame the platform. They
demanded a reversal of the position assigned to human thought in
the Marxist–Leninist scheme. Marxism–Leninism taught that
public consciousness is a superstructure of the underlying relations
of production; public thought under socialism, therefore, must be
an instrument of the Party controlling Socialist production.

The meetings rejected this doctrine. They affirmed that truth
must be recognized as an independent power in public life. The
press must be set free to tell the truth. The murderous trials based
on faked charges were to be publicly condemned and their per-
petrators punished; the rule of law must be restored. And, above
all, the arts corrupted by subservience to the Party must be set

free to rouse the imagination and to tell the truth. It was this outbreak that created the centre of opposition which later overthrew
the Communist government of Hungary.

*

Has the response of the West to these events been adequate? I
am not asking whether we ought to have aided the Hungarian
Revolution by money or the force of arms. I am asking about our
intellectual and moral responses.

What did we think, what do we think today, of this change of
mind among many of the most devoted Hungarian Stalinists? Do
we realize that this was a wholesale return to the ideals of nineteenth-century liberalism? In the Hungarian Revolution of 1956
its fighters were clearly going back to the ideals of 1848, to Liberty,
Equality, Fraternity. After the French Revolution the ideas of
liberty had filtered through the whole of Europe, and in 1848
these ideas aroused a chain of insurgences. Starting from Paris,
rebellions swept through the German states and through Austria
into Hungary. The Hungarian revolutionaries of 1956 revived
these same ideas; they believed that the ideals of truth, justice and
liberty were valid, and they were resolved to fight and conquer in
their names.

I ask you again: what do we say to this? It has been a long time
since history was last written in the English language as the inevitable progress of truth, justice, and liberty. I think J. B. Bury
was the last to do so fifty years ago. Our current interpretations of
social change and of the rise of new ideas are nearer to the theories
of Marx than to the views of Bury, or those of J. S. Mill, or of
Jefferson, or Condorcet and Gibbon. Our interpretations are
couched in terms of a value-free sociology, of an historicist histo-
riography, or of depth psychology. We can then hardly be expected to acknowledge the aims which the Hungarian rebels pro-
fessed to be fighting for. Our most popular explanation of unrest
in the Soviet countries is sociological. It says that the methods of
Stalin had fulfilled their purpose of carrying out the rapid indus-
trialization of the Soviet Union, but that these methods were no
longer suited to a more complex society and hence the need had
arisen for new ideals, more appropriate to the new situation. This
is said to have caused the renewal of thought in the Soviet
countries since Stalin's death.

Such theories are put forward without any supporting evidence, and nobody asks for evidence. It is ignored that two of the most highly industrialized regions of Europe, namely Eastern Germany and Czechoslovakia, have produced the hardest Stalinist governments and resisted reform the longest. Any mechanical explanation of human affairs, however absurd, is accepted today unquestioningly.

Listen to the story told four years ago in *Encounter* by a distinguished expert on Soviet countries, Professor Richard Pipes, then Associate Director of Harvard's Russian Research Centre. Professor Pipes wrote:

> Four years ago, when writing an essay on the Russian intelligentsia for the journal *Daedalus*, I wanted to conclude it with a brief statement to the effect that the modern Russian intellectual had a very special mission to fulfil: 'to fight for truth.' On the advice of friends I omitted this passage since it sounded naive and unscientific. Now I regret having done so. . . .[1]

Thus at the most influential academic centre studying Soviet affairs, it took three years after the rebellion of writers at the Petöfi Circle for it to be mooted for the first time that this kind of unrest was due to craving for truth. Even then this suggestion was suppressed in deference to expert opinion, because to speak of intellectuals fighting for truth was held to be 'naive and unscientific'.

Professor Pipes continues this passage by explaining why he thinks now (four years later) that in the case of Russian intellectuals it is not unscientific to attribute to them a craving for truth. The reasons for this apply equally to the conditions under which Hungarian intellectuals rebelled, and thus the argument applies to them too. Professor Pipes writes:

> The reason the word 'truth' is in disrepute among us is because we attach to it generally moral connotations; that is, we understand it as a concept which implies the existence of a single criterion of right and wrong—something we are not willing to concede. We react thus because in the environment in which we live our right to perceive is not usually questioned; what can be questioned is our interpretation of the perceived reality. But in an environment where the very right to perception of reality is inhibited by claims of the State, the word 'truth' acquires a very different meaning. It signifies not true value

but true experience: the right to surrender to one's impressions without being compelled for some extraneous reason to interpret and distort them.[2]

We are told here that it is unscientific to speak of 'truth' in our society and that the word merits its current discredit because we attach moral values to it. It is legitimate to recognize that the Soviet intellectuals fight for truth because they are demanding merely the right to perceive reality and not to convey any interpretation of it in terms of values believed to be true. However, the writers who rebelled in the Petöfi Circle ten years ago were not demanding the right to have certain 'perceptions of reality'. They demanded that the execution of Rajk, based on faked charges, be publicly admitted and that they be free to denounce the tyranny forcing its false values on the people; they were demanding the right to write the truth in novels, in poetry and in the newspapers.

I think that to understand this rebellion we must see it as part of a major historical progression, composed of three stages to be seen jointly. The first was the defection of leading intellectuals of the West, abandoning 'the God that failed'. Some turned away during the trials of 1937–38, others after the Stalin–Hitler pact of 1939, others still later. But by the end of the Second World War there was an ardent band of former Communists desperately warning against the Soviets, whose philosophy made them impervious to our values.

The next decisive change occurred in Soviet Russia itself on the day Stalin died. The first act of his successors was to release the thirteen doctors of the Kremlin who had recently been sentenced to death on their own false confessions of murderous attempts against Stalin and other members of the government. This action had a shattering effect on the Party. If Party-truth was to be refuted by mere bourgeois objectivism, then Stalin's whole fictitious universe would presently dissolve.

The alarm was justified. After the further revelations of the Twentieth Party Congress, it became clear that the new masters of the Kremlin had acted as they did because they felt that their position would be safer if they had more truth on their side and less against them. They sacrificed the most powerful weapon of terror for this end—the weapon of faked trials; no such trial was held in the Soviet empire after the Jewish doctors were set free. A radical change of the foundations had begun.

The third major step in the growth of the power to vindicate the truth—and the values resting on the right to tell the truth—was the rebellion of Hungarian writers. We can see this now as part of the historical process which had started with the numerous defections from Communism among Western intellectuals about fifteen years earlier.

The rebellion of the Petöfi Circle was a change of mind by dedicated Communists forming an intellectual *avant-garde*. Though undertaken against the still ruling Stalinism, it spread under the very eyes of the secret police, until one day it brought the workers out into the streets and won over the army to its support. The government was overthrown. And, though a few days later the Russians moved in with new tanks, they did not restore the Stalinists to power. Since October 23, 1956, ideas had never ceased to circulate freely in Hungary. You cannot fully print them, but you can spread them effectively by word of mouth.

*

When seen in this context these events might appear self-explanatory. They would indeed be so if the truth of the Enlightenment appeared self-evident today. But though these truths still dominate our public statements and largely dominate also the day-to-day judgments of men, they are, for the most part, ignored by social scientists. Most academic experts will refuse to recognize today that the mere thirst for truth and justice has caused the revolts now transforming the Soviet countries. They are not Marxists, but their views are akin to Marxism in claiming that the scientific explanation of history must be based on more tangible forces than the fact that people change their minds.

Such a split between the laity and the learned is not unusual in the history of thought, and has at times been beneficent. But I think that the major responsibilities of our time require a clarification of these inconsistencies. I have quoted the hesitation of Professor Pipes of Harvard and have criticized the advisers mentioned by him for their reluctance to acknowledge the fight for truth among Soviet intellectuals. I will now take a look at the principles governing this attitude. I shall use as my source a distinguished textbook entitled *Politics and Social Life: An Introduction to Political Behaviour*, published in 1963.[3] This textbook, composed of seventy contributions by well-known academic scholars, covers 830 large pages, It claims to teach the 'Science of Social Behaviour', both its principles and its application to several subjects. The introduction, by Robert A. Dahl of Yale University, declares that the proper subjects of science are 'events which may be observed with the senses and their extension'. This excludes from science any statements of value. Values admittedly enter into the *lives* of social scientists, but in the pursuit of science the scientist makes only statements of fact that can be observed by our senses. To state, for example, that the Supreme Court of the United States has nine members is to state a fact, while to say that its decisions are impartial is not to state a fact; this kind of statement is to be excluded from the science of political behaviour.

Professor Dahl follows up these principles by an attack on traditional political science. He says—and in this he is right—that this kind of inquiry is concerned with such questions as 'what is a good society?'. He derides such a pursuit by calling it mere 'political theology'.

To see how these scientific principles work in our case, I shall now quote some detailed evidence of the mental transformation among Hungarian Communists and other Soviet intellectuals. Take first the passage written at the beginning of October, 1956 (that is, a few weeks before the outbreak of the revolution) by Miklos Gimes, until lately a firm Stalinist, and quoted at length in the preceding essay:

> Slowly we had come to believe . . . that there are two kinds of truth, that the truth of the Party and the people can be different and can be more important than the objective truth and that truth and political expediency are in fact identical . . . And so we arrived at the outlook . . . which poisoned our whole public life, penetrated the remotest corners of our thinking, obscured our vision, paralysed our critical faculties and finally rendered many of us incapable of simply sensing or apprehending truth. This is how it was, it is no use denying it.[4]

Speaking of faked trials, Gimes must have had foremost in mind the trial and hanging of Laszlo Rajk. The grave of Rajk was visited at about this time by a procession of many thousands, led by Communists. The pilgrimage took place on October 6, the day that traditionally commemorates in Hungary the hanging (at the orders of the Austrian Emperor) of thirteen revolutionary generals in 1849.

Let me add here some extracts from a later (non-Hungarian)

document. It is a long poem by a leading Bulgarian Communist, Dimitar Metodiev, published in the official Party organ of Bulgaria in January 1962.[5] It describes in passionate terms the great change that by this time was universally imposed by the Party. The poem, entitled 'Song of Our Faith', starts with the verse:

> If one had told me yesterday:
> —Friend take off your glasses!—
> I would have laughed
> in a black rage
> at the mortal insult.

and it continues later:

> On the ground now
> The glasses lie smashed
> And I look at them stunned.

*

> Friends!
> the great hour of the twentieth congress
> has struck our earth.
> Oh let its holy justice
> solemnly, inexorably go forth today.

*

Returning once more to Hungary, look at a case in which 'the smashing of the glasses' happened, long before its official enforcement by the Party and even before any public manifestations by the Hungarian intellectuals. It happened to the Hungarian Communist writer Paloczi-Horvath, while imprisoned at the orders of Rakosi, as described in his book *The Undefeated*.[6] Since his arrest in September 1949, Paloczi had suffered incessant cruelties, inflicted on him to make him confess to false charges; yet he had never wavered in his Communist faith. Then suddenly, after two years in prison, in a matter of a few days, he changed his mind and rejected the Party. His sufferings in prison continued unchanged, but from this moment he felt free, even happy—a new person.

Let me now confront the science of political behaviour with these pieces of evidence and see what such a science can make of them. Let us take a generous view of the range included among 'events which may be observed by the senses and their extension'. Thus we may accept it as a scientifically observed fact that two very different ways of seeing political affairs have been current in the Soviet countries: one until Stalin's death in March 1953 and another from about two years later, after the Twentieth Party Congress. A pair of hitherto indubitable spectacles were smashed, and everything looked different from then on. Science can record this fact.

But does it account for *the act of smashing the spectacles?* Does it explain this act, which in Hungary amounted to a revolution? Our science could acknowledge this fundamental change of outlook as a fact—and perhaps even class it as an intellectual achievement—if the change could be regarded as the correction of a hitherto current theory by the discovery of new factual evidence. But this is not what happened. Paloczi-Horvath acknowledges with amazement that all the facts he was seeing in a new light after his defection from Communism had already been known to him as facts before his change of mind. Arthur Koestler has described this phenomenon in looking back on his time as a Communist. 'My party education had equipped my mind (he wrote) with such elaborate shock absorbing buffers and elastic defences that everything seen and heard became automatically transformed to fit a pre-conceived pattern.'[7] Stalinism was a closed system, a system of the kind I have described in *Personal Knowledge* as capable of accommodating any conceivable new piece of evidence. Such a system (one that can interpret in its own terms any possible fact) can be shaken only by preference for a total change of outlook. The Bulgarian Dimitar Metodiev was right in describing it as the smashing of one's spectacles.

Remember that the whole person is involved in trusting a particular comprehensive outlook. Any criticism of it is angrily rejected. To question it is felt to be an attack on an existential assurance protected by the dread of mental disintegration. We have many testimonies by Communists that their minds clung to Marxism–Leninism for fear of being cast into the darkness of a meaningless, purposeless universe. Paloczi-Horvath himself describes how, after his abandonment of the Communist faith, he at first felt lost, incapable of coherent thought. It was only after a few days that he began to experience a new way of making sense,

D

which he felt to be a more honest, decenter way of thinking, bringing him a happiness that transcended his sufferings in prison.

Gimes confirms this emotional value of a comprehensive framework. Looking back on his time as a devoted member of the Party
when he believed that advantage to the revolution was the
criterion of truth and of all other human values, he feels horrified
by the mental corruption caused by this doctrine. The scornful
rejection of objectivity as a bourgeois delusion and fraud, which
he had previously accepted as an intellectual triumph, now appears
to him as an abysmal loss, the loss of the capacity to see any truth
at all.

We have many descriptions also of conversions in the opposite
direction. Thousands of leading intellectuals have joined the
Communist Party because they found in Marxism an interpretation of history and a 'guide to action far superior to the outlook predominant since the French Revolution among progressive circles in the West. In 1917, when President Wilson was
confronted by Lenin on the world scene, these people laughed
Wilson's language to scorn and dedicated themselves instead to
Lenin's doctrine, which they felt to be intellectually and morally
superior.

We may take it, then, as an established fact that during the past
half century radical changes of mind have taken place, which were
motivated each time by passionate affirmations of value. And we
can return again, with these facts before us, to the science of
political behaviour and ask how this science deals with such conversions from one basic conviction to another.

I shall admit once more the widest possible interpretation of
this scientific method, and shall concentrate on the question of
how the method treats the moral motives of men when they
smash their spectacles and put on new spectacles instead.

The behavioural scientist acknowledges that moral values
motivate him in private life. He may meaningfully observe that
moral motives are claimed by people for their actions. Such
reference to alleged values was sanctioned by Rickert in 1902 in
his book *Die Grenzen der Naturwissenschaftlichen Begriffsbildung*.[8]
When he taught here that value judgments are beyond the competence of science, he excluded *Werturteile* from science but
allowed that *Wertbezogenheit* is observable by science. Through
the mediation of Max Weber this doctrine has since been used to

reconcile moral neutralism in science with observing the experience of moral motivation in persons studied by the scientist. According to this theory the scientific method can establish, for example, that the rebellious Hungarian intellectuals attributed moral value to the freedom of truth and felt that the doctrine of Party-truth caused a moral corruption of public life; but it cannot observe whether this moral judgment was right or not, since this observation would constitute a moral judgment which science is not competent to make.

However, this doctrine can be proved to be inconsistent by two complementary arguments, one starting from the existence of the scientist as a moral agent (outside the range, as he alleges, of his scientific activity) and examining the implications of his (extra-scientific) moral judgments for the statements he makes as a scientist; the other moving from his allegedly value-free scientific pronouncements to his (extra-scientific) moral judgments.

The first argument is as follows: (1) All men, whatever their professions, make moral judgments. (2) When we claim that an action of ours is prompted by moral motives, or else when we make moral judgments of others—as in recognizing the impartiality of a court of law—we invariably refer to moral standards *which we hold to be valid.* Our submission to a standard has universal intent. We do not prefer courts of law to be unbiased in the same sense in which we prefer a steak to be rare rather than well-done; our appeal to moral standards necessarily claims to be *right*, that is, binding on all men.[9] (3) Such a claim entails a distinction between *moral truth* and *moral illusion.* (4) This distinction in turn entails a distinction between two types of motivation. The awareness of moral truth is founded on the recognition of a valid claim, which can be reasonably argued for and supported by evidence; moral illusion, in contrast, is compulsive, like a sensory illusion. (5) Thus once we admit, as we do when we acknowledge the existence anywhere of valid moral judgments, that true human values exist and that people can be motivated by their knowledge of them, *we have implicitly denied the claim that all human actions can be explained without any reference to the exercise of moral judgment.* For to observe—in our present case—that the Hungarian writers rebelled against the practice of faked trials because they *believed* this practice to be wrong, leaves open the question *why* they believed this. If true human values exist, the Hungarians may not have been driven by economic necessity, propaganda, or any other compulsion; they may have been rebelling against a *real evil*, and may have done so *because they knew it to be evil*. But this cannot be decided without first establishing whether faked trials are in fact evil or not. Therefore: (6) *This value judgment proves indispensable* to the political scientist's explanation of their behaviour.

The inconsistency of a science professing that it can explain all human action without making value judgments, while the scientist's private actions are said to be often motivated by moral motives, can be more simply demonstrated the other way round. If the social scientist can explain all human actions by value-free observations, then none of his own actions can claim to be motivated by moral values. Either he exempts himself from his own theory of human motivation, or he must conclude that all reference to moral values—or any other values—are meaningless: are empty sounds.

Such a conclusion, though repulsive, would at least appear consistent.[10] But there exists another consistent position that makes better sense, namely the kind of position affirmed by the Hungarian revolutionaries. They expressed their horror of a philosophy which taught that truth, justice, and morality must be subservient to the Party, and demanded that these values be recognized as free powers of the mind. Their moral motives were confirmed by their claim that the standards of truth, justice, and morality must be recognized as independent powers in public affairs. A passion for freedom thus confirms the existence of the freedom it fights for.

This analysis shows that a science that claims to explain all human action without making a value judgment not merely discredits the moral motives of those fighting for freedom, but also discredits their aims. This is why the Hungarian revolutionary movement, which revived the ideals of 1848 and which claimed that truth and justice should be granted power over public affairs, has met with such a cold reception by the science of political behaviour. Modern academic theories of politics give support, on the contrary, to the doctrine which denies that human ideas can be an independent power in public affairs.

It goes without saying that these implications of their science were contrary to the sympathies of the scholars wedded to this science. It is true that Professor Pipes hesitated for three years before he first tried to state the obvious fact that Soviet intellectuals were fighting for truth. But when he was stopped from doing so by his more fastidious colleagues, he did not give up; after another four years he produced a labyrinthine theory which allowed him to state this fact.

Such scholarly prevarications may appear harmless, but they are not, for they obscure great events which dominate our history. No vision of these events can then arise to guide us. We are bogged down in meaningless details. Think of the great figures of the Enlightenment. Think of Condorcet hiding in Paris from the Jacobins and completing before his death his triumphant forecast of universal progress. And then look at the article in the volume on the *Science of Political Behaviour* which deals with 'Soviet Domestic Politics Since the Twentieth Party Congress', an article originally published in 1958.[11] Its author expects to see a growing influence of indoctrination in Russia on the grounds that extreme measures to secure ideological conformity, like those of the Zsdanov period, have been given renewed prominence since mid-1957. This is the kind of hand-to-mouth foresight which the science of social behaviour has produced, for lack of vision of what is actually going on.

\*

Remember now the contemptuous rejection by the science of social behaviour of such questions as 'What is a good society?' Such inquiries, belonging to traditional political science, were derided as 'social theology'. But what the revolution in Hungary —and the whole movement of thought of which it formed a part— declared was a doctrine of political science in the traditional sense of the term. The movement condemned a society in which thought —the thought of science, morality, art, justice, religion—is not recognized as an autonomous power. It rejected life in such a society as corrupt, suffocating and stupid. This was clearly to raise, and to answer up to a point, the question 'What is a good society?' It was to establish a doctrine of political science.

Actually the current transformation of thought in the Soviet countries had added to political science new and remarkable insights. We have seen that this social transformation was achieved by a smashing of spectacles. Its typical utterances, such as those I have quoted, manifest the deep emotional upheaval caused by recognizing once more that truth, justice, and morality have an intrinsic reality; and this is the decisive fact. Paloczi-Horvath remained in prison, but his conversion made him free; and that symbolizes the character of this whole immense political movement. It was not started by demands for institutional reform, and it went on without materially changing the institutional framework of the countries it transformed.

I know how very peculiar was this transformation of the Soviet countries, for I have often been challenged about it during the past years. When I spoke of the radical changes going on in the Soviet countries, I was faced sharply with the objection that these movements had brought no constitutional changes and could therefore be reversed at any moment. But this argument misconceives the foundations of power in this age ruled by rival philosophies. I myself yielded in a way to this error when, at the beginning of this talk, I called Stalin's regime 'insane'. His regime was actually well founded on the strange assumption that neither truth nor justice, nor art, nor human feeling exist except in the service of the Party and subject to its rule. This conviction went so deep, was so fully accepted even by its victims, that when faithful Communists were executed on trumped-up charges, they went to their death shouting 'Long live Stalin!' And this logic works also in reverse: Stalin's regime virtually ceased to exist when its basic conceptions of intellectual and moral reality lost their hold on thought.

But we may yet ask, why trust this change of basic conceptions? Could people not go back to their previous outlook, which supported Stalin for so long? There is indeed nothing to prevent them from doing so, except the fact that their present conception of mental reality is far nearer to the truth, and they feel this and enjoy it. In this sense, and in this sense alone, can we say that what has happened has not been merely a *changing* of spectacles, but a *smashing* of spectacles. And this is a change more radical and more lasting than any constitutional reforms could be.

*

We have seen that the vagaries of philosophy, which have hardly ever been followed literally among men before, often control our fate today. The Soviet people have gone through a philosophical experiment which revealed to them the nature of mental reality in a way not recognized in our universities. They are turning away from the site of their calamities and seek support in the West. This we fail to give them. Our scientific methods search for truth by turning a blind eye on the values which the rebellious Communists have recognized, and our traditional schools of political science fail to take the chance that history has given them to vindicate these values. They are disabled by the anti-metaphysical pressure surrounding them.

Meanwhile, in the Soviet countries, the ideas of mental independence are not only renewing the grounds of thought, but are daily revealing new sights previously blocked by official fictions. Hungarian newspapers have published complaints by Party members that scant respect is paid to them. They say that the government itself prefers non-Party members. We can understand what is happening here. Those who still hotly profess the Marxist interpretation of history, who proclaim the surpassing achievements of revolutionary socialism and predict the proximate coming of Communism—these people are increasingly looked upon as ignorant fools. The young are immune against their teachings. The Old Believers' authority is drained away by the superior intelligence surrounding them. Everywhere outside China this change is clearly in progress.

The change is bound to be accelerated by the gradual acceptance, since 1963, of Liberman's critique of detailed planning as inferior to market operations controlled by profit. It is becoming clear that there is in fact no viable socialist alternative to the market. Thus the Russian Revolution, which had conquered power in order to achieve a radically distinct form of economic organization, one that would be far more productive and also morally superior to commercial management, has now demonstrated the fact that there is no such possibility. By the time its fiftieth anniversary is celebrated, the Revolution may be widely recognized by its very successors as having been virtually pointless. It may live on henceforth in its emblems, as the Mexican Revolution has lived on, without making much difference in substance.

*

On the fortieth anniversary of the Russian Revolution, close on nine years ago, I published an article in *Encounter* under the title 'The Foolishness of History'. I complained that our scientific approach to history debars us from envisaging the part of folly in shaping history. I wrote that:

> ... volume upon volume of excellent scholarship is rapidly accumulating on the history of the Russian Revolution, but as I read these books I find my own recollection of the event dissolving bit by bit ... The Revolution is about to be quietly enshrined under a pyramid of monographs.
>
> Yet I know that it was something quite different. Not only when it actually happened; but all along, up to this day—for it still lives in our own blood. It was boundless; it was infinitely potent; it was an act of madness. A great number of men—led by one man possessing genius—set themselves limitless aims that had no bearing at all on reality. They detested everything in existence and were convinced therefore that the total destruction of existing society and the establishment of their own absolute power on its ruins would bring total happiness to humanity. That was—unbelievable as it may seem —*literally* the whole substance of their projects for a new economic, political, and social system of mankind.[12]

I think that this is now dawning on the minds of people all over the planet. The realization of the fact that we have wasted half a century of European history and in the process well-nigh destroyed our civilization may lead to terrible thoughts beyond my horizon. On the other hand, the final dissolution of the bogus salvation promised by our revolutions may exorcise at last the bogey of its hellish powers. Once the disasters of the past fifty years are clearly seen to have been pointless, Europeans may turn once more to cultivate their own garden. Such a new flowering of Europe may yet save this planet from the familiar mortal danger threatening us all today and for future times to come.

---

[1] R. PIPES, 'Russia's Intellectuals', *Encounter*, 22 (1964), pp. 79–84.

[2] *Ibid.*

[3] N. W. POLSBY, R. A. DENTLER, P. S. SMITH (Eds.), *Politics and Social Life*, Boston: Houghton Mifflin, 1963.

[4] M. GIMES, in a Budapest periodical, October 3, 1956. See p. 29 above.

[5] D. METODIEV, 'Song of Our Faith', *East Europe*, *11* (1962), pp. 8–11.

[6] G. PALOCZI-HORVATH, *The Undefeated*, Boston: Little, Brown, 1959.

[7] A. KOESTLER, *The God That Failed*, London: Hamilton, 1950, p. 68.

[8] H. RICKERT, *Die Grenzen der Naturwissenschaftlichen Begriffsbildung*, Tübingen: Mohr, 1902.

[9] This claim is not impaired by the fact that the application of true values may be subject to exceptions. Arsenic is rightly known as a poison, and aspirin, as a harmless drug, though some people are immune to arsenic and every year a few people die from taking a tablet of aspirin.

And let me note that, contrary to Kant, the universality of moral standards applies only to the judgments of men and not to their behaviour, for men's situations are often incommensurable.

[10] Once it is acknowledged, however, that *any* claim to truth entails a recognition of standards, even the scientist's 'value-free' statements of fact are seen to be unable to claim their own truth in the light of his own theory. For the purpose of the present argument, however, it is not necessary to follow through the epistemological implications of the doctrine to this ultimate self-contradiction.

[11] See note 3 above.

[12] M. POLANYI, 'The Foolishness of History', *Encounter*, 9 (1957), no. 5, pp. 33–37

# 3
# The Two Cultures
# 1959

Sir Charles Snow complains about the gap between science and the rest of our culture. I concur. But I see the problem in a different perspective. I don't agree that the influence of science on the rest of our thoughts is too feeble. On the contrary, the claims made today on the minds of men in the name of science are comprehensive. Freud and Marx—little of modern culture is unaffected by the teachings of one or both of these two, and both derived their authority by speaking for science. Yet these teachings are but two streams of a wider flow descending from the Romantics and Utilitarians, themselves originating from the philosophers of the Enlightenment who were inspired by Newton's discoveries.

Admittedly, Greek thought was rationalist before the rise of science, and a trickle of this rationalism has continued to flow through all the succeeding centuries. But it was the impact of seventeenth-century science that evoked modern rationalism and endowed it with overwhelming powers. 'One day', writes Paul Hazard, 'the French people, almost to a man, were thinking like Bossuet. The day after, they were thinking like Voltaire.' [1]

This is exaggerated, but the picture is dramatically true. We might add that just as the three centuries following on the calling of the apostles sufficed to establish Christianity as the state religion of the Roman Empire, so the three centuries after the founding of the Royal Society sufficed for science to establish itself as the supreme intellectual authority of the post-Christian age. 'It is contrary to religion!'—the objection ruled supreme in the seventeenth century. 'It is unscientific!' is its equivalent in the twentieth.

If I yet agree that there is a gap, and a dangerous gap, between science and the rest of our culture, it is not such deficiencies as the ignorance of thermodynamics shown by literary people, mentioned by Charles Snow, that I have in mind. Even mature scientists know little more than the names of most branches of science. This is inherent in the division of labour on which the progress of modern science is based, and which is likewise indispensable to the advancement of all our modern culture. The amplitude of our cultural heritage exceeds ten thousand times the carrying capacity of any human brain, and hence we must have ten thousand specialists to transmit it. To do away with the specialization of knowledge would be to produce a race of quiz winners and destroy our culture in favour of a universal dilettantism.

Our task is not to suppress the specialization of knowledge but to achieve harmony and truth over the whole range of knowledge. This is where I see the trouble, where a deep-seated disturbance between science and all other culture appears to lie. I believe that this disturbance was inherent originally in the liberating impact of modern science on medieval thought and has only later turned pathological.

Science rebelled against authority. It rejected deduction from first causes in favour of empirical generalizations. Its ultimate ideal was a mechanistic theory of the universe, though in respect of man it aimed only at a naturalistic explanation of his moral and social responsibilities.

Set free by these principles, scientific genius has extended man's intellectual control over nature far beyond previous horizons. And by secularizing man's moral passions, scientific rationalism has evoked a movement of reform which has improved almost every human relationship, both private and public. The rationalist ideals of welfare and of an educated and responsible citizenry have created an active mutual concern among millions of submerged and isolated individuals. In short, scientific rationalism has been the chief guide towards all the intellectual, moral, and social progress on which the nineteenth century prided itself—and to the great progress achieved since then as well.

Yet it would be easy to show that the principles of scientific rationalism are strictly speaking nonsensical. No human mind can function without accepting authority, custom, and tradition: it must rely on them for the mere use of a language. Empirical induction, strictly applied, can yield no knowledge at all, and the mechanistic explanation of the universe is a meaningless ideal. Not because of the much invoked Principle of Indeterminacy, which is irrelevant, but because the prediction of all atomic positions in the universe would not answer any question of interest to anybody. And as to the naturalistic explanation of morality, it must ignore, and so by implication deny, the very existence of human responsibility. It too is absurd.

Scientific rationalism did serve man well as long as it was moving towards its false ideals from a great distance. But this could not last. Eventually the truth-bearing power of its absurd ideals was bound to be spent and its stark absurdity to assert itself.

This is what has happened in the twentieth century. Scientific obscurantism has pervaded our culture and now distorts even science itself by imposing on it false ideals of exactitude. Whenever they speak of organs and their functions in the organism, biologists are haunted by the ghost of 'teleology'. They try to exorcise such conceptions by affirming that eventually all of them will be reduced to physics and chemistry. The fact that such a suggestion is meaningless does not worry them. Neurologists follow suit by asserting that all mental processes too will be explained by physics and chemistry. The difficulty of dealing with consciousness is eliminated by declaring:

> 'The existence of something called consciousness is a venerable *hypothesis*: not a datum, not directly observable. . . .' (Hebb). 'Although we cannot get along without the concept of consciousness actually there is no such thing' (Kubie). 'The knower as an entity is an unnecessary postulate' (Lashley).[2]

The manifest absurdity of such a position is accepted by these distinguished men as the burden of their scientific calling. Neurologists, like all the rest of us, know the difference between consciousness and unconsciousness; when they deny it, they mean that, since it eludes explanation in terms of science, its existence endangers science and must be denied in the interest of science. Indeed, any neurologist who would seriously challenge this bigotry would be regarded as a nuisance to science.

The shadow of these absurdities lies deep on the current theory of evolution by natural selection. The selectionist must assume, and does in fact usually assume, that consciousness is *useful* since otherwise it would have been suppressed by natural selection; but since all bodily processes must be explained by physics and chemistry, he cannot admit that consciousness can set a living body in motion, which means that he assumes it to be *strictly ineffectual*.[3] I have searched the literature for a reply to this decisive self-contradiction, but in vain. Scientists do not enlarge on such questions if they want to be taken seriously as scientists.

Examples of such double-talk and double-think could be multiplied from the whole range of biological sciences. But I do not think that this denial of the true nature of things for the sake of scientific standards has yet caused widespread harm to science itself; it mostly remains on paper. In any case, I am primarily concerned in this note with the effect of current scientific principles on our culture at large, where the disregard of truth in favour of hard-boiled scientific ideals has spread confusion and led eventually to sinister results.

This process has run its course along a variety of lines. Take, once more, Freud and Marx. Their thoughts have transformed the heritage of the eighteenth century in parallel ways. The Enlightenment believed that man's moral responsibility would be safely grounded in nature. Rousseau trusted natural man uncorrupted by society; he established the intrinsic rights of great passions, of creative spontaneity and unique individuality. A drier, more mechanistic version of naturalism was developed by Helvetius and Bentham; it reduced man to a bundle of appetites feeding themselves according to a mathematical formula.

Like Rousseau's noble savagery, Freud's libido is restrained by society. But no noble features are ascribed to it; on the contrary, morality is imposed on the libido externally, and this restraint is actually condemned because it produces sickness. Good and evil are replaced by health and sickness.

The parallel movement from Bentham to Marx is determined by the denial of common interests between different social classes. Rightness is no longer achieved then by the triumph of utility over prejudice, but by the triumph of one class over another; good is what contributes to the victory of the proletariat, and evil is the contrary. Naturalism is thus transformed from a moral command into a doctrine of moral scepticism.

Yet it is not this scepticism by itself that is distinctive of the modern mind. For moral scepticism, and the ensuing hedonism, libertinism, Machiavellism, etc., have been current before now, and are only about as effective today as they were in former times. The decisive step in forming the modern mind takes place at the next move *when moral scepticism is combined with moral indignation.* It is the fusion of these two—logically incompatible—attitudes that produces modern nihilism.*

To the typical modern revolutionary the degree of evil he is prepared to commit or condone in the name of humanity is the measure of his moral force. He gives effect to his *immanent* morality by his *manifest* immorality. But such moral inversion is never absolute; at some point men will recoil from the demands of inversion and seek to re-establish truth and human ideals in their own right. This is when we hear of the god that failed.

Yet those who recoil from an inverted to a straight morality will still feel that their inversion had been a sign of a more intense passion for social justice. And in a sense they are right. Unfeeling people have remained immune to moral inversion simply because they had little social zeal seeking active manifestation.

In our age it is impossible therefore to speak simply of men as noble or ignoble. When Snow writes that 'jam tomorrow' often brings out the noblest in man, one must ask which morality he means, the 'immanent' or the 'manifest'. Acts that are glorious by one of these standards are utterly repulsive by the other.

This conflict of standards has divided human masses, split up families, and ruined friendships throughout the world, as no conflict has done before. 'If ever in history there was a time,' writes Tillich, 'when human objectives supported by an infinite amount of good-will heaped catastrophe upon catastrophe upon mankind, it was the twentieth century.' [4] And yet greater disaster menaces us from the continuing disarray of moral standards. For in spite of recent improvement, there is still hardly enough common ground between the great revolutionary powers, on the one hand, and the traditional powers, on the other, to secure the survival of man armed with atom bombs.

True, the consummation of scientific rationalism which has corrupted the public life of our century has opened up wide avenues of discovery to the arts. The line of modern writing descending from Dostoievsky undertook to explore the limits of nihilism, in search of an authentic residue of moral reality. While this quest has sometimes led to meaningless despair, the movement has, as a whole, hardened the moral tone of our century and cleared the ground for re-laying the foundations of morality.

* Editor's note: see Essay One for development of this thesis.

A parallel inquiry has explored the chaos created by the rejection of all existing forms. This too has sometimes led to inanities (like dada-ism), but the broad movement has been rich in discoveries. It has produced a world of harmonies responding to unsuspected sensibilities. It is enough to recall the magic domain of surrealism to which a deliberate absurdity of narrative content opened the way.

This movement was in fact but the culmination of an earlier, less radical, emancipation. Starting with the Impressionism of the 1860s, the past century has achieved the feat of pulling itself up out of a universal descent into realism and sentimentalism, towards the vigour of a new primitive culture. Such rejuvenation has, I believe, never before been achieved without the previous intermission of a long Dark Age.

Recently, a profound change has taken place in the temper of the European and American mind. Since about 1950 a general decline of social zeal has set in. In the West this change of mood has reduced utopian aspirations to more concrete projects of betterment, while throughout Russia and its follower States it has caused a recoil from the most monstrous forms of moral inversion. In Poland the reversion of the Communist intellectuals went much further than this, and in the abortive Hungarian revolution it would have gone all the way. In these two countries morally inverted man turned himself violently right way up. No such movement has ever taken place in previous history.

The corresponding intellectual movement, condemned as 'revisionism' by the Soviet Government, has its counterpart in the West in a tendency to reinterpret the masters who had impelled the exploration of nihilism in a purely idealistic sense. Thus, in his widely read book, *The Sane Society*, Erich Fromm is led by a discussion of Freud and Marx to conclude that the mentally healthy person is the person who lives by love, reason, and faith, who respects life, his own and that of his fellow man—a condition which is said to produce a Humanistic Communitarian Socialism.[5]

But, though yet without a clear doctrine, the revisionism of the West is as strong as that of the Soviet empire and pursues parallel lines. Just as rebellious Communists reverted to popular nationalism, so did also the French people in moving towards de Gaulle; and everywhere, the recoil from a nihilistic rationalism was supported by religion—even while humanitarian rationalists of the eighteenth-century type supported this recoil in their own quite different way.

This, I believe, is the context in which the relation of science to the rest of our culture has to be reconsidered today. Science remains the only uncontested intellectual authority, and yet it can as little sanction the claims of nationalism, religion, or natural ethics as ever it could before. In fact, its criteria of objectivity must deny reality to any moral claims. No chemical analysis or microscopic examination can prove that a man who bears false witness is immoral. Nor can the logic of scientific rationalism, which has once already worked itself out among us to its last sinister conclusions, be suspended again by the inertia of custom. We cannot recover a previous state of innocence.

No, a humanistic revisionism can be secured only by revising the claims of science itself. The first task must be to emancipate the biological sciences, including psychology, from the scourge of physicalism; the absurdities now imposed on the sciences of life must be eliminated. The task is difficult, for it calls in question an ideal of impersonal objectivity on which alone we feel it safe to rely. Yet this absurd ideal must be discarded. And if once we succeed in this, we shall find that science no longer threatens man's responsible existence and that we can re-start the great work of the Enlightenment without danger of the traps that have so disastrously ensnared its progress in the present century.

[1] PAUL HAZARD, *The European Mind, 1680–1715*, trs. J. L. May, London: Hollis & Carter, 1953, p. xv.
[2] These quotations are taken from the review by SIR RUSSELL BRAIN [*Brain, 78* (1955), pp. 669–70] of *Brain Mechanism and Consciousness: A Symposium*, J. F. DELAFRESNAYE (ed.), Oxford: Blackwell Scientific Publications, 1954. The views expressed by the famous three neurologists are not criticized by Sir Russell in this review.
[3] When I urged a meeting of the American Association of the Advancement of Science (held in New York at Christmas, 1956) to recognize the absurdity of regarding human beings as insentient automata, the distinguished neurologist, R. W. Gerard, answered me passionately: 'One thing we know, ideas don't move muscles!' I could not believe my ears.
[4] PAUL TILLICH, 'The Dilemma of Our Period', *i.e. The Cambridge Review*, no. 4, September, 1955.
[5] ERICH FROMM, *The Sane Society*, New York: Rinehart and Toronto: Clarke, Irwin and Co., 1955, p. 275.

# PART TWO

# The Nature of Science

# 4
# The Republic of Science:
# Its Political and
# Economic Theory
## 1962

My title is intended to suggest that the community of scientists is organized in a way which resembles certain features of a body politic and works according to economic principles similar to those by which the production of material goods is regulated. Much of what I will have to say will be common knowledge among scientists, but I believe that it will recast the subject from a novel point of view which can both profit from and have a lesson for political and economic theory. For in the free co-operation of independent scientists we shall find a highly simplified model of a free society, which presents in isolation certain basic features of it that are more difficult to identify within the comprehensive functions of a national body.

The first thing to make clear is that scientists, freely making their own choice of problems and pursuing them in the light of their own personal judgment, are in fact co-operating as members of a closely knit organization. The point can be settled by considering the opposite case where individuals are engaged in a joint task without being in any way co-ordinated. A group of women shelling peas work at the same task, but their individual efforts are not co-ordinated. The same is true of a team of chess players. This is shown by the fact that the total amount of peas shelled and the total number of games won will not be affected if the members of the group are isolated from each other. Consider by contrast the effect which a complete isolation of scientists would have on the progress of science. Each scientist would go on for a while developing problems derived from the information initially available to all. But these problems would soon be exhausted, and in the absence of further information about the results achieved by others, new problems of any value would cease to arise, and scientific progress would come to a standstill.

This shows that the activities of scientists are in fact co-ordinated, and it also reveals the principle of their co-ordination. This consists in the adjustment of the efforts of each to the hitherto achieved results of the others. We may call this a co-ordination by mutual adjustment of independent initiatives—of initiatives which are co-ordinated because each takes into account all the other initiatives operating within the same system.

*

When put in these abstract terms the principle of spontaneous co-ordination of independent initiatives may sound obscure. So let me illustrate it by a simple example. Imagine that we are given the pieces of a very large jigsaw puzzle, and suppose that for some reason it is important that our giant puzzle be put together in the shortest possible time. We would naturally try to speed this up by engaging a number of helpers; the question is in what manner these could be best employed. Suppose we share out the pieces of the jigsaw puzzle equally among the helpers and let each of them work on his lot separately. It is easy to see that this method, which would be quite appropriate to a number of women shelling peas, would be totally ineffectual in this case, since few of the pieces allocated to one particular assistant would be found to fit to-gether. We could do a little better by providing duplicates of all the pieces to each helper separately, and eventually somehow bring together their several results. But even by this method the team would not much surpass the performance of a single individual at his best. The only way the assistants can effectively co-operate, and surpass by far what any single one of them could do, is to let them work on putting the puzzle together in sight of the others, so that every time a piece of it is fitted in by one helper, all the others will immediately watch out for the next step that becomes possible in consequence. Under this system, each helper will act on his own initiative, by responding to the latest achievements of the others, and the completion of their joint task will be greatly accelerated. We have here in a nutshell the way in which a series of independent initiatives are organized to a joint achievement by mutually adjusting themselves at every successive stage to the situation created by all the others who are acting likewise.

Such self-co-ordination of independent initiatives leads to a joint result which is unpremeditated by any of those who bring it about. Their co-ordination is guided as by 'an invisible hand' towards the joint discovery of a hidden system of things. Since its end-result is unknown, this kind of co-operation can only advance stepwise, and the total performance will be the best possible if each consecutive step is decided upon by the person most competent to do so. We may imagine this condition to be fulfilled for the fitting together of a jigsaw puzzle if each helper watches out for any new opportunities arising along a particular section of the hitherto completed patch of the puzzle, and also keeps an eye on a particular lot of pieces, so as to fit them in wherever a chance presents itself. The effectiveness of a group of helpers will then exceed that of any isolated member, to the extent to which some member of the group will always discover a new chance for adding a piece to the puzzle more quickly than any one isolated person could have done by himself.

Any attempt to organize the group of helpers under a single authority would eliminate their independent initiatives and thus reduce their joint effectiveness to that of the single person directing them from the centre. It would, in effect, paralyse their co-operation.

Essentially the same is true for the advancement of science by independent initiatives adjusting themselves consecutively to the results achieved by all the others. So long as each scientist keeps making the best contribution of which he is capable, and on which no one could improve (except by abandoning the problem of his own choice and thus causing an overall loss to the advancement of science), we may affirm that the pursuit of science by independent self-co-ordinated initiatives assures the most efficient possible organization of scientific progress. And we may add, again, that any authority which would undertake to direct the work of the scientist centrally would bring the progress of science virtually to a standstill.

\*

What I have said here about the highest possible co-ordination of individual scientific efforts by a process of self-co-ordination may recall the self-co-ordination achieved by producers and consumers operating in a market. It was, indeed, with this in mind that I spoke of 'the invisible hand' guiding the co-ordination of independent initiatives to a maximum advancement of science, just as Adam Smith invoked 'the invisible hand' to describe the achievement of greatest joint material satisfaction when independent producers and consumers are guided by the prices of goods in a market. I am suggesting, in fact, that the co-ordinating functions of the market are but a special case of co-ordination by mutual adjustment. In the case of science, adjustment takes place by taking note of the published results of other scientists; while in the case of the market, mutual adjustment is mediated by a system of prices broadcasting current exchange relations, which make supply meet demand.

But the system of prices ruling the market not only transmits information in the light of which economic agents can mutually adjust their actions, it also provides them with an incentive to exercise economy in terms of money. We shall see that, by contrast, the scientist responding directly to the intellectual situation created by the published results of other scientists is motivated by current professional standards.

Yet in a wider sense of the term, the decisions of a scientist choosing a problem and pursuing it to the exclusion of other possible avenues of inquiry may be said to have an economic character. For his decisions are designed to produce the highest possible result by the use of a limited stock of intellectual and material resources. The scientist fulfils this purpose by choosing a problem that is neither too hard nor too easy for him. For to apply himself to a problem that does not tax his faculties to the full is to waste some of his faculties; while to attack a problem that is too hard for him would waste his faculties altogether. The psychologist K. Lewin has observed that one's person never becomes fully involved either in a problem that is much too hard, nor in one that is much too easy. The line the scientist must choose turns out, therefore, to be that of greatest ego-involvement; it is the line of greatest excitement, sustaining the most intense attention and effort of thought. The choice will be conditioned to some extent by the resources available to the scientist in terms of materials and assistants, but he will be ill-advised to choose his problem with a view to guaranteeing that none of these resources be wasted. He should not hesitate to incur such a loss, if it leads him to deeper and more important problems.

*

This is where professional standards enter into the scientist's motivation. He assesses the depth of a problem and the importance of its prospective solution primarily by the standards of scientific merit accepted by the scientific community—though his own work may demand these standards to be modified. Scientific merit depends on a number of criteria which I shall enumerate here under three headings. These criteria are not altogether independent of each other, but I cannot analyse here their mutual relationship.

(1) The first criterion that a contribution to science must fulfil in order to be accepted is a sufficient degree of plausibility. Scientific publications are continuously beset by cranks, frauds and bunglers whose contributions must be rejected if journals are not to be swamped by them. This censorship will not only eliminate obvious absurdities but must often refuse publication merely because the conclusions of a paper appear to be unsound in the light of current scientific knowledge. It is indeed difficult even to start an experimental inquiry if its problem is considered scientifically unsound. Few laboratories would accept today a student of extrasensory perception, and even a project for testing once more the hereditary transmission of acquired characters would be severely discouraged from the start. Besides, even when all these obstacles have been overcome, and a paper has come out signed by an author of high distinction in science, it may be totally disregarded, simply for the reason that its results conflict sharply with the current scientific opinion about the nature of things.

I shall illustrate this by an example which I have used elsewhere.[1] A series of simple experiments were published in June 1947 in the *Proceedings of the Royal Society* by Lord Rayleigh—a distinguished Fellow of the Society—purporting to show that hydrogen atoms striking a metal wire transmit to it energies up to a hundred electron volts. This, if true, would have been far more revolutionary than the discovery of atomic fission by Otto Hahn. Yet, when I asked physicists what they thought about it, they only shrugged their shoulders. They could not find fault with the experiment yet not one believed in its results, nor thought it

worth while to repeat it. They just ignored it. A possible explanation of Lord Rayleigh's experiments is given in my *Personal
Knowledge*.[2] It appears that the physicists missed nothing by disregarding these findings.

(2) The second criterion by which the merit of a contribution is
assessed may be described as its scientific value, a value that is
composed of the following three coefficients: (a) its accuracy,
(b) its systematic importance, (c) the intrinsic interest of its subject-matter. You can see these three gradings entering jointly into
the value of a paper in physics compared with one in biology. The
inanimate things studied by physics are much less interesting than
the living beings which are the subject of biology. But physics
makes up by its great accuracy and wide theoretical scope for the
dullness of its subject, while biology compensates for its lack of
accuracy and theoretical beauty by its exciting matter.

(3) A contribution of sufficient plausibility and of a given
scientific value may yet vary in respect of its originality; this is the
third criterion of scientific merit. The originality of technical
inventions is assessed, for the purpose of claiming a patent, in
terms of the degree of surprise which the invention would cause
among those familiar with the art. Similarly, the originality of a
discovery is assessed by the degree of surprise which its communication should arouse among scientists. The unexpectedness of a
discovery will overlap with its systematic importance, yet the surprise caused by a discovery, which causes us to admire its daring
and ingenuity, is something different from this. It pertains to the
act of producing the discovery. There are discoveries of the
highest daring and ingenuity, as for example the discovery of
Neptune, which have no great systematic importance.

*

Both the criteria of plausibility and of scientific value tend to enforce conformity, while the value attached to originality en-
courages dissent. This internal tension is essential in guiding and
motivating scientific work. The professional standards of science
must impose a framework of discipline and at the same time encourage rebellion against it. They must demand that, in order to
be taken seriously, an investigation should largely conform to the
currently predominant beliefs about the nature of things, while
allowing that in order to be original it may to some extent go

against these. Thus, the authority of scientific opinion enforces the teachings of science in general, for the very purpose of fostering their subversion in particular points.

This dual function of professional standards in science is but the logical outcome of the belief that scientific truth is an aspect of reality and that the orthodoxy of science is taught as a guide that should enable the novice eventually to make his own contacts with this reality. The authority of scientific standards is thus exercised for the very purpose of providing those guided by it with independent grounds for opposing it. The capacity to renew itself by evoking and assimilating opposition to itself appears to be logically inherent in the sources of the authority wielded by scientific orthodoxy.

But who is it, exactly, who exercises the authority of this orthodoxy? I have mentioned scientific opinion as its agent. But this raises a serious problem. No single scientist has a sound understanding of more than a tiny fraction of the total domain of science. How can an aggregate of such specialists possibly form a joint opinion? How can they possibly exercise jointly the delicate function of imposing a current scientific view about the nature of things, and the current scientific valuation of proposed contributions, even while encouraging an originality which would modify this orthodoxy? In seeking the answer to this question we shall discover yet another organizational principle that is essential for the control of a multitude of independent scientific initiatives. This principle is based on the fact that, while scientists can admittedly exercise competent judgment only over a small part of science, they can usually judge an area adjoining their own special studies that is broad enough to include some fields on which other scientists have specialized. We thus have a considerable degree of overlapping between the areas over which a scientist can exercise a sound critical judgment. And, of course, each scientist who is a member of a group of overlapping competences will also be a member of other groups of the same kind, so that the whole of science will be covered by chains and networks of overlapping neighbourhoods. Each link in these chains and networks will establish agreement between the valuations made by scientists overlooking the same overlapping fields, and so, from one overlapping neighbourhood to the other, agreement will be established on the valuation of scientific merit throughout all the domains of science. Indeed, through these overlapping neighbourhoods uniform standards of scientific merit will prevail over the entire range of science, all the way from astronomy to medicine. This network is the seat of scientific opinion. Scientific opinion is an opinion not held by any single human mind, but one which, split into thousands of fragments, is held by a multitude of individuals, each of whom endorses the others' opinion at second hand, by relying on the consensual chains which link him to all the others through a sequence of overlapping neighbourhoods.

*

Admittedly, scientific authority is not distributed evenly throughout the body of scientists; some distinguished members of the profession predominate over others of a more junior standing. But the authority of scientific opinion remains essentially mutual; it is established *between* scientists, not above them. Scientists exercise their authority over each other. Admittedly, the body of scientists, as a whole, does uphold the authority of science over the lay public. It controls thereby also the process by which young men are trained to become members of the scientific profession. But once the novice has reached the grade of an independent scientist, there is no longer any superior above him. His submission to scientific opinion is entailed now in his joining a chain of mutual appreciations, within which he is called upon to bear his equal share of responsibility for the authority to which he submits.

Let me make it clear, even without going into detail, how great and varied are the powers exercised by this authority. Appointments to positions in universities and elsewhere, which offer opportunity for independent research, are filled in accordance with the appreciation of candidates by scientific opinion. Referees reporting on papers submitted to journals are charged with keeping out contributions which current scientific opinion condemns as unsound, and scientific opinion is in control, once more, over the issue of textbooks, as it can make or mar their influence through reviews in scientific journals. Representatives of scientific opinion will pounce upon newspaper articles or other popular literature which would venture to spread views contrary to scientific opinion. The teaching of science in schools is controlled likewise. And, indeed, the whole outlook of man on the universe is conditioned by an implicit recognition of the authority of scientific opinion.

I have mentioned earlier that the uniformity of scientific standards throughout science makes possible the comparison between the value of discoveries in fields as different as astronomy and medicine. This possibility is of great value for the rational distribution of efforts and material resources throughout the various branches of science. If the minimum merit by which a contribution would be qualified for acceptance by journals were much lower in one branch of science than in another, this would clearly cause too much effort to be spent on the former branch as compared with the latter. Such is in fact the principle which underlies the rational distribution of grants for the pursuit of research. Subsidies should be curtailed in areas where their yields in terms of scientific merit tend to be low, and should be channelled instead to the growing points of science, where increased financial means may be expected to produce a work of higher scientific value. It does not matter for this purpose whether the money comes from a public authority or from private sources, nor whether it is disbursed by a few sources or a large number of benefactors. So long as each allocation follows the guidance of scientific opinion, by giving preference to the most promising scientists and subjects, the distribution of grants will automatically yield the maximum advantage for the advancement of science as a whole. It will do so, at any rate, to the extent to which scientific opinion offers the best possible appreciation of scientific merit and of the prospects for the further development of scientific talent.

For scientific opinion may, of course, sometimes be mistaken, and as a result unorthodox work of high originality and merit may be discouraged or altogether suppressed for a time. But these risks have to be taken. Only the discipline imposed by an effective scientific opinion can prevent the adulteration of science by cranks and dabblers. In parts of the world where no sound and authoritative scientific opinion is established, research stagnates for lack of stimulus, while unsound reputations grow up based on commonplace achievements or mere empty boasts. Politics and business play havoc with appointments and the granting of subsidies for research; journals are made unreadable by including much trash.

Moreover, only a strong and united scientific opinion imposing the intrinsic value of scientific progress on society at large can elicit the support of scientific inquiry by the general public. Only by securing popular respect for its own authority can scientific opinion safeguard the complete independence of mature scientists and the unhindered publicity of their results, which jointly assure the spontaneous co-ordination of scientific efforts throughout the world. These are the principles of organization under which the unprecedented advancement of science has been achieved in the twentieth century. Though it is easy to find flaws in their operation, they yet remain the only principles by which this vast domain of collective creativity can be effectively promoted and co-ordinated.

*

During the last twenty to thirty years, there have been many suggestions and pressures towards guiding the progress of scientific inquiry in the direction of public welfare. I shall speak mainly of those I have witnessed in England. In August 1938, the British Association for the Advancement of Science founded a new division for the social and international relations of science, which was largely motivated by the desire to offer deliberate social guidance to the progress of science. This programme was given more extreme expression by the Association of Scientific Workers in Britain. In January 1943, the Association filled a large hall in London with a meeting attended by many of the most distinguished scientists of the country, and it decided—in the words officially summing up the conference—that research would no longer be conducted for itself as an end in itself. Reports from Soviet Russia describing the successful conduct of scientific research according to plans laid down by the Academy of Science with a view to supporting the economic Five-Year Plans encouraged this resolution.

I appreciate the generous sentiments which actuate the aspiration of guiding the progress of science into socially beneficent channels, but I hold its aim to be impossible and indeed nonsensical.

An example will show what I mean by this impossibility. In January 1945, Lord Russell and I were together on the BBC Brains Trust. We were asked about the possible technical uses of Einstein's theory of relativity, and neither of us could think of any. This was forty years after the publication of the theory and fifty years after the inception by Einstein of the work which led to its discovery. It was fifty-eight years after the Michelson–Morley experiment. But, actually, the technical application of relativity, which neither Russell nor I could think of, was to be revealed within a few months by the explosion of the first atomic bomb. For the energy of the explosion was released at the expense of mass in accordance with the relativistic equation $e = mc^2$, an equation which was soon to be found splashed over the cover of *Time* magazine, as a token of its supreme practical importance.

Perhaps Russell and I should have done better in foreseeing these applications of relativity in January 1945, but it is obvious that Einstein could not possibly take these future consequences into account when he started on the problem which led to the discovery of relativity at the turn of the century. For one thing, another dozen or more major discoveries had yet to be made before relativity could be combined with them to yield the technical process which opened the atomic age.

Any attempt at guiding scientific research towards a purpose other than its own is an attempt to deflect it from the advancement of science. Emergencies may arise in which all scientists willingly apply their gifts to tasks of public interest. It is conceivable that we may come to abhor the progress of science and stop all scientific research, or at least whole branches of it, as the Soviets stopped research in genetics for twenty-five years. You can kill or mutilate the advance of science, you cannot shape it. For it can advance only by essentially unpredictable steps, pursuing problems of its own, and the practical benefits of these advances will be incidental and hence doubly unpredictable.

In saying this, I have *not* forgotten, but merely set aside, the vast amount of scientific work currently conducted in industrial and governmental laboratories.[3] In describing here the autonomous growth of science, I have taken the relation of science to technology fully into account.

\*

But even those who accept the autonomy of scientific progress may feel irked by allowing such an important process to go on without trying to control the co-ordination of its fragmentary initiatives. The period of high aspirations following the last war produced an event to illustrate the impracticability of this more limited task.

The incident originated in the University Grants Committee, which sent a memorandum to the Royal Society in the summer of 1945. The document, signed by Sir Charles Darwin, requested the aid of the Royal Society to secure 'The Balanced Development of Science in the United Kingdom'; this was its title.

The proposal excluded undergraduate studies and aimed at the higher subjects that are taught through the pursuit of research. Its main concern was with the lack of co-ordination between universities in taking up 'rare' subjects, 'which call for expert study at only a few places, or in some cases perhaps only one'. This was linked with the apprehension that appointments are filled according to the dictates of fashion, as a result of which some subjects of greater importance are being pursued with less vigour than others of lesser importance. It proposed that a co-ordinating machinery should be set up for levelling out these gaps and re-dundancies. The Royal Society was asked to compile, through its Sectional Committees covering the main divisions of science, lists of subjects deserving preference in order to fill gaps. Such surveys were to be renewed in the future to guide the University Grants Committee in maintaining balanced proportions of scientific effort throughout all fields of inquiry.

Sir Charles Darwin's proposal was circulated by the Secretaries of the Royal Society and the members of the Sectional Committees along with a report of previous discussions of proposals by the Council and other groups of Fellows. The report acknowledged that the co-ordination of the pursuit of higher studies in the universities was defective ('haphazard') and endorsed the project for periodic, most likely annual, surveys of gaps and redundancies by the Royal Society. The members of the Sectional Committees were asked to prepare, for consideration by a forthcoming meeting of the Council, lists of subjects suffering from neglect.

Faced with this request, which I considered at the best pointless, I wrote to the Physical Secretary (the late Sir Alfred Egerton) to express my doubts. I argued that the present practice of filling vacant chairs by the most eminent candidate that the university can attract was the best safeguard for rational distribution of efforts over rival lines of scientific research. As an example (which should appeal to Sir Charles Darwin as a physicist) I recalled the successive appointments to the chair of physics in Manchester during the past thirty years. Manchester had elected to this chair Schuster, Rutherford, W. L. Bragg and Blackett, in this sequence, each of whom represented at the time a 'rare' section of physics: spectroscopy, radioactivity, X-ray crystallography, and cosmic-rays, respectively. I affirmed that Manchester had acted rightly and that they would have been ill-advised to pay attention to the claims of subjects which had not produced at the time men of comparable ability. For the principal criterion for offering increased opportunities to a new subject was the rise of a growing number of distinguished scientists in that subject and the falling off of creative initiative in other subjects, indicating that resources should be withdrawn from them. While admitting that on certain occasions it may be necessary to depart from this policy, I urged that it should be recognized as the essential agency for maintaining a balanced development of scientific research.

Sir Alfred Egerton's response was sympathetic, and, through him, my views were brought to the notice of the members of Sectional Committees. Yet the Committees met, and I duly took part in compiling a list of 'neglected subjects' in chemistry. The result, however, appeared so vague and trivial (as I will illustrate by an example in a moment) that I wrote to the Chairman of the Chemistry Committee that I would not support the Committee's recommendations if they should be submitted to the Senate of my university.

However, my worries were to prove unnecessary. Already the view was spreading among the Chairmen of the Sectional Committees 'that a satisfactory condition in each science would come about naturally, provided that each university always chose the most distinguished leaders for its post, irrespective of his specialization'. While others still expressed the fear that this would make for an excessive pursuit of fashionable subjects, the upshot was, at the best, inconclusive. Darwin himself had, in fact, already declared the reports of the Sectional Committees 'rather disappointing'.

The whole action was brought to a close, one year after it had started, with a circular letter to the Vice-Chancellors of the British universities signed by Sir Alfred Egerton, as secretary, on behalf of the Council of the Royal Society, a copy being sent to the University Grants Committee. The circular included copies of the reports received from the Sectional Committees and endorsed these in general. But in the body of the letter only a small number of these recommendations were specified as being of special importance. This list contained seven recommendations for the establishment of new schools of research, but said nothing about the way these new schools should be co-ordinated with existing activities all over the United Kingdom. The impact of this document on the universities seems to have been negligible. The Chemistry Committee's recommendation for the establishment of 'a strong school of analytic chemistry', which should have concerned me as Professor of Physical Chemistry, was never even brought to my notice in Manchester.

*

I have not recorded this incident in order to expose its error. It is an important historical event. Most major principles of physics are founded on the recognition of an impossibility, and no body of scientists was better qualified than the Royal Society to demonstrate that a central authority cannot effectively improve on the spontaneous emergence of growing points in science. It has proved that little more can, or need, be done towards the advancement of science than to assist spontaneous movements towards new fields of distinguished discovery, at the expense of fields that have become exhausted. Though special considerations may deviate from it, this procedure must be acknowledged as the major principle for maintaining a balanced development of scientific research.[4]

Let me recall yet another striking incident of the post-war period which bears on these principles. I have said that the distribution of subsidies to pure science should not depend on the sources of money, whether they are public or private. This will hold to a considerable extent also for subsidies given to universities as a whole. But after the war, when in England the cost of expanding universities was largely taken over by the state, it was felt that this must be repaid by a more direct support for the national interest. This thought was expressed in July 1946 by the Committee of Vice-Chancellors in a memorandum sent out to all universities, which Sir Ernest Simon (as he then was), as Chairman of the Council of Manchester University, declared to be of 'almost revolutionary' importance. I shall quote a few extracts:

The universities entirely accept the view that the Government has not only the right, but the duty, to satisfy itself that every field of study which in the national interest ought to be cultivated in Great Britain, is in fact being adequately cultivated in the universities. . . .

In the view of the Vice-Chancellors, therefore, the universities may properly be expected not only individually to make proper use of the resources entrusted to them, but collectively to devise and execute policies calculated to serve the national interest. And in that task, both individually and collectively, they will be glad to have a greater measure of guidance from the Government than, until quite recent days, they have been accustomed to receive. . . .

Hence the Vice-Chancellors would be glad if the University Grants Committee were formally authorised and equipped to undertake surveys of all main fields of university activity designed to secure that as a whole universities are meeting the whole range of national need for higher teaching and research. . . .

We meet here again with a passionate desire for accepting collective organization for cultural activities, though these actually depend for their vigorous development on the initiative of individuals adjusting themselves to the advances of their rivals and guided by a cultural opinion in seeking support, be it public or private. It is true that competition between universities was getting increasingly concentrated on gaining the approval of the Treasury, and that its outcome came to determine to a considerable extent the framework within which the several universities could operate. But the most important administrative decisions, which determine the work of universities, as for example the selection of candidates for new vacancies, remained free and not arranged collectively by universities, but by competition between them. For they cannot be made otherwise. The Vice-Chancellors' memorandum has, in consequence, made no impression on the life of the universities and is, by this time, pretty well forgotten by the few who had ever seen it.[5]

\*

We may sum up by saying that the movements for guiding science towards a more direct service of the public interest, as well as for co-ordinating the pursuit of science more effectively from a centre, have all petered out. Science continues to be conducted in British universities as was done before the movement for the social guidance of science ever started. And I believe that all scientific

F

progress achieved in the Soviet Union was also due—as everywhere else—to the initiative of original minds, choosing their own problems and carrying out their investigations, according to their own lights. This does not mean that society is asked to subsidize the private intellectual pleasure of scientists. It is true that the beauty of a particular discovery can be fully enjoyed only by the expert. But wide responses can be evoked by the purely scientific interest of discovery. Popular response, overflowing into the daily press, was aroused in recent years in England and elsewhere by the astronomical observations and theories of Hoyle and Lovell, and more recently by Ryle, and the popular interest was not essentially different from that which these advances had for scientists themselves.

And this is hardly surprising, since for the last three hundred years the progress of science has increasingly controlled the outlook of man on the universe, and has profoundly modified (for better and for worse) the accepted meaning of human existence. Its theoretic and philosophic influence was pervasive.

Those who think that the public is interested in science only as a source of wealth and power are gravely misjudging the situation. There is no reason to suppose that an electorate would be less inclined to support science for the purpose of exploring the nature of things than were the private benefactors who previously supported the universities. Universities should have the courage to appeal to the electorate, and to the public in general, on their own genuine grounds. Honesty should demand this at least. For the only justification for the pursuit of scientific research in universities lies in the fact that the universities provide an intimate communion for the formation of scientific opinion, free from corrupting intrusions and distractions. For though scientific discoveries eventually diffuse into all people's thinking, the general public cannnot participate in the intellectual milieu in which discoveries are made. Discovery comes only to a mind immersed in its pursuit. For such work the scientist needs a secluded place among like-minded colleagues who keenly share his aims and sharply control his performances. The soil of academic science must be exterritorial in order to secure its rule by scientific opinion.

*

The existence of this paramount authority, fostering, controlling and protecting the pursuit of a free scientific inquiry, contradicts the generally accepted opinion that modern science is founded on a total rejection of authority. This view is rooted in a sequence of important historical antecedents which we must acknowledge here. It is a fact that the Copernicans had to struggle with the authority of Aristotle upheld by the Roman Church, and by the Lutherans invoking the Bible; that Vesalius founded the modern study of human anatomy by breaking the authority of Galen. Throughout the formative centuries of modern science, the rejection of authority was its battle-cry; it was sounded by Bacon, by Descartes and collectively by the founders of the Royal Society of London. These great men were clearly saying something that was profoundly true and important, but we should take into account today the sense in which they have meant their rejection of authority. They aimed at adversaries who have since been defeated. And although other adversaries may have arisen in their places, it is misleading to assert that science is still based on the rejection of any kind of authority. The more widely the republic of science extends over the globe, the more numerous become its members in each country, and the greater the material resources at its command, the more there clearly emerges the need for a strong and effective scientific authority to reign over this republic. When we reject today the interference of political or religious authorities with the pursuit of science, we must do this in the name of the established scientific authority which safeguards the pursuit of science.

Let it also be quite clear that what we have described as the functions of scientific authority go far beyond a mere confirmation of facts asserted by science. For one thing, there are no mere facts in science. A scientific fact is one that has been accepted as such by scientific opinion, both on the grounds of the evidence in favour of it and because it appears sufficiently plausible in view of the current scientific conception of the nature of things. Besides, science is not a mere collection of facts, but a system of facts based on their scientific interpretation. It is this system that is endorsed by a scientific authority. And within this system this authority endorses a particular distribution of scientific interest intrinsic to the system; a distribution of interest established by the delicate value-judgments exercised by scientific opinion in sifting and rewarding current contributions to science. Science *is what it is*, in virtue of the way in which scientific authority constantly eliminates, or else recognizes at various levels of merit, contributions offered to science. In accepting the authority of science, we accept the totality of all these value-judgments.

Consider, also, the fact that these scientific evaluations are exercised by a multitude of scientists, each of whom is competent to assess only a tiny fragment of current scientific work, so that no single person is responsible at first hand for the announcements made by science at any time. And remember that each scientist originally established himself as such by joining at some point a network of mutual appreciation extending far beyond his own horizon. Each such acceptance appears then as a submission to a vast range of value-judgments exercised over all the domains of science, which the newly accepted citizen of science henceforth endorses, although he knows hardly anything about their subject-matter. Thus, the standards of scientific merit are seen to be transmitted from generation to generation by the affiliation of individuals at a great variety of widely disparate points, in the same way as artistic, moral or legal traditions are transmitted. We may conclude, therefore, that the appreciation of scientific merit too is based on a tradition which succeeding generations accept and develop as their own scientific opinion. This conclusion gains important support from the fact that the methods of scientific inquiry cannot be explicitly formulated and hence can be transmitted only in the same way as an art, by the affiliation of apprentices to a master. The authority of science is essentially traditional.

*

But this tradition upholds an authority which cultivates originality. Scientific opinion imposes an immense range of authoritative pronouncements on the student of science, but at the same time it grants the highest encouragement to dissent from them in some particular. While the whole machinery of scientific institutions is engaged in suppressing apparent evidence as unsound, on the ground that it contradicts the currently accepted view about the nature of things, the same scientific authorities pay their highest homage to discoveries which deeply modify the accepted view about the nature of things. It took eleven years for the quantum theory, discovered by Planck in 1900, to gain final acceptance. Yet by the time another thirty years had passed, Planck's position in science was approaching that hitherto accorded only to Newton. Scientific tradition enforces its teachings in general, for the very purpose of cultivating their subversion in the particular.

I have said this here at the cost of some repetition, for it opens a vista of analogies in other intellectual pursuits. The relation of originality to tradition in science has its counterpart in modern literary culture. 'Seldom does the word [tradition] appear except in a phrase of censure,' writes T. S. Eliot.[6] And he then tells how our exclusive appreciation of originality conflicts with the true sources of literary merit actually recognized by us:

> We dwell with satisfaction upon the poet's difference from his predecessors, especially his immediate predecessors; we endeavour to find something that can be isolated in order to be enjoyed. Whereas if we approach a poet without this prejudice, we shall often find that not only the best, but the most individual parts of his work may be those in which the dead poets, his ancestors, assert their immortality most vigorously.[7]

Eliot has also said, in *Little Gidding*, that ancestral ideas reveal their full scope only much later, to their successors:

> And what the dead had no speech for, when living,
> They can tell you, being dead: the communication
> Of the dead is tongued with fire beyond the language of the living.

And this is so in science: Copernicus and Kepler told Newton where to find discoveries unthinkable to themselves.

\*

At this point we meet a major problem of political theory: the question whether a modern society can be bound by tradition. Faced with the outbreak of the French Revolution, Edmund Burke denounced its attempt to refashion at one stroke all the institutions of a great nation and predicted that this total break with tradition must lead to a descent into despotism. In reply to this, Tom Paine passionately proclaimed the right of absolute self-determination for every generation. The controversy has continued ever since. It has been revived in America in recent years by a new defence of Burke against Tom Paine, whose teachings had hitherto been predominant. I do not wish to intervene in the American discussion, but I think I can sum up briefly the situation

in England during the past 170 years. To the most influential
political writers of England, from Bentham to John Stuart Mill,
and recently to Isaiah Berlin, liberty consists in doing what one
likes, provided one leaves other people free to do likewise. In this
view there is nothing to restrict the English nation *as a whole* in
doing with itself at any moment whatever it likes. On Burke's
vision of 'a partnership of those who are living, those who are
dead and those who are to be born', these leading British theorists
turn a blind eye. But practice is different. In actual practice it is
Burke's vision that controls the British nation; the voice is Esau's,
but the hand is Jacob's.

The situation is strange. But there must be some deep reason
for it, since it is much the same as that which we have described
in the organization of science. This analogy seems indeed to reveal
the reason for this curious situation. Modern man claims that he
will believe nothing unless it is unassailable by doubt; Descartes,
Kant, John Stuart Mill and Bertrand Russell have unanimously
taught him this. They leave us no grounds for accepting any
tradition. But we see now that science itself can be pursued and
transmitted to succeeding generations only within an elaborate
system of traditional beliefs and values, just as traditional beliefs
have proved indispensable throughout the life of society. What
can one do then? The dilemma is disposed of by continuing to
profess the right of absolute self-determination in *political theory*
and relying on the guidance of tradition in *political practice*.

But this dubious solution is unstable. A modern dynamic
society, born of the French Revolution, will not remain satisfied
indefinitely with accepting, be it only *de facto*, a traditional framework as its guide and master. The French Revolution, which, for
the first time in history, had set up a government resolved on the
indefinite improvement of human society, is still present in us. Its
most far-reaching aspirations were embodied in the ideas of
socialism, which rebelled against the whole structure of society
and demanded its total renewal. In the twentieth century this
demand went into action in Russia in an upheaval exceeding by
far the range of the French Revolution. The boundless claims of
the Russian Revolution have evoked passionate responses
throughout the world. Whether accepted as a fervent conviction
or repudiated as a menace, the ideas of the Russian Revolution
have challenged everywhere the traditional framework which

modern society had kept observing in practice, even though claiming absolute self-determination in theory.

\*

I have described how this movement evoked among many British scientists a desire to give deliberate social purpose to the pursuit of science. It offended their social conscience that the advancement of science, which affects the interests of society as a whole, should be carried on by individual scientists pursuing their own personal interests. They argued that all public welfare must be safeguarded by public authorities and that scientific activities should therefore be directed by the government in the interest of the public. This reform should replace by deliberate action towards a declared aim the present growth of scientific knowledge intended as a whole by no one, and in fact not even known in its totality, except quite dimly, to any single person. To demand the right of scientists to choose their own problems appeared to them petty and unsocial, as against the right of society deliberately to determine its own fate.

But have I not said that this movement has virtually petered out by this time? Have not even the socialist parties throughout Europe endorsed by now the usefulness of the market? Do we not hear the freedom and the independence of scientific inquiry openly demanded today even in important centres within the Soviet domain? Why renew this discussion when it seems about to lose its point?

My answer is that you cannot base social wisdom on political disillusion. The more sober mood of public life today can be consolidated only if it is used as an opportunity for establishing the principles of a free society on firmer grounds. What does our political and economic analysis of the Republic of Science tell us for this purpose?

It appears, at first sight, that I have assimilated the pursuit of science to the market. But the emphasis should be in the opposite direction. The self-co-ordination of independent scientists embodies a higher principle, a principle which is *reduced* to the mechanism of the market when applied to the production and distribution of material goods.

\*

Let me sketch out briefly this higher principle in more general terms. The Republic of Science shows us an association of independent initiatives, combined towards an indeterminate achievement. It is disciplined and motivated by serving a traditional authority, but this authority is dynamic; its continued existence depends on its constant self-renewal through the originality of its followers.

The Republic of Science is a Society of Explorers. Such a society strives towards an unknown future, which it believes to be accessible and worth achieving. In the case of scientists, the explorers strive towards a hidden reality, for the sake of intellectual satisfaction. And as they satisfy themselves, they enlighten all men and are thus helping society to fulfil its obligation towards intellectual self-improvement.

A free society may be seen to be bent in its entirety on exploring self-improvement—every kind of self-improvement. This suggests a generalization of the principles governing the Republic of Science. It appears that a society bent on discovery must advance by supporting independent initiatives, co-ordinating themselves mutually to each other. Such adjustment may include rivalries and opposing responses which, in society as a whole, will be far more frequent than they are within science. Even so, all these independent initiatives must accept for their guidance a traditional authority, enforcing its own self-renewal by cultivating originality among its followers.

Since a dynamic orthodoxy claims to be a guide in search of truth, it implicitly grants the right to opposition in the name of truth—truth being taken to comprise here, for brevity, all manner of excellence that we recognize as the ideal of self-improvement. The freedom of the individual safeguarded by such a society is therefore—to use the term of Hegel—of a positive kind. It has no bearing on the right of men to do as they please; but assures them the right to speak the truth as they know it. Such a society does not offer particularly wide private freedoms. It is the cultivation of public liberties that distinguishes a free society, as defined here.

\*

In this view of a free society, both its liberties and its servitudes are determined by its striving for self-improvement, which in its turn is determined by the intimations of truths yet to be revealed, calling on men to reveal them.

This view transcends the conflict between Edmund Burke and Tom Paine. It rejects Paine's demand for the absolute self-determination of each generation, but does so for the sake of its own ideal of unlimited human and social improvement. It accepts Burke's thesis that freedom must be rooted in tradition, but transposes it into a system cultivating radical progress. It rejects the dream of a society in which all will labour for a common purpose, determined by the will of the people. For in the pursuit of excellence it offers no part to the popular will and accepts instead a condition of society in which the public interest is known only fragmentarily and is left to be achieved as the outcome of individual initiatives aiming at fragmentary problems. Viewed through the eyes of socialism, this ideal of a free society is conservative and fragmented, and hence adrift, irresponsible, selfish, apparently chaotic. A free society conceived as a society of explorers is open to these charges, in the sense that they do refer to characteristic features of it. But if we recognize that these features are indispensable to the pursuit of social self-improvement, we may be prepared to accept them as perhaps less attractive aspects of a noble enterprise.

These features are certainly characteristic of the proper cultivation of science and are present throughout society as it pursues other kinds of truth. They are, indeed, likely to become ever more marked, as the intellectual and moral endeavours to which society is dedicated enlarge in range and branch out into ever new specialized directions. For this must lead to further fragmentation of initiatives and thus increase resistance to any deliberate total renewal of society.

---

[1] M. POLANYI, *The Logic of Liberty*, London: Routledge & Kegan Paul, and Chicago: University of Chicago Press, 1951, p. 12.

[2] M. POLANYI, *Personal Knowledge*, London: Routledge & Kegan Paul, and Chicago: University of Chicago Press, 1958, p. 276.

[3] I have analysed the relation between academic and industrial science elsewhere in some detail, see *Journal of the Institute of Metallurgy*, *89* (1961), pp. 401 ff. Cf. *Personal Knowledge*, pp. 174–84.

[4] Here is the point at which this analysis of the principles by which funds are to be distributed between different branches of science may have a lesson for economic theory. It suggests a way in which resources can be rationally distributed between *any* rival purposes that cannot be valued in terms of money. All cases of public expenditure serving purely collective interests are of this kind. A comparison of

such values by a network of overlapping competences may offer a possibility for a true collective assessment of the relative claims of thousands of government departments of which no single person can know well more than a tiny fraction.

⁵ I have never heard the memorandum mentioned in the University of Manchester. I knew about it only from Sir Ernest Simon's article entitled 'A Historical University Document', *Universities Quarterly*, *1–2* (1946–48), pp. 189–92. My quotations referring to the memorandum are taken from this article.

⁶ T. S. Eliot, *Selected Essays*, London: Faber, 1941, p. 13.

⁷ *Ibid.*, p. 14.

# $\int$
# The Growth of Science
# in Society
# 1967

*The Warrant of Scientific Judgment*
The current situation in the philosophy of science is a strange one. The movement of logical positivism, which aimed at a strict definition of validity and meaning, reached the height of its claims and prestige about twenty years ago. Since then it has become clearer year by year that this aim was unattainable. And since (to my knowledge) no alternative has been offered to the desired strict criteria of scientific truth, we have no accepted theory of scientific knowledge today.

Most writers on science now accept the validity of science as unquestionable and neither in need of philosophic justification nor capable of justification. You will rarely find this spelled out, but it is revealed by current practice. Take Ernest Nagel's widely accepted account of science.[1] He writes that we do not know whether the premises assumed in the explanation of the sciences are true; and that were the requirement that these premises must be known to be true adopted, most of the widely accepted explanations in current science would have to be rejected as unsatisfactory. In effect, Nagel implies that we must save our belief in the truth of scientific explanations by refraining from asking what they are based upon. Scientific truth is defined, then, as that which scientists affirm and believe to be true.

Yet this lack of philosophic justification has not damaged the public authority of science, but rather increased it. Modern philosophers have excused our unaccountable belief in science, by declaring that the claims of science are only tentative and ever open to refutation by adverse evidence. And this has added to the authority of science. It was taken to show that, while scientific knowledge was supremely reliable, scientists were at the same time supremely open-minded, setting thereby an example of incomparable modesty and tolerance.

## The Velikovsky Affair

Still, there have been some occasions in this century when the very foundations of science have been challenged. Sporadic attacks came in the form of laws against teaching the theory of evolution and in a papal encyclical warning against the evolutionary theory. An attack on a broad front was made in the Soviet Union. But a more personal challenge to the foundations of science came from Dr Velikovsky's highly unorthodox book, *Worlds in Collision*, published about fifteen years ago.[2] This book was emphatically rejected by scientists, and yet it had a wide response among the lay public, who much resented the summary dismissal of the book by the experts. Moreover, the conflict widened when some three years ago new evidence turned up supporting Velikovsky's theory and this was again bluntly rejected by scientists. This seemed utterly unjustified to many people, and a group of social scientists took up the matter. In *The American Behavioral Scientist*,[3] under the leadership of its editor, Dr Alfred de Grazia (Professor of Social Theory and Government in New York University), they launched a systematic attack on the whole procedure by which contributions to science are tested, accepted or rejected.

A few words may cover Velikovsky's theory for my present purpose. The theory is based on the acceptance of evidence from the Old Testament, the Hindu Vedas, and Graeco-Roman mythology about the occurrence of catastrophic events in the earth's history from the fifteenth to the seventh century B.C. It interprets these disasters and upheavals as due to the repeated passage of the earth through the tail of a comet. This comet, Velikovsky claims, subsequently collided with Mars and by losing its tail transformed its head into the planet Venus. Further terrestrial upheavals ensued when in the year 687 B.C. Mars nearly collided with the earth; on one occasion the earth turned completely over, so that the sun rose in the west and set in the east. To account for these events Velikovsky supplements Newtonian gravitation by the assumption of powerful electrical and magnetic fields acting between planets.

As I said before, these ideas were rejected by astronomers, but

they appealed to a wide circle of laymen: the book actually became a best-seller. And so bitter was the reaction of astronomers and other scientists to this, and such was the pressure they exercised, that Macmillan, who had published Velikovsky's book, felt compelled to give up their rights to it. They passed them on to Doubleday who felt less vulnerable to the hostility of scientific opinion.

When eventually, in September 1963, *The American Behavioral Scientist* published its protest against the treatment of Velikovsky, the editor of the journal, Professor de Grazia, stated the aim of the inquiry undertaken by him as follows: 'The central problems are clear: Who determines scientific truth? What is their warrant?' and he added that 'some judgment must be passed upon the behaviour of scientists and, if adverse, some remedies must be proposed'.[4] Referring to the three articles in this issue of his journal de Grazia went on to say:

> If the judgment of the authors is correct, the scientific establishment is gravely inadequate to its professed aims, commits injustices as a matter of course, and is badly in need of research and reform.[5]

Now, if we accepted the modern critique of science, which leaves us today no other ultimate criterion of a scientific teaching than that scientists accept it as valid, the answer to de Grazia's first question, 'Who determines scientific truth?' would be simply: 'The scientists.' And to the second question, 'What is their warrant?' we would answer that the decisions of scientists cannot be accounted for.

But this is unacceptable. We must be able to say whether the reception of Velikovsky's ideas by scientists was fair and, if not, what went wrong? To find out this, Professor de Grazia sets out some points of a rational procedure for testing a proposed contribution to science: A contribution must not be rejected unread; its author may claim that it be tested and publicly discussed with him; if the contribution suggests radical innovations, these should be welcomed; if its ideas were at first rejected, the author should have a chance to return with additional proof, and his claims should be once more cordially examined; and no authority should prevail against experimental evidence.

Professor de Grazia shows that all these rules were broken in Velikovsky's treatment by scientists. His work was condemned as

utter nonsense by distinguished astronomers who frankly said that they had not read his book. He asked to be admitted to a public discussion of his views, and this was refused. He had concluded that the surface of Venus was hot and its atmosphere heavy with hydrocarbons and asked the Harvard Observatory to test this prediction; this was refused. This happened in 1956. In February 1963, the American space explorer, Mariner II, confirmed Velikovsky's predictions about Venus: its surface temperature was 800° F., and its clouds appeared replete with hydrocarbons.[6] But this confirmation of the theory did not succeed in causing its discussion to be reopened by scientists; it was rated as a curious coincidence. Authority prevailed against facts.

It is understandable that Professor de Grazia was disappointed by the failure of scientists to live up to their professions to give a ready hearing to any new ideas and to submit humbly to the test of any evidence contradicting their current views. No wonder, perhaps, that he then went on to suggest that the acceptance of a new contribution by science may not depend on the evidence of its truth, but takes place either at random, or in the service of ruling powers, or in response to economic or political interests, or simply as dictated by accepted dogma.

De Grazia was right in contrasting the principles which scientists profess to follow in treating a novel contribution to science with the way they treated Velikovsky's ideas; but these principles must not be applied literally. They should be qualified by their tacit assumptions, and, once done, this resolves not only the anomalies of the Velikovsky case, but also the dilemma that the current philosophic critique of science leaves the validity of science unexplained. For both these anomalies are due to the fact that the demand for strict criteria of scientific truth causes us to overlook the tacit principles on which science is actually founded. Let me show these tacit operations.

### The Tacit Component in Scientific Judgment

A vital judgment practised in science is the assessment of *plausibility*. Only plausible ideas are taken up, discussed and tested by scientists. Such a decision may later be proved right, but at the time that it is made, the assessment of plausibility is based on a broad exercise of intuition guided by many subtle indications, and *thus it is altogether undemonstrable. It is tacit.*

To show what I mean, let me recall an example of a claim lacking plausibility to the point of being absurd: I found it many years ago in a letter published in *Nature*. The author of this letter had observed that the average gestation period of different animals ranging from rabbits to cows was an integer multiple of the number $\pi$. The evidence he produced was ample, the agreement good. Yet the acceptance of this contribution by the journal was only meant as a joke. No amount of evidence could convince a modern biologist that gestation periods are equal to integer multiples of $\pi$. Our conception of the nature of things tells us that such a relationship is absurd.

A more technical example from physics can be found in a paper by Lord Rayleigh published in the *Proceedings of the Royal Society* in 1947[7]; this case is discussed in the preceding paper. I have also had occasion to describe how the possible reality of a certain type of observation which had long been denied, was for a time accepted, then again rejected, only to be soon accepted again and presently rejected once more—these two consecutive alternations of acceptance and rejection taking place within twenty-five years. The observations in question were the apparent transformations of elements. Ever since the immutability of elements had been accepted, such observations had been cast aside as 'dirt effects'. After Rutherford and Soddy established the fact of radioactive disintegration, such effects were taken seriously and accepted for publication—but disappeared from the journals again when it was recognized that radioactivity occurs only in a very few, comparatively rare elements. But new reports of apparently well-authenticated cases appeared in journals once more in response to Rutherford's discovery of the artificial disintegration of elements; and these presently vanished again, as the nature of such disintegration became clear and showed that it could not happen in a chemical laboratory. Apparent chemical transformations of elements have no doubt continued to turn up, and have been unhesitatingly ignored as they had been for so long until the advent of radioactivity.

*The Tacit Component and the Dangers of Misjudgment*
Suppose then that Velikovsky's claims were as implausible as the parallelism between periods of gestation and the number $\pi$; or as implausible as Lord Rayleigh's results published in the *Proceedings*

*of the Royal Society*; or, again, as implausible as the chemical transformation of elements now appears to be—or that they were to
appear even more absurd than these claims—then it would certainly correspond to the current custom of science to reject them
at a glance unread and to refuse to discuss them publicly with the
author. Indeed, to drop one's work in order to test some of
Velikovsky's claims, as requested by him, would appear a culpable
waste of time, expense, and effort.

But how about the predictions of Velikovsky which came true?
Should these not have caused his book to be reconsidered? No, a
theory rejected as absurd will not always be made plausible by the
confirmation of some of its predictions. The fate of Eddington's
cosmic theories may illustrate this. In 1946, I put on record an
anxious remark by a distinguished mathematician (then professor
at the University of Manchester) who complained that recent
measurements had much strengthened the evidence for Eddington's equation relating the masses of a proton and an electron. He
feared that this confirmation of Eddington's theory (which he
held to be absurd) might gain acceptance for it. His anxiety
proved unjustified. A few years later I could note that a quite
different set of new measurements had recently improved thirty-
fold the accuracy of another prediction of Eddington's theory and
that this, too, was disregarded as fortuitous by the great majority of
physicists. The theory has since passed into limbo—from which
no conceivable future confirmation can retrieve it. In refusing to
take notice of the fact that some of Velikovsky's predictions came
true, scientists acted on the same lines as they did—and did
rightly—in the case of Eddington's theories and in many other
similar instances.[8]

This does not mean, of course, that scientists have *always* been
right in so doing. I have myself suffered from the mistake of such
judgments. In the same month that *The American Behavioral Scientist* came out protesting against the treatment of Velikovsky at the
hand of scientific opinion, I published in *Science*[9] an account of the
way my theory of adsorption was disregarded for half a century
because its presuppositions were contrary to the current views
about the nature of inter-molecular forces, even though it has
turned out that my theory was right. But I did not complain
about this mistaken exercise of authority. Hard cases make bad
law. The kind of discipline which had gone wrong in my case was

indispensable. Journals are bombarded with contributions offering fundamental discoveries in physics, chemistry, biology or
medicine, most of which are nonsensical. Science cannot survive
unless it can keep out such contributions and safeguard the basic
soundness of its publications. This may lead to the neglect or even
suppression of valuable contributions, but I think this risk is un-
avoidable. If it turned out that scientific discipline was keeping out
a large number of important ideas, a relaxation of its severity might
become necessary. But if this would lead to the intrusion of a
great many bogus contributions, the situation could indeed become
desperate. The pursuit of science can go on only so long as scientific
judgments of plausibility are not too often badly mistaken.

### The Consensual Ground of Scientific Judgment

Yet we may well wonder how the continuity enforced by current
judgments of plausibility can allow the appearance of any true
originality. For it certainly does allow it: science presents a panorama of surprising developments. How can such surprises be
produced on effectively dogmatic grounds?

A phrase often heard in science may point towards the explanation. We speak of 'surprising confirmations' of a theory. The
discovery of America by Columbus was a surprising confirmation
of the earth's sphericity; the discovery of electron diffraction was
a surprising confirmation of de Broglie's wave-theory of matter;
the discoveries of genetics brought a surprising confirmation of
the Mendelian principles of heredity. We have here the paradigm
of all progress in science: discoveries are made by pursuing unsuspected possibilities suggested by existing knowledge. And this is
how science retains its identity through a sequence of successive
revolutions.

This achievement is grounded on a tacit dimension of science,
which science shares with all empirical observations. The sight of
a solid object before me indicates that it has both another side
and a hidden interior, which I could explore. The sight of another
person indicates unlimited hidden workings of his mind and body.
Perception has this inexhaustible profundity because what we
perceive is *an aspect of reality*, and aspects of reality are clues to yet
boundless undisclosed and perhaps as yet unthinkable experiences.
This is what the existing body of scientific thought offers to the
productive scientist: he sees in it an aspect of reality which as such

G

is an inexhaustible source of new and promising problems. And his work bears this out; science continues to be fruitful, because it offers an insight into the nature of reality.

This view of science merely recognizes something all scientists actually believe. For they must believe that science offers us an aspect of reality and may therefore manifest its truth inexhaustibly and often surprisingly in the future. Only in this belief can the scientist conceive problems, pursue inquiries, claim discoveries; this belief is the ground on which he teaches his students and exercises his authority over the public. And it is by transmitting this belief to succeeding generations that scientists grant their pupils independent grounds from which to start on their own discoveries and innovations—sometimes in opposition to their own teachers. This belief both justifies the discipline of scientific soundness and safeguards the freedom of scientific originality.

Admittedly, this constitution of science can work only so long as scientists have similar conceptions of the nature of things. Indeed, reasoned discussion breaks down in science between two opinions based on different foundations. Neither side can then produce an argument which the other can interpret in his own terms, as has happened in the course of a number of important scientific polemics. A famous case was the violent controversy over the question whether fermentation is caused by living cells or by inanimate catalysts. It went on for more than half a century, involving such great chemists as Woehler and Liebig on the side of 'inanimate catalysts' and including Pasteur on the side of 'living germ cells'. Effective argument being impossible, it was often displaced by ridicule and scorn for the opponent's views. The controversy was resolved only after the contestants had died— through the discovery in 1897 of enzymes (inanimate bodies) pressed out of living cells; in a way both sides had been right. But I can see no guarantee that such a happy resolution of a conflict will always be possible and that it would come in time to avoid a fatal break in the rational procedure of scientific argument. The continued pursuit of science would break down, if scientists came widely to disagree about the nature of things.

*Implications for Scientific Policy*
This brings me back to the origins of the Velikovsky case. Basic assumptions about the nature of things will tend to lie most

widely apart between persons inside and outside of science. Laymen normally accept the teachings of science not because they share its conception of reality, but because they submit to the authority of science. Hence, if they ever venture seriously to dissent from scientific opinion, a regular argument may not prove feasible. It will almost certainly prove impracticable when the question at issue is whether a certain set of evidence is to be taken seriously or not. There may be nothing strange to the layman in the suggestion that the average periods of pregnancy of various animals are integer multiples of the number $\pi$, but he will only drive the scientist to despair if he challenges him to show why this is absurd. So he will be confronted with the scientist's blunt, unreasoning judgment, which rejects at a glance a set of data that seem convincing to the layman. He will demand in vain that the evidence should at least be properly examined and will not understand why the scientist, who prides himself on welcoming any novel idea with an open mind and on holding his own scientific theories only tentatively, sharply refuses his request.

Such conflicts between science and the general public may imperil science. It is generally supposed that science will always be protected from destructive lay interference on account of its economic benefits; but this is not so. The Soviet Government adopted the theories of Lysenko and gravely hampered all branches of biological research for thirty years, overlooking altogether the damage to its agriculture. The ruling party believed in fact that it was improving the cultivation of grain through Lysenko's use of the hereditary transmission of acquired characters, an operation which scientific genetics declared impossible. Far from preventing the attack on science, the economic motive reinforced it—and this may frequently be the case. The great fallacies that have misled mankind for centuries were mostly practical.

Hence, to defend science against lay rebellions on the grounds of its technical achievements may be precarious. To pretend that science is open-minded, when it is not, may prove equally perilous. But to declare that the purpose of science is to understand nature may seem old fashioned and ineffectual. And to confess further how greatly such explanations of nature rely on vague and undemonstrable conceptions of reality may sound positively scandalous. But since all this is in fact true, might it not prove safest to say so?

In any case, it is only on these grounds that the rules governing scientific life can be understood. They alone can explain how an immense number of independent scientists, largely unknown to each other, co-operate step by step, holding the same indefinable assumptions and submitting to the same severe unwritten standards. Let us see how this works.

For a scientific community, comprising great numbers, to function, there must exist a large area of hidden and yet accessible truths, far exceeding the capacity of one man to fathom; there must be work for thousands. Each scientist starts then by sensing a point of deepening coherence, and continues by feeling his way towards such coherence. His questing imagination, guided by intuition, forges ahead until he has achieved success or admitted failure. The clues supporting his surmises are largely unspecifiable, his feeling of their potentialities hardly definable. Scientific research is one continued act of tacit integration—like making out an obscure sight, or being engaged in painting a picture, or in writing a poem. It is rare, therefore, for two scientists to contribute to one inquiry on equal terms or for one scientist to be engaged in more than one problem at a time. But it is not rare for two or more scientists to make the same discovery independently—because different scientists can actualize only the same available potentialities, and they can indeed be relied on fully to exploit such chances.

This is why the initiative to scientific inquiry and its pursuit must be left to the free decision of the individual scientist; the scientist must be granted independence because only his personal vision can achieve essential progress in science. Inquiries can be conducted as surveys according to plan, but these will never add up to new ideas.

Independence will safeguard originality, which is the essence of progress in science. But there is another requirement, which must be sustained, on the contrary, by the authority of scientific opinion over scientists. We have seen scientific opinion watching that unreliable contributions should not be disseminated among scientists. But to form part of science a statement must not only be *true*, but also *interesting* and, more particularly, be interesting to science. Reliability—or exactitude—is only one factor contributing scientific interest; it is not enough. Two further important factors enter into the assessment of scientific values. One is the way a new fact enters into the systematic structure of science, correcting or expanding this structure. The other factor is independent both of the reliability and the systematic interest of a scientific discovery, for it lies in its subject matter as it was known originally, before it was investigated by science. It consists in the intrinsic *pre-scientific* interest of the object studied by science.

The scientific interest—or the scientific value—of a contribution to science is thus jointly formed by three factors: its *exactitude*, its *systematic importance*, and the *intrinsic interest of its subject matter*. The proportion in which these factors enter into scientific value varies greatly over the different domains of science; deficiency in one factor may be balanced by greater excellence in another. The highest degree of exactitude and widest range of systematization are found in mathematical physics, and this compensates for the lesser intrinsic interest of its inanimate subject. At the other end of the sciences, we have domains like zoology and botany which lack exactitude and have no systematic structure comparable in range and beauty to that of physics, but which make up for this deficiency by the far greater intrinsic interest of living things compared with inanimate matter.

A scientist engaged in research must have a keen sense of scientific value. He must be attracted by problems promising a result of scientific value and must be capable of feeling his way towards it. A great discovery may depend on realizing the importance of some fact one has hit upon. Slowness in abandoning a line of inquiry which would bring only unimportant results is part of the same weakness, and most scientists who have conducted a research school have known such mortifying mistakes; they do indeed mark a deficiency in one's scientific ability.

The assessment of scientific value is also the principal standard by which the institutional structure of the scientific community is determined. Funds and appointments serving scientific research must be distributed in a way that promises the highest total increment to science. Authority at influential centres must be given to scientists distinguished by their exceptional capacity for advancing science, and rewards must be distributed at these centres in such a way as will encourage the greatest total advancement of science. Every decision of this kind requires comparisons of scientific value; it can be made in a rational manner only if there exist true standards for comparing the value of contributions to science all along the range of science from astronomy to medicine.

This does not mean that one has to compare the scientific value of one *entire branch of science* with another. It requires only that we be able to compare the value of *scientific increments* achieved in the various branches of science at similar costs of effort and money. The marginal principle of economics offers the conceptual model for this: we must try to keep equal the marginal yield, in terms of scientific value, all along the advancing borders of the sciences.

But how can anybody compare the scientific value of discoveries (and expected discoveries) in, say, astronomy with those in medicine? Nobody can, but nobody needs to. All that is required is that we compare these values in closely neighbouring fields of science. Judgments extending over neighbourhoods will overlap and form a chain spanning the entire range of sciences. This principle—*the principle of overlapping neighbourhoods*—here fulfils the functions which a capital market performs in comparing the profitability of competing enterprises among the thousand branches of an economic system.

But the two great principles of scientific growth, the granting of independence to mature scientists and the imposition of scientific values on their performances, leave open two important questions. The first question is, how can the initiatives of scientists independently choosing their problems be co-ordinated? The second, how can a true scientific opinion be formed that will subject scientists to proper scientific rigour, instruct them in scientific values and cause their merits to be rightly assessed and rewarded? All these aims are achieved by two twin principles; namely, *self-co-ordination by mutual adjustment* and *discipline under mutual authority*.

Of *self-co-ordination by mutual adjustment* I have written often in the past twenty years.[10] Each scientist sets himself a problem and pursues it with a view to the results already achieved by all other scientists, who had likewise set themselves problems and pursued them with a view to the results achieved by others before. Such self-co-ordination represents practically the highest possible efficiency in the use of scientific talent and material resources, provided only that the professional opportunities for research and the money for its pursuit are rationally distributed.

This brings us to the principle of *mutual authority*. It consists in the fact that scientists keep watch over each other; each scientist is both subject to criticism by others and is encouraged by their appreciation. This is how scientific opinion is formed, both enforcing scientific standards and regulating the distribution of professional opportunities and research grants. Naturally, only fellow scientists working in closely related fields are competent to exercise authority over each other; but their restricted fields form chains of overlapping neighbourhoods extending over the entire range of sciences.[11]

Thus an *indirect consensus* is formed between scientists so far apart that they could not understand more than a small part of each other's subjects. It is enough that the standards of plausibility and worthwhileness be equal around every single point for this will keep them equal over all the sciences. Scientists from the most distant branches of science will rely then on each other's results and will blindly support each other against any laymen seriously challenging a scientist's professional authority.

This is the way the scientific community is organized. These are the grounds on which science rests. This the way in which discoveries are made. Science is governed by common beliefs, by values and practices transmitted to succeeding generations. Each new independent member of the scientific community adheres to this tradition, assuming at the same time the responsibility shared by all members for re-interpreting the tradition and, possibly, revolutionizing its teachings.

The opportunities for discovery offered by nature to the human mind are not of our making. We have developed a body of thought capable of exploiting these opportunities and have organized a body of men for this task. The laws of this community are determined by the nature of its task. But the task itself is indeterminate: it merely demands that we advance into the unknown. And even this done, the advances are not known to any single man, for no man can know more than a tiny fragment of science.

The chances offered by nature to our minds have evoked a response over which we have little control, and this is the growth of science in society. Should we rejoice to be servants of such great transcendent powers? Perhaps we are becoming—and even ought to become in other ways—a society of explorers dedicated to the pursuit of aims unknown to us. Perhaps the freedom of thought in which we take pride has such awesome implications. I cannot tell.

[1] ERNEST NAGEL, *The Structure of Science*, New York: Harcourt, Brace and World, 1961, p. 43.

[2] IMMANUEL VELIKOVSKY, *Worlds in Collision*, New York: Doubleday, 1950.

[3] *The American Behavioral Scientist*, *VII* (1963) contains a foreword by ALFRED DE GRAZIA on 'The Politics of Science and Dr Velikovsky', p. 3; and articles by R. E. JUERGENS on 'Minds in Chaos: A Recital of the Velikovsky Story', pp. 4–17, L. C. STECCHINI on 'The Inconstant Heavens: Velikovsky in Relation to Some Past Cosmic Perplexities', pp. 19–44, and ALFRED DE GRAZIA on 'The Scientific Reception System and Dr Velikovsky', pp. 45–49.

[4] *Ibid.*, p. 3.

[5] *Loc. cit.* The present paper was completed before the publication of Alfred de Grazia (ed.), *The Velikovsky Affair*, New York: University Books, 1966, which expands the contributions to the *American Behavioral Scientist*. The article by Professor de Grazia, to which I have referred in my essay, is revised, and the passages on 'the central problems' are now to be found in de Grazia's introduction to the book, while the other passage I quoted verbatim is absent. Though I can find no substantial shift from the position stated in the *American Behavioral Scientist*, I would say that I have come to appreciate better the merit of Professor de Grazia in raising the question concerning the grounds on which contributions to science are accepted by scientists.

[6] Cf., JUERGENS, *op. cit.*, p. 7.

[7] LORD RAYLEIGH, 'The Surprising Amount of Energy which can be Collected from Gases after the Electric Discharge has Passed', *Proceedings of the Royal Society*, 189 (1947), pp. 296–99.

[8] The historical cases quoted here and in the previous four paragraphs are from my books: *Science, Faith and Society*, London: Oxford University Press, 1946; and *The Logic of Liberty*, London: Routledge and Chicago: University of Chicago Press, 1951.

[9] See Essay 6.

[10] The theory of mutual adjustment in society was first fully stated in my essay, 'The Growth of Thought in Society', *Economica*, *8* n.s. (1941), and developed further in the books mentioned in footnote 8 above, as well as in my latest book, *The Tacit Dimension*, New York: Doubleday, 1966. For a summary see the preceding essay.

[11] Mutual authority, based on overlapping competence, will also apply to other cultural fields and, indeed, to a wide range of consensual activities of which the participants know only a small fragment. It is a way by which resources can be rationally distributed between purposes that cannot be valued in terms of money. All cases of public expenditure serving collective interests are of this kind. This is, I believe, how the claims of a thousand government departments can be reasonably adjudicated, though no single person can know intimately more than a tiny fraction of them.

# 6
# The Potential Theory of Adsorption
## 1963

Since 1948, when I retired from the professional pursuit of science to take up philosophy, occasional reports have reached me that my theory of adsorption, which hitherto had been rejected, was gradually gaining acceptance. Assuming that this outcome is no longer in doubt,[1] I think it worthwhile to look back on the reasons why this fairly simple matter has so long been left undecided. The story also throws light on an interesting aspect of the scientific method.

I wrote my first paper on adsorption over fifty years ago; it was published in 1914. In it I assumed (i) that the adsorption of gases on solids is due to an attraction that derives from a potential which is uniquely determined by the spatial position of the gas molecule and therefore independent of the presence of any other molecules in the field of the adsorption potential; and (ii) that, when subject to the field of adsorption, the gas behaves in accordance with its normal equation of state. When compressed to its normal vapour density, it condenses to a liquid.

These principles were first fully developed in a paper published in 1916, which also supplied a wide range of experimental verification, as follows. From a complete adsorption isotherm of a vapour, a distribution of the adsorption potential was derived, in the form $\varepsilon = f(\phi)$, $\varepsilon$ being the adsorption potential and $\phi$ the space enclosed by the level having this potential, and from this adsorption-potential curve all other measured isotherms were computed and found to agree with the theory. This result was confirmed later in a number of papers by my pupils and by other authors.[2]

The result was impressive. Herbert Freundlich, then the most authoritative writer on this subject, gave a full account of my theory in the next edition of his *Kapillarchemie*, published in 1922. He told me, 'I am heavily committed now to your theory myself; I hope it is correct.'

Actually, his words already expressed an uneasiness, and soon my theory was almost universally rejected. How did this happen?

During the very years in which the theory was born, there occurred a dazzling series of insights into the nature of things. Debye's discovery of fixed dipoles, Bohr's atomic model, and the ionic structure of sodium chloride found by W. H. Bragg and W. L. Bragg, established the pervasive function of electrical forces in the architecture of matter. It seemed obvious that, in consequence, cohesive forces must be explained by electrical interaction. A number of theories were put forward on these lines. Keesom suggested an electrostatic interaction of fixed quadrupoles; Debye, an interaction of quadrupoles with induced dipoles. Kossel's attempt to explain all chemical bonds as attraction between positive and negative ions also belongs to this period.

This view of atomic forces made my theory of adsorption untenable. Electrical interactions could not be derivable from a spatially fixed potential; they would be screened off by the presence of other molecules in the field.

The weight of these theoretical objections was greatly increased by three experimental claims put forward by Irving Langmuir in the years 1916 to 1918. (i) Langmuir reported that the adsorption of gases on mica surfaces reached saturation with the formation of an adsorbed layer of less than monomolecular strength. (ii) He claimed that isotherms could be accounted for by an equation that has since been known as 'Langmuir's isotherm'—an equation in which it is presupposed that molecules are adsorbed at scattered centres by forces that render attraction between adsorbed molecules negligible. (iii) Langmuir proved by beautiful experiments that surface layers on water are monomolecular and that their structure is determined by electrostatic interaction with the underlying water. For this work he was awarded the Nobel prize.

All this evidence seemed to bear out the picture of short-range electrical forces, or valences, originating at discrete points of the atomic lattice forming the wall—a picture which would render my theory of adsorption untenable.

I myself was protected for a while against any knowledge of these developments by serving as a medical officer in the Austro-Hungarian Army, from August 1914 to October 1918, and by the subsequent revolutions and counter-revolutions that lasted until the end of 1919. Members of less well-informed circles elsewhere continued to be impressed for some time by the simplicity of my theory and its wide experimental verifications. But its downfall had become inevitable.

The turning point came when I was invited by Fritz Haber to give a full account of my theory in the Kaiser Wilhelm Institute for Physical Chemistry, in Berlin. Einstein was specially invited to attend my lecture. Some scientists present who had not yet fully accepted the electrical concept of interatomic forces congratulated me on the 'flood of light' I had thrown on the subject, but Einstein and Haber decided I had displayed a total disregard for the scientifically established structure of matter. Professionally, I survived the occasion only by the skin of my teeth.

However, my belief in my theory was quite unshaken, and I proceeded to undertake a series of experiments with a view to proving its validity. These experiments offered good supporting evidence for the theory, even though there were some systematic deviations from it. These I attributed to the fact that the surface tension of the very thin, *possibly* monomolecular, adsorbed layer vitiates to some extent the assumption that the adsorbed substance behaves according to the equation of state for the substance observed in bulk. Once more I reported my results to a meeting presided over by Haber in Berlin. When I finished, Haber declared that, by my admission of systematic deviations from the theory and of the possibly monomolecular thickness of the adsorbed layer as an explanation of these deviations, I had actually given up my theory. I had, of course, done nothing of the kind, but I had certainly become quite isolated in my belief in it, at least from the leading scientists of the time.[3]

And yet deliverance was approaching. In 1930, F. London put forward a new theory of cohesive forces, based on quantum mechanical resonance between the polarization of electronic systems. I immediately fired the following question at London: 'Are these forces subject to screening by intervening molecules? Would a solid acting by these forces possess a spatially fixed adsorption potential?' London carried out the computation, and we published the result jointly (in 1930): adsorptive forces behave exactly in accordance with the assumptions of my theory. Having found this, we inferred that the adsorption potential of a solid wall decreases with the third power of the distance from the wall. (I refer to this inference hereafter as the 'inverse third power law'.)

The following year I was invited to give an introductory lecture before the Faraday Society on the subject of adsorption. In this lecture I showed that application of the inverse third power law to determine adsorption potential for a wedge-shaped crevice yields $\varepsilon = f(\phi)$ curves of the characteristic type observed for charcoal.

I thought I had now won the battle I had fought for fifteen years. But my paper before the Faraday Society actually made no impression.[4] It seems that by this time the opinion that my theory was false had hardened to a point where the reasons for which it had been rejected were forgotten. Hence my refutation of these objections had no effect.

There were, of course, still some objections to be met. To Langmuir's claims, developed along the lines I have mentioned, new evidence had been added by the adsorption of cesium vapour on tungsten. Attention was also drawn from adsorption by cohesive forces to chemisorption, because of its bearing on heterogenous catalysis, even though it rarely produces equilibria for the study of adsorption isotherms. In addition, the suitability of my experimental material was questioned on the grounds that it was porous, with unknown irregular surface configurations. These objections have continued to exercise some influence up to the present.

However, Langmuir's extrapolation of his isotherms on mica (from observations made in 1917) was soon to prove erroneous: saturation was found to take place at a multimolecular thickness of the adsorbed layer. That the Langmuir isotherm itself is theoretically false still seems to be insufficiently appreciated today. It is not applicable to any adsorption by cohesive forces, for the differences in the molecular energy of such adsorption along a solid surface are very small and can never outweigh the cohesive energy of the adsorbed molecules. The Langmuir isotherm might conceivably be applicable to chemisorption when chemisorption is reversible. But the only instance I know of in which it clearly applies is the deposition of cesium cations on a negatively charged tungsten surface, a very untypical case of adsorption. To represent the Langmuir isotherm as a proper approximation to the adsorption equilibrium is therefore misleading. The formula should be dropped altogether.

Work in recent years has shown that the isotherm of adsorption on plane surfaces can be derived, beyond the point at which the first one or two layers of molecules are adsorbed, from an adsorption potential that obeys the inverse third power law, while the part of the isotherm that corresponds to the deposition of the first layers does not obey my theory. This follows, in my view, from the fact that the surface tension of the adsorbed layer keeps it from behaving in accordance with the normal equation of state at the early stages of adsorption. Confirmation of the inferred inverse third power law for plane surfaces is a beautiful experimental achievement, yet porous adsorbents retain the advantage that the adsorbed layer is accumulated on them in such a way that surface tension is reduced, and makes the normal equation of state applicable to the entire observed isotherm. The discrediting of my verification of my theory on the grounds that the verification was based on experiments with porous adsorbents proved to be unjustified.

This historical survey may be of interest to scientists puzzled by the fact that the acceptance of the correct theory of adsorption was delayed by almost half a century; but I think its main interest lies in the bearing of the story on the scientific method.

The first point to mention is the fact that I would never have conceived my theory, let alone have made a great effort to verify it, if I had been more familiar with major developments in physics that were taking place. Moreover, my initial ignorance of the powerful false objections that were raised against my ideas protected those ideas from being nipped in the bud. Later, by undertaking the labour necessary to verify my theory, I became immune to these objections, but I remained powerless to refute them. My verification could make no impression on minds convinced that it was bound to be specious. Since electrical forces could not produce an adsorption potential of the kind I was postulating, and since no principle was conceivable at the time which could account for such an adsorption potential, Langmuir's claims supporting the then current view of matter were firmly accepted, though they were false (or irrelevant to adsorption on solid surfaces), and my evidence was rejected unexamined, though it was valid. I could do nothing about it.

Could this miscarriage of the scientific method have been avoided? I do not think so. There must be at all times a predominantly accepted scientific view of the nature of things, in the light of which research is jointly conducted by members of the community of scientists. A strong presumption that any evidence which contradicts this view is invalid must prevail. Such evidence has to be disregarded, even if it cannot be accounted for, in the hope that it will eventually turn out to be false or irrelevant.

I shall repeat here some comments that I made in an earlier essay on the way in which current views of plausibility properly serve to suppress evidence that runs counter to them.[5] Observations which can be interpreted as a transmutation of chemical elements frequently occur in the laboratory. But published claims, by reputable investigators, of having achieved transmutation appear only at times when the possibility of such a process is for some reason considered plausible. Such was the case when suddenly, under the stimulus of Rutherford's and Soddy's discovery of radioactive transmutations (1902-3), careful observers made a series of erroneous claims that they had achieved a transmutation of elements. A. T. Cameron (1907) and Sir William Ramsay (1908) announced the transformation of copper into lithium as a result of the action of $\alpha$-particles.

In 1913 Collie and Patterson claimed that they had formed helium and neon by electric discharge through hydrogen. After these claims had been disproved, no new ones were made until 1922, when as a result of the discovery, made three years earlier by Rutherford, of certain forms of artificial transmutation, there was a new wave of similar claims based on erroneous evidence. The transmutation of mercury into gold under the effect of electric discharge was reported independently by Miethe and Stammreich in Germany and Nagaoka in Japan. Smits and Karssen reported the transformation of lead into mercury and thallium. Paneth and Peters claimed that hydrogen had been transformed into helium under the influence of a platinum catalyst. All these claims had to be abandoned in the end; the last was given up in 1928. A year later came the establishment of the theory of radioactive disintegration, which showed that these attempts to transform elements had been futile. Since then I have so far seen no such claims published, although evidence of transformation of the kind put forward by Ramsey, Paneth, and others must be turning up all the time. It is disregarded and would not be accepted for publication, because it is no longer considered sufficiently plausible. Remember, also, D. C. Miller's observations, contradicting the result of the Michelson–Morley experiment. They were properly set aside for a period of about fifty years, though they were not explained and shown to be erroneous until 1955.[6]

I am making, therefore, no complaint about the suppression of my theory for reasons which must have seemed well founded at the time, though they have now been proved false. It is perhaps more difficult to understand why more than fifteen years passed after the presentation of my paper of 1932, in which the original objections had been proved unfounded, before the rediscovery and gradual rehabilitation of the theory set in. I suppose so much confusion was left over from the previous period that it took some time for scientists to take cognizance of the new situation, and that meanwhile my own work, which had been so long discredited, remained suspect. If the problem had been more important, this period of latency would no doubt have been shorter.

The dangers of suppressing or disregarding evidence that runs counter to orthodox views about the nature of things are, of course, notorious, and they have often proved disastrous. Science guards against these dangers, up to a point, by allowing some measure of dissent from its orthodoxy. But scientific opinion has to consider and decide, at its own ultimate risk, how far it can allow such tolerance to go, if it is not to admit for publication so much nonsense that scientific journals are rendered worthless thereby.

Discipline *must* remain severe and *is* in fact severe. I doubt that I could have got my theory of adsorption passed by the referees of any scientific journal had I presented it five years later than 1916. I was lucky enough to profit by the relative ignorance of referees in 1916, and also by the complete ignorance of the professor of theoretical physics at the University of Budapest, who accepted the substance of my theory as a Ph.D. thesis in 1917 (may his departed spirit forgive me these ungrateful remarks!).

Even so, the opposition to my theory would have cut off any hope I had of a scientific career—on which, having left medicine,

I was embarking belatedly—had I not done other scientific work that brought me recognition which outweighed the discredit brought upon me by my theory of adsorption.

Even as professor of physical chemistry at the Victoria University of Manchester, I was unable to teach my theory. Undergraduates would have expected to be examined on it. But examinations were set and marked by a committee that included an external examiner and members of the teaching staff junior to myself. I could not undertake to force on them views totally opposed to generally accepted opinion. A system of collegiate examinations severely curtails the teaching of views that conflict with currently dominant scientific opinion.

I repeat here that I am not arguing against the present balance between the powers of orthodoxy and the rights of dissent in science. I merely insist on acknowledgement of the fact that the scientific method is, and must be, disciplined by an orthodoxy which can permit only a limited degree of dissent, and that such dissent is fraught with grave risks to the dissenter. I demand a clear recognition of this situation for the sake of our intellectual honesty as scientists, and I charge that this situation is not recognized today but is, on the contrary, obscured by current declarations about science. Take this by Bertrand Russell:

> The triumphs of science are due to the substitution of observation and inference for authority. Every attempt to revive authority in intellectual matters is a retrograde step. And it is part of the scientific attitude that the pronouncements of science do not claim to be certain, but only the most probable on the basis of present evidence. One of the great benefits that science confers upon those who understand its spirit is that it enables them to live without the delusive support of subjective authority.[7]

Such statements obscure the fact that the authority of current scientific opinion is indispensable to the discipline of scientific institutions; that its functions are invaluable, even though its dangers are an unceasing menace to scientific progress. I have seen no evidence that this authority is exercised without claims of certainty for its own teachings. In any case, it is a mistake to assume that it is easier to justify a scientific opinion that merely makes claims of probability than one that makes claims of certainty. Both express a commitment, and to this extent both must go beyond the evidence.

The instance of the miscarriage of science of which I have told the story may not have been important in itself, but it makes me ponder the perils of a particular dangerous mode of scientific explanation. The physicists of the period from 1912 to 1930 considered it as established beyond reasonable doubt that only electrical forces could account for intramolecular attraction. Arguments for the insufficiency of this explanation were rejected as unscientific, because no other principles of molecular interaction appeared conceivable. This reminds me of the impatience with which most biologists set aside today all the difficulties of the current selectionist theory of evolution, because no other explanation that can be accepted as scientific appears conceivable. This kind of argument, based on the absence of any alternative that is accepted as scientific, may often be valid, but it seems to me the most dangerous application of scientific authority.

---

[1] I am relying for this assumption on the following surveys: M. M. DUBININ, 'The Potential Theory of Adsorption of Gases and Vapors for Adsorpents with Energetically Non-Uniform Surfaces', *Chemical Reviews*, *60* (1960), pp. 235–41, and R. S. HANSEN and C. A. SMOLDERS, 'Coloid and Surface Chemistry in the Mainstream of Modern Chemistry', *Journal of Chemical Education*, *391* (1962), pp. 167–78.

[2] In my paper of 1914 I calculated from the adsorption isotherm of a vapour the potential energy of an adsorbed molecule as a function of the amount absorbed, which I identified with the distance from the surface of the adsorbent, assumed to be plane. (The fact that the adsorbent was actually porous did not affect the predictions of the theory: in the paper of 1916 I introduced the concept that the volume enclosed by a potential surface is the variable on which the potential depends.) The term *Adsorptionspotential* was first introduced by Eucken [EUCKEN, A., 'Zur Theorie der Adsorption', *Deutsche Physikaliche Gesellschaft*, *10* n.s. (1914), pp. 345–62] a few months before publication of my paper of 1914. Eucken computed, from a hypothetical formula for the decrease of the adsorption potential with the distance from a plane adsorbent, the temperature dependence of the linear part of the adsorption isotherm. This procedure was erroneous in four respects. (i) Insufficient account was taken of the porosity of the adsorbents; such porosity profoundly alters the potential distribution relative to that on a plane surface. (ii) The inclination of the hypothetical linear part of the isotherms was assessed from the initial slope of a curved isotherm taken from the literature—a procedure which was not justifiable. (iii) The procedure was self-contradictory, for the ideal gas laws were applied to conditions in which, according to the theory itself, the ideal gas laws could not possibly hold. (iv) The hypothetical formula used for the adsorption potential of a plane solid wall was incorrect. Eight years later, Eucken ['Über die Theorie der Adsorptionsvorgänge', *Zeitschrift für Elecktrochemie*, *28* (1922), pp. 6–16] attacked my theory while modifying his own assumptions to include some of those I had made.

[3] One of the papers published in 1928 [*Z. Phys. Chem.*, *132* (1928), p. 321] lent strong support to my theory from a new angle. It showed that, below the melting point of a substance, the quantity adsorbed at saturation steadily increases with rising temperature up to the melting point. The nature and magnitude of this effect could be

H

derived from the fact, assumed in my theory, that the adsorbed layer is an amorphous modification of the adsorbed substance. This paper seems to have gone entirely unnoticed.

[4] M. POLANYI, 'Theories of the Adsorption of Gases', *Transactions of the Faraday Society*, 28 (1932), pp. 316–33.

[5] M. POLANYI, *Science, Faith and Society*, Oxford: Oxford University Press, 1946, pp. 75–76.

[6] See M. POLANYI, *Personal Knowledge*, London: Routledge & Kegan Paul, and Chicago: University of Chicago Press, 1958, p. 13; for other cases, see *ibid.*, p. 276, and M. POLANYI, *The Logic of Liberty*, London: Routledge & Kegan Paul, and Chicago: University of Chicago Press, 1951, p. 17.

[7] B. RUSSELL, *The Impact of Science on Society*, London: Allen and Unwin, 1952, pp. 110–11.

# 7
# My Time with X-rays
# and Crystals
## 1962

A great poet and scholar once said, 'Where kings build palaces, carters find jobs.' Most of history is written about kings, and that is as it should be, but the work of carters has its own history too, and that too is important. For great discoverers would achieve little unless followed by enterprising settlers. I shall recollect here a brief phase of the early colonization of the immense domain of knowledge on which Max von Laue first set foot fifty years ago, followed by W. H. and W. L. Bragg, whose discoveries first revealed its major treasures.

The example of great scientists is the light which guides all workers in science, but we must guard against being blinded by it. There has been too much talk about the flash of discovery, and this has tended to obscure the fact that discoveries, however great, can only give effect to some intrinsic potentiality of the intellectual situation in which scientists find themselves. It is easier to see this for the kind of work that I have done than it is for major discoveries, and this may justify my telling this story.

In Germany there was established at the time when I started this work, a chain of research institutes supported by the Kaiser Wilhelm Gesellschaft. One of these was the newly founded Institute of Fibre Chemistry in Berlin–Dahlem, to which I was appointed in the autumn of 1920. My first contacts revealed the peculiar character of the profession I had joined. Following German custom, I called on the directors of the other institutes in Dahlem, and first of all on the great Fritz Haber, Director of the Institute of Physical Chemistry. Haber, who had seen my speculative papers on reaction kinetics, referred to them with a stern admonishment: 'Reaction velocity,' said he, 'is a world problem. You should cook a piece of meat.' He meant that first of all I should prove my capacity as a craftsman; the rest would follow. Rather different was the impression conveyed by Carl Neuberg, Director of the Institute of Biochemistry. 'Don't stay here, dear colleague,' he said, 'Accept the first offer of a Chair at a university. If you don't make a discovery for a couple of years here, you are just an old ass; at a university you have always your academic laurels to rest upon.'

Discovery requires in fact something beyond craftsmanship, namely the gift of recognizing a problem ripe for solution by your own powers, large enough to engage your powers to the full, and worth the expenditure of this effort. Haber had admonished me, because he thought I had taken on a problem that was not yet ripe, and in any case too large for me. Perhaps he was right, but at any rate, my new job with the Institute of Fibre Chemistry led me in a different direction. On my arrival at the institute its Director, Reginald Oliver Herzog—whom I remember warmly for his kindness and wide intellectual sensibility—immediately gave me, what Haber said I needed, a piece of meat to cook. Following his discovery of the crystalline nature of cellulose (paralleled by Scherrer), Herzog—aided by his assistant Jancke—had just found that a bundle of ramie fibres irradiated by an X-ray beam at right angles produced a diffraction pattern composed of sets of four equivalent dots symmetrical to two mirror-planes, one passing through the primary beam and the axes of the fibres, and the other vertical to the former. There was excitement about this diagram, and I was asked to solve the mystery. In the next few days I made my first acquaintance with the theory of X-ray diffraction, of which, owing to wars and revolutions and my exclusive interest in thermo-dynamics and kinetics, I had heard little before. However, I soon returned the result that the four-point diagram was caused by a group of parallel crystals arranged at random around one axis, and this interpretation was included in a joint publication with the work of Herzog and Jancke. So I had cooked a piece of meat—and this transformed my position. Herzog, with kindly enthusiasm, showered me with every facility for experimental work, most precious of which were funds for employing assistants and financing research students. In this I was incredibly lucky. I was joined by Herrmann Mark, Erich Schmid, Karl

Weissenberg, all three from Vienna, by Erwin von Gomperz and some others; the place was soon humming. It was the time of runaway inflation, and poor Herzog found it difficult to pay all these people. Protest meetings were held, resolutions passed, Weissenberg in the lead; the Institute earned the name of an Assistenten-Republik. We had a glorious time.

I shall now try to give an account from memory—without access even to my own papers—of the way some of my further contributions were born in those days. I found that all the dots forming the fibre diagram lay on a series of hyperbolae, each hyperbola comprising dots reflected by planes having identical indices with respect to the crystal axis parallel to the fibre. I established the formula determining the series of these hyperbolae, as a function of the identity period parallel to the axis of the fibre. Thus equipped, I evaluated the elementary cell of cellulose and drew the conclusion that the structure of cellulose was either one straight giant molecule composed of a single file of linked hexoses or else an aggregate of hexobiose-anhydrids; both structures were compatible with the symmetry and size of the elementary cell—but unfortunately I lacked the chemical sense for eliminating the second alternative.

This foolishness also had an amusing consequence. When I first stated my conclusions in the Colloquium presided over by Haber, there was a storm of protest from all sides. The assertion appeared scandalous, the more so, since I said that it was compatible both with an infinitely large molecular weight or an absurdly small one. I was gleefully witnessing the chemists at cross-purposes with a conceptual reform, when I should have been better occupied in definitely establishing the chain structure as the only one compatible with the known chemical and physical properties of cellulose. I failed to see the importance of the problem.

A failure of the same kind was my treatment of sero-fibroin. Herzog had discovered its fibre diagram and handed it to me for evaluation. I determined its elementary cell and observed that there was only room for glycine and alanine in it. But I could not make up my mind what to think of the other observed decomposition products. I did not recognize the immense importance of the question and passed it on half-baked to Brill, for the doctoral thesis he was doing under my supervision.

Such failures are worth recording, in order to correct the current theories of the scientific method, based altogether on success stories. It is interesting to recall in this connection that the weakness of my initiative was due in part to the fact that my confidence in this line of inference was impaired by a slight deviation of the position of two dots on the equator of the cellulose diagram from the theoretical values predicted by my analysis. These loose ends were debilitating, but I am glad that at least I did not obey the current Sunday school precepts of the scientific method, which would command one to reject a theory if a single piece of evidence contradicts it. (I still don't know what caused the discrepancy in those dots.)

Following my discovery of the hyperbolae in the fibre diagram of cellulose and my evaluation of its elementary cell on this basis, the principles thus established were transposed into the rotating crystal method in collaboration with Weissenberg and Mark. The former far surpassed me in mathematics, while the latter lent me his manipulative skill bordering on genius. To the best of my recollection, the project, including the suggestion of using an elongated Debye-camera for the purpose of including the higher layer lines, came from me. Weissenberg generalized the layer line relationship, which I had only established for the directions of the crystal axes to include identity periods in any direction; Mark carried out the first experiments with the new method. The first use of the rotating crystal apparatus for the determination of an unknown crystal structure was made, I think, by Mark and myself in 1923 on white tin. It was used in the first place by Mark, Schmid and myself for elucidating the plastic flow of zinc crystals.

The strength of solids had now become my principal interest. The technological purpose of the Institute had thrown this great problem into my lap. I saw that the characteristic feature of the solid state, namely its solidity, was yet unexplained and, indeed, hardly explored by physicists. I found that in the light of the recently discovered structure of rock salt, such a crystal should be thousands of times stronger in resisting rigid rupture or plastic deformation than it actually was. In facing this paradox I appealed to two features of modern physics, (1) that a crystal of rock salt was one giant molecule, and (2) that inside a molecule energy could be transferred by quantum jumps not controlled by the laws of classical mechanics. From a calculation based on the actual strength of rock salt I concluded that the energy required for producing the new surface formed by breaking the crystal would have to be supplied from the stress stored up on either side of the future break, in an area extending two or three millimetres in both directions of it. So I set out to show experimentally that crystals shorter than a few millimetres were stronger than those of greater length. The result was inconclusive, and the whole idea may have been wrong; but in pursuing it I stumbled on an important aspect of the strength of materials which seemed to reflect my original paradox and to encourage the way I was trying to solve it: I came to know about the hardening of materials by cold working.

I was deeply struck by the fact that every process that destroyed the ideal structure of crystals (and thus reduced the areas which could be regarded as single molecules) increased the resistance of crystalline materials. This seemed to confirm the principle by which I explained the low resistance of crystals to stress and to refute the rival theory—inspired by the work of Griffiths on quartz threads—that the weakness of crystals was due to cracks or other imperfections of structure. The cold working of rock salt crystals by vigorously scraping their sides and of tungsten crystals (obtained from filaments for incandescent lamps) by drawing them through a nozzle confirmed this. The results, presented in September, 1921 under the title 'The Hardening of Crystals by Cold Working' to the meeting of the Bunsen Gesellschaft, were received with uneasy surprise. Gustav Tammann, speaking as an elder statesman, expressed this in the discussion. Yet, as later work was to show, my observations were fundamentally sound.

Meanwhile, I took up antecedent questions. Some metallurgists, interested in my work on the hardening of single crystals, told me of a method invented by Czochralski for producing metal crystals in the form of wires. It consisted in pulling out a thread from a pool of molten metal so that the thread continued to solidify at the rate at which you were pulling it out. Erwin von Gomperz, who was doing his thesis with me, was charged to make single crystals of tin and zinc in this way. Unfortunately, the metal tended to come out in lumps, and the project was saved only by the intervention of Herrmann Mark, who covered the liquid metal by a sheet of mica with a hole in the middle, through which the thread came out in a smooth cylindrical wire. But for this ingenious intervention, our subsequent investigations of the plastic flow of metals might not have come about.

The next stage of our work elucidated the crystallographic laws of plastic flow in zinc and tin. These are now well known. Of this work I should like to say only that it is a rare instance of something supposed to be a common occurrence, namely, of the participation of as many as three scientists as equals in a fairly important piece of work. We were lucky in hitting on a problem ripe for solution, big enough to engage our combined faculties, and the solution of which was worth this effort. The ripeness of the problem was confirmed when, a few months after our paper on zinc came out, a similar investigation was published by G. I. Taylor and Miss Elam in England, solving the same problem for an entirely different system, namely aluminium. Though these two parallel papers applied very different methods, they both evaluated identical possibilities concealed in a common intellectual situation.

The following episode might illustrate this principle on a smaller scale and show incidentally also how crude was the knowledge of crystal lattices on which we were relying at the time. Shortly after Mark and I had published the structure of white tin, we received a visit from the Dutch scientist van Arkel, who told us that our result was wrong, for he had established an entirely different structure of the metal. Only after hours of discussion did it transpire that his structure was actually the same as ours, but looked different because he represented it from axes turned by 45 degrees relative to ours.

Most of this work was completed in a little over two years from the day when I first 'cooked a piece of meat' in Dahlem— all of it being supported as a rather odd kind of fibre chemistry by our noble-hearted director, R. O. Herzog. Having established the geometrical mechanism of deformation in crystalline solids, we could now take up effectively the physical problems of deformation that had first attracted me into this field. But Mark had become engrossed in structure analysis, and Weissenberg had also taken up problems of his own. It fell, therefore, mainly to Schmid and myself to embark on the physics of solid strength, equipped with the crystallographic results to which our whole group had previously contributed. Schmid established his law of shearing stress at the yield point. Together we observed that minimal deformation of crystals can lead to noticeable hardening and discovered the fact of 'recovery' which cancelled hardening without recrystallization. Schmid established hardening for greater deformations by applying his law of shearing stress. Jointly we proved, by strains applied under hydrostatic pressure, that stress vertical to a slip plane leaves its resistance to heating unaffected. Experiments with W. Meissner and E. Schmid, at the temperature of $1°$ K, demonstrated the athermal quality of gliding in crystals, and this brought out the fundamental contrast of crystal plasticity to the deformation of amorphous solids, which become perfectly rigid at absolute zero. Observations with G. Masing on fine-grained zinc ruptured at liquid air temperature confirmed the fact that the internal fragmentation of a crystalline material increased its resistance to brittle rupture. In every instance so far the strength of crystals was found rising from its paradoxically low value towards the much higher theoretical strength which Griffiths had observed in amorphous quartz threads —just as the disturbance of the crystalline order shifted the condition of the crystal towards the amorphous state. This was also the explanation I found for the curious Joffe-effect: I showed, by experiments with W. Ewald, that the water dissolving the surface of a rock salt prism reduces its resistance against plastic flow and that it is the onset of this flow, acting as cold working, that increases the crystal's resistance to brittle rupture, as observed by Joffe.

I shall pass by our inquiries starting from the discovery of fibre structure in cold worked polycrystalline metals, by merely mentioning that it was nice to be able to account for this phenomenon by the crystallography of plastic deformation as observed in single crystals. More interesting, perhaps, was the fact (found with P. Beck) that the annealing of a bent aluminium crystal caused it to recrystallize, while, if it were straightened out before annealing, no recrystallization took place. These were sidelines, for they threw no light on the nature of solid strength, which remained shrouded in the paradox that all effects which would tend to restore the ideal crystal structure appeared to weaken the material far below its ideal strength, whereas every disturbance of this structure tended to raise its strength towards its ideal value.

My fascination with this fact had borne fruit—but it proved excessive. From a paper written by Erich Schmid on the occasion of my seventieth birthday, I gather that the picture I had formed of the hardening and weakening of crystals made me overlook an important clue for modifying it. My experiments with W. Ewald (1924) show that bending a rock salt crystal in one direction hardens it only for further bending in the same direction and actually weakens it for bending it back. Schmid says that such mechanical recovery has subsequently been effected in various crystals, including those of metals. Had I noticed the fact that deformation may actually weaken a crystal, my mind would have been more hospitable to the idea that the extremely low resistance of crystals against plastic deformation might be due to the kind of irregularity in the structure of the crystals that is now known as *dislocation*. However, the idea of dislocations causing a high degree of plasticity did gradually take shape in my thoughts. I gave a full account of this theory in April, 1932 in a lecture addressed to the members of Joffe's institute in Leningrad, who received it well. On returning to Berlin I talked about my theory to Orowan, who told me that he had developed a similar idea in his thesis about to be submitted for a degree. He urged me to publish my paper without considering his rival claim, but I preferred to delay this until he too was free to publish. (This explains why my communication came out in Germany and in German a year after I had left the country and had already published many papers in England.)

Meanwhile the principle that scientists only reveal hidden knowledge which has been made accessible by the intellectual situation of the moment reasserted itself. Once more the same intimations had matured into the same solutions in another, totally different, mind, the mind of G. I. Taylor in England. What I had published as 'Versetzung' in German, he published simultaneously as 'dislocation' in English.

By the autumn of 1923 I left the Institute for Fibre Chemistry through promotion to independent membership in the Institute of Physical Chemistry. Haber received me now with full confidence in my ability to work as a scientist, and I immediately plunged back into reaction kinetics. My time with X-rays and crystals had lasted three years.

# 8
# The Unaccountable
# Element in Science
## 1962

I hope that it will become clear in the course of this paper what I mean by calling some elements of science unaccountable. Let me now say only that I shall speak of the contributions made to scientific thought by acts of personal judgment which cannot be replaced by the operation of explicit reasoning. I shall try to show that such tacit operations play a decisive part not only in the discovery, but in the very holding of scientific knowledge. I shall outline the structure of these acts and indicate to what extent this structure offers a justification for relying on such acts.

Let me start by recalling that even a writer like Kant, so powerfully bent on strictly determining the rules of pure reason, occasionally admitted that into all acts of judgment there enters, and must enter, a personal decision which cannot be accounted for by any rules. Kant says that no system of rules can prescribe the procedure by which the rules themselves are to be applied. There is an ultimate agency which, unfettered by any explicit rules, decides on the subsumption of a particular instance under any general rule or a general concept. And of this agency Kant says only that it 'is what constitutes our so-called mother-wit'. (*Critique of Pure Reason*, A.133.) Indeed, at another point he declares that this faculty, indispensable to the exercise of any judgment, is quite inscrutable. He says that the way our intelligence forms and applies the schema of a class to particulars 'is a skill so deeply hidden in the human soul that we shall hardly guess the secret trick that Nature here employs'. (*Critique of Pure Reason*, A.141.) We are told, in effect, that every time we speak of dogs, trees or tables in general, or else identify something as a dog, a tree or a table, we are performing a secret trick which is unlikely ever to be revealed to our understanding.

One may wonder how a critique of pure reason could accept the operations of such a powerful mental agency, exempt from any analysis, and make no more than a few scattered references to it. And one may wonder too that generations of scholars have left such an ultimate submission of reason to unaccountable decisions unchallenged. Perhaps both Kant and his successors instinctively preferred to let such sleeping monsters lie, for fear that, once awakened, they might destroy their fundamental conception of knowledge. For, once you face up to the ubiquitous controlling position of unformalizable mental skills, you do meet difficulties for the justification of knowledge that cannot be disposed of within the framework of rationalism.

\*

I shall deal here only with the most attenuated traces of un-formalizable mental skills which we meet even in that citadel of exact science, that show-piece of strict objectivity, the classical theory of mechanics. Mechanics are the mathematical formulae by which the motions of the planets are governed. The theory is perfectly strict, and is usually said to predict strictly the observed positions and velocities of the planets. But such is not the case. For the observed readings will never coincide with theoretically predicted values, and the disparities will not only necessarily lie beyond the scope of the theory but, according to Kant's argument about the application of rules to individual instances of experience, can ultimately be interpreted only by unformalizable mental activities. Let us see what happens in practice.

When comparing observations with theoretical predictions, the first thing to decide is whether the deviations are wholly random or else show some significant trend. I shall place this question into a broader context. The picking out of significant shapes from a multitude of disorderly impressions is a task we perform un-ceasingly by looking at things in front of us. Usually this process of making sense of what we see goes on automatically and cor-rectly. But there is evidence (of which I shall give examples later) that the capacity to see objects has to be acquired during infancy by a process of learning; and of course it is common knowledge that students of science have to learn laboriously to see things through a telescope, a microscope, or in the vague shadows of a radiogram. Indeed, occasionally, we all have to strain our eyes in order to pick out a vaguely visible object. Remember also that camouflage may conceal normally visible objects from the eye by breaking up their contours. And that, of course, our eyes may be misguided into seeing objects which apparently hang firmly together but actually don't exist. For many centuries people regarded heavenly constellations as highly significant objects, though they are in fact purely accidental, illusory aggregates.

In general, therefore, to perceive an object is to solve a problem; it is to answer the question whether there is anything there, and if so, what. We first stare at something we cannot quite make out. We strain our attention trying to make a guess, but as we gradually begin to feel sure of our guess, we may actually have been deceived by a shape which happens to simulate a real object. Such is also the way the astronomer has to decide whether the observed deviations from the theoretical path of a planet show any regularity. He must try to perceive the presence, or else make sure of the absence, of a significant shape in these deviations.

Decisions thus arrived at can of course be subject to further tests, and I shall come back to this. But ulterior tests cannot produce a discovery. The astronomer would spend his whole life in futile checkings, unless he had the faculty for picking out regularities which are quite likely to prove significant. This gift of seeing things where others see nothing is indeed the mark of scientific genius, a faculty guided by vague criteria, just as are the feats of keen eyesight. This is what the members of the first scientific society boasted of by calling themselves the *Academia dei Lincei*.

It is true that in certain cases you can apply a statistical analysis to decide between regularity and randomness. This method does work by strict mathematical rules. But actually its application depends both at the start and at its conclusion on decisions that cannot be prescribed by strict rules. We must start off by suggesting some regularity which the deviations seem to possess— for example, that they are all in one direction or that they show a definite periodicity—and there exist no rules for reasonably picking out such regularities. When a suspected pattern has been fixed upon, we can compute the chances that it might have arisen accidentally, and this will yield a numerical value (for example

1 in 10 or 1 in 100) for the probability that the pattern was formed by mere chance and is therefore illusory. But having got this result, we have still to make up our minds informally whether the numerical value of the probability that the suspected regularity was formed by chance warrants us in accepting it as real or else in rejecting it as accidental.

Admittedly, rules for setting a limit to the improbability of the chances which a scientist might properly assume to have occurred have been widely accepted among scientists. But these rules have no other foundation than a vague feeling for what a scientist may regard as unreasonable chances. The late Enrico Fermi is reported to have said that a miracle is an event the chances of which are less than one in ten. The rule which Sir Ronald Fisher has made widely current in his book, *The Design of Experiments*, is a little more cautious; it rejects as illusory only patterns for which the odds of having been formed by chance is less than one in twenty. But if anyone were to suggest that the limit should be set at one in five or at one in two hundred, nothing more could be said against this than that it does not seem reasonable. So the mathematical analysis of observed deviations from a theoretical equation can do no more than partially to formalize the process of identifying significant shapes—the process that perception carries out for us informally whenever we look at things. Mathematics only inserts a formalized link in a procedure which starts with the intuitive surmise of a significant shape, and ends with an equally informal decision to reject or accept it as truly significant by considering the computed numerical probability of its being accidental.

There is one field where we can take formalization one step further. If we call the numerical improbability that a surmised pattern had arisen by chance its distinctiveness, we find that it is this quality that communication theory defines as the amount of information conveyed by a set of signals. We note, for example, that a series of twenty dots and dashes can present $2^{20}$ different configurations, each of which may convey a distinctive message. And this is the same as to say that the distinctiveness of any single configuration of twenty consecutive dots and dashes is $2^{20}$—in view of the fact that the probability of the sequence having turned up by chance is $2^{-20}$. So now both the distinctiveness of the pattern (if true), and the probability of its occurrence by chance (if specious) have a numerical value attached to them. But the physical fact of twenty consecutive dots and dashes does not reveal whether it is distinctive or whether it means nothing. It is only by our interpretation of the sequence as a coded message that it acquires its distinctive character; it is endowed with its distinctiveness of $2^{-20}$ by our effective use of it as a set of symbols. Only when we have thus attributed a meaning to a sequence, can we assess the probability of the sequence having occurred by chance, and find that the odds against this are 1 to $2^{20}$.

So we see that while communication theory does make the distinctiveness of certain patterns vividly explicit, it brings out also clearly that this quality is the result of an informal act of our own. And this can be seen to exemplify also once more the fact that randomness can be conceived only in relation to a potential order, so that both randomness and order express the outcome of an informal act of personal interpretation. For if the twenty signals had in fact flowed through the channel at random, we could attribute no probability to their particular arrangement. The sequence would then be described technically as a mere 'noise', within which any particular configuration of signals would have to be identified with any other of its $2^{20}-1$ alternatives. In fact, any ordinary noise is a noise only by virtue of the fact that we indiscriminately identify any particular configuration of its elements with any other configuration of them and thus interpret them all as the same noise. This is the philosophy of noise.

It brings out a new aspect of the task facing the astronomer in pondering on any particular set of deviations from the theoretical path of a planet. All channels of communication are affected by a certain amount of noise, and we have to read the signals against the disturbing background of this noise. If the noise level is high and the true signals scanty, we must strain our attention to pick out the significant sequence, while indiscriminately lumping together, as mere background, the signals which form the noise. And this is precisely what the astronomer must try to do if he wants to distinguish a slight but significant perturbation in the path of a planet from a background of random observational errors.

Moreover, to equate noise with background offers an illuminating transition to a more general principle entering into the recognition of significant shapes. A communication distinguished from the accompanying noise may be looked upon as a particular instance of the contrast between figure and background, a relation extensively explored by gestalt psychology. Remember the famous ambiguous pictures, such as Rubin's 'vase or faces'. You may look at this picture in one way and see two faces in profile with an empty space between them, and then look at it in another way and see a vase in the middle, with an empty background on either side where you saw the faces before. This experience shows that when an area is seen as a figure, it acquires significance and solidity, which it instantly loses when it is made to function as background —while at the same time the area which a moment ago was mere background now becomes a significant and substantial figure. We may generalize this by saying that the figure is something distinctive seen against a background that is indeterminate. Let me elaborate this.

Mimicry renders an insect invisible against its background by repeating on its wings the pattern of the leaves or blades of grass among which it lives. Camouflage acts in a similar way. In both instances, patterns will be particularly effective if they divert attention from the object's outlines. The opposite result, of rendering an object conspicuous, is achieved by covering it with a distinctive pattern which emphasizes its contours. And of course, this clear pattern will be most effective when set against a background of blurred, randomly scattered features. Indeed, an object cannot be strictly distinguished from its background unless its particulars lack any definite correlation with those of the background, and this condition is necessarily fulfilled if the particulars of the background are themselves random. Once more then, randomness is shown to safeguard the indeterminacy of a background. Insufficient randomness of background is represented in science by systematic errors which, by simulating a real effect, obscure the outline of any real effect actually present. Systematic observational errors obscure, for example, any real deviation of a planet's course from its theoretical orbit, by introducing a specious regularity from which the real deviation cannot be readily distinguished. A figure can also be concealed, as in puzzles, by covering it with random scribblings; this corresponds to a message being drowned by noise, as mentioned above.

But I must leave for a moment the subject of observational errors in order to enlarge the whole conception of a background as distinct from an object. I have said before that we see the ambiguous figure of Rubin quite differently, depending on 'how we look at it'. I must explore a little further our curious capacity for looking at a thing so effectively in two different ways, and shall pass on for this purpose to an object rendered distinctive by moving against its background. We see a cow strolling in a field. The field, and indeed the whole landscape, with the entire universe as far as the eye can reach and even beyond it to infinity—are seen, or thought, as being at rest, with the cow trotting along in the midst of it all. The background extending indefinitely and comprising an infinite range of unknown or at least unheeded particulars is seen to be at absolute rest, while certain circumscribed objects may be seen to move—as we too may feel ourselves moving—against this background.

This relation holds in fact also in reverse. An area which fills our field of vision up to the horizon will in general be seen at rest. If you look down from a bridge on the waters of a broad river like the Danube, you see the water fixed rigidly at rest while you feel yourself and the parapet over which you are leaning flying over it. If you are looking upstream, you fly forward; if downstream, backward. But the moment you lift your eyes so that your vision includes the borders of the river, the motion of the bridge stops, and the water starts once more streaming below it. So each time the area which extends indefinitely beyond the horizon functions as a background—even when as a result of it we are compelled to see a racing river stand still and the bridge on which we stand fly through the air above it.

This shows how very effective can be the act of looking at an area one way rather than another: to see it as a background to a neighbouring area which we look upon as an object—or to see the two areas the other way round. It is becoming clear also that the different ways of looking at neighbouring areas are correlated. An object is seen as such *by virtue* of our seeing its surroundings as its background—and vice versa. This has come out now strikingly in the fact that the perception of an object *in motion* appears functionally related to seeing around it an indefinitely extended background at absolute rest. It suggests that we are performing one single mental act in jointly seeing an object against its background, and that this seeing may be right or illusory; indeed, that *we are aware of the background in terms of the object's appearance*—e.g. of its being in motion—and that this view of the object *may be true or false*.

This gives us the first inkling of the structure of that mother-wit to which Kant surrenders the application of rules to experience and of that inscrutable power hidden in the bosom of Nature, by which he accounts for our capacity to form and apply universal conceptions—the tacit power which I shall try to identify and justify as the unaccountable element in science.

Our next step towards this aim leads us to the beautiful experiments of Ames in which figures were seen against the background of a room—a room of a very special kind. Opposite each other in two corners of this room stood a grown man and a young boy, and the boy looked taller than the man. This was due to the fact that the shape of the room was distorted so that at the two corners where the figures stood, the height of the ceiling and the distances from the opposite wall differed greatly. The boy standing at the corner with the lower ceiling and closer to the observer was seen taller than the grown man seen further away at the opposite corner, where the ceiling was higher.

This result is due to an illusion in two stages, both of which are relevant to us. (1) Viewed (with one eye) from the position prescribed for the experiment, the irregularly shaped room appears normal. (2) Against the background of this apparently normal but actually skew-angled room we see the sizes of persons standing in two opposite corners mistakenly as if they were standing in the opposite corners of a normal room. The illusory appearance of the room serves as a background to the illusory appearance of the figures; and the room itself is seen illusorily against another background, namely our life-long experience that rooms have regular rectangular shapes.

Both illusions are compelling when the room is seen, as prescribed, with one eye placed at a point from which the angles subtended by the edges of the skew-shaped room are the same as those of a normal room. The impression made by the room is then determined—in the absence of any striking clues to the contrary—by the past experience of normal rooms; and once the room is seen as normal, it functions as the background to the figures and thus determines their apparent size in the way a normal room would.

But the flow of this account conceals a decisive gap. It describes a sequence of two stages in which clues operate to make us see two figures at absurd sizes. But why do clues not operate in the opposite direction? The fact that young boys are smaller than adults could form a clue to correct our illusory perception of the room and controvert thereby the rule that all rooms are right-angled parallelepipeds.

We must admit that clues *might* in fact operate in this way. This does happen when you look at the experimental arrangement from a forbidden angle. Other 'give-away' clues have the same effect, for example clues collected by tapping the walls of the irregular room with a long stick. Such a scrutiny may destroy the illusion and make us see the two figures once more at their proper size. But the effort needed to achieve this shows how great is the power that operates in the opposite direction. This power resides in the area which tends to function as a background because it extends indeterminately around the central object of our attention. Seen thus from the corner of our eyes, or remembered at the back of our minds, this area compellingly affects the way we see the object on which we are focusing. We may indeed go so far as to say that we are aware of this subsidiarily noticed area mainly in the appearance of the object to which we are attending.

This interplay of background and figure illustrates a general principle: the principle that whenever we are focusing our attention on a particular object, we are relying for doing so on our awareness of many things to which we are not attending directly at the moment, but which are yet functioning as compelling clues for the way the object of our attention will appear to our senses. An obvious and often commented instance of this is our tendency to overlook things that are unprecedented. Having no clue to them, we do not see them. Charles Darwin has described how the Fuegians crowded wonderingly around the rowing boat which took his party on shore from the *Beagle*, but failed to notice the ship itself lying at anchor in front of them. Scientists are of course as subject to this failing as these Fuegians were: even astronomers observing planets, to whom I have so far restricted myself. When Neptune was discovered by Galle in 1846 by following up the predictions of Leverrier, the past positions of the new planet were computed and their identity established with a star recorded by Lalande in Paris in May 1795. This being communicated to the Paris observatory, an examination of Lalande's notebook showed that he made two observations of the planet, on the 8th and 10th May, and finding them discordant (since the planet had moved) had rejected one as probably in error and marked the other as questionable. The Cambridge astronomer Challis who undertook to test the predictions of Leverrier and Adams sighted the planet four times during the summer 1846 and once even noticed that it had a disc, but these facts made no impression on him since he doubted the hypothesis he was testing. Before its discovery as a planet by Sir William Herschel in 1781, Uranus had been recorded as a fixed star at least seventeen times: seventeen times its motion had gone unnoticed. What is more, it would be idle to reproach these astronomers for succumbing to this Fuegian attitude to the unprecedented. For the craving to find strands of permanence in the tumult of changing appearances is the supreme organon for bringing our experience under intellectual control. In fact, if astronomers had gone on testing every new star on the possibility of its being a very slowly moving planet, they might well have wasted all their time in obtaining an immense mass of meaningless observations.

Yes, the principle which misguided the Fuegians is of inestimable value. The boundless variety of raw experiences is devoid of all meaning, and our perceptive powers can render it intelligible only by identifying very different appearances as the same objects and qualities. How do our eyes do this? Snow at dusk throws less light into our eyes than a dinner jacket in sunshine, and if you look at the surface of these objects through a blackened tube, snow may appear dark and the black cloth light. But when we look at them in the usual way, snow will always be seen to be white, and a dinner jacket to be black. It is the supreme achievement of our eyes to show us objects as having a constant colour, size and shape, irrespective of their distance, position and illumination. The experiment with the blackened tube shows that this is done by taking in clues from the whole field of vision, coming from the utmost corners of our eyes, and relying on our awareness of these peripheral clues for the way we see the object which occupies the centre of our attention.

Such is the function of peripheral impressions when used as clues, and it is our powers of comprehension that bring them into action by looking at them with a bearing on the object of our attention. It is this art, the art of seeing infinite varieties of clues in terms of relatively few and enduring objects, by which we make sense of the world. It is this process of skilful integration that a monkey brought up in darkness has to learn slowly when faced with the task of recognizing its feeding bottle by the help of its eyes, and which the human baby has probably to learn likewise when acquiring the skill of looking at things. It is the same kind of learning which students have laboriously to pursue on a higher level in the practical classes of anatomy and microscopy, of radiology and clinical observation, the kind of study by which the zoologist and botanist acquires his expert capacity for identifying individual specimens of different species.

The main clues on which perception relies are in fact deeply hidden *inside the body* and cannot be experienced in themselves by the perceiver. Though we may notice the strain in our eyes and are aware of the posture of our head, the intricate pattern of internal stimuli arising from the adjustment of the lenses in our eyes, from the muscles controlling the convergence of the eyeballs, from the inner ear, etc., and the elaborate system by which our perception makes us aware of these data in the appearance of the objects we are looking at, these can hardly be experienced in themselves at all. Moreover, gestalt psychology has shown how much ingenuity is required to track down even the clues within sight of the eyes, since they are seen only incidentally and their effect on the appearance of the object perceived can be revealed only by elaborate experimental investigations. Most of the clues used in seeing objects may therefore never be identified, and besides, if identified and seen in themselves would lose their suggestive power as clues, and bereft of this function would tend to be lost among other meaningless details. Yet all these hidden evaluations of not identifiable clues are conducted, particularly when perception is strained, by the full powers of our intelligence, relying on operations which, as experiments have proved, must be acquired by efforts which in certain cases may prove so strenuous that their persistent pursuit leads to mental breakdown.

We are at last facing here fully that secret power of our nature which Kant despaired of elucidating. We see that a great deal can be known about the way it works, but we realize also that the better we know it, the less it appears capable of definition by precise objective rules. On the contrary, it is ever more clearly seen to be an intrinsically personal effort, guided by unspecifiable clues towards the achievement of a coherence sensed by ourselves in pursuing it.

Let me return with this in mind to the astronomer making up his mind whether the observed deviations from the theoretical path of a planet show any real regularity against the background of random—or perhaps somewhat systematic—observational errors. We have left him having to realize that in his inquiry he must rely on a personal interpretation of the evidence since neither order nor randomness can be measured or otherwise strictly ascertained, so that he must recognize order by his own sense of orderliness and identify randomness by his sense of randomness. The astronomer might find support for acquiescing in this situation by reflecting on the system of crystallography, a thoroughly respectable part of the exact sciences, which can be controverted by no experimental facts, since it only sets up a system of perfect order to which solids might conform; so that observed deviations from crystallography are not seen as failures of crystallography but as imperfections of the specimens in question. And as to the assessment of random chances, he might have found consolation in the fact that the laws of quantum mechanics, as well as those of thermodynamics, being statements of probabilities, are controvertible only by using some arbitrary rejection rule for denying the possibility of very odd chances.

But now the astronomer pondering on his observed data has to face further methodological worries. He must realize that the in-intellectual framework acquired in his scientific training will induce him to see what conforms to this framework and to ignore what does not; and he will be aware also of the dilemma that this evident menace to his originality is also the indispensable guide of all scientific thinking, the very safeguard of true scientific discipline. Yet he wants to get on with his inquiry. Looking at his data, he must try to make out whether they show any significant shape, perhaps a deviation from existing theory as important as Kepler found in Tycho's data of the path of Mars, or Leverrier found in the perturbations of the planet Uranus—a new feature that, if rightly interpreted, would bring him immortal fame, but if claimed mistakenly, would stamp him as a fool forever. Judging by the structure of perception, there is no explicit rule by which he can proceed to solve his problem. He must strain his attention towards any signs of regularity, but his effort must be based on an awareness of peripheral data, noticed only from the corner of his eye or remembered only at the back of his mind —while it may also require the appreciation of novel kinds of order, never met before.

But I had now better leave the astronomer to deal with his particular worries and try to widen the question facing him to include other lines of scientific research. Remember that the efforts of perception are evoked by scattered features of raw experience suggesting the presence of a hidden pattern which will make sense of the experience. Such a suggestion, if true, is itself knowledge, the kind of foreknowledge we call a good problem. Problems are the goad and the guide of all intellectual effort, which harass and beguile us into the search for an ever deeper understanding of things. The knowledge of a true problem is indeed a paradigm of all knowing. For knowing is always a tension alerted by largely unspecifiable clues and directed by them towards a focus at which we sense the presence of a thing—a thing that, like a problem, embodies the clues on which we rely for attending to it. This is the lesson derived from perception, which we have now to apply generally to the pursuit of knowledge by scientific inquiry. We shall see that it covers the unaccountable elements of science from the dawn of discovery to the holding of established scientific knowledge.

All research starts by a process of collecting clues that intrigue the inquiring mind, clues that will largely be like the peripheric clues of perception, not noticed or not even noticeable in themselves. And a good problem is half a discovery. In the case of the diffraction of X-rays by crystals, Laue's discovery followed almost immediately on the stating of the problem. Lee and Yang recently earned the Nobel prize by merely pointing out in practical terms the question whether the two directions of helicity are equivalent in nature. It took only forty-eight hours of experimental work to discover that they were not. But the elucidation of some problems may take years or even centuries. The question raised by Aristarchus of Samos whether, contrary to appearance, it was perhaps the earth that moves round the sun was not finally settled till Newton's discovery of general gravitation.

A problem is something that is puzzling and promising, and research carries this excitement into action, which in discovery culminates in triumphant satisfaction. A scientist must have the gift of seeing a problem where others see none, of sensing the direction towards a solution where others find no bearings, and of eventually revealing a solution that is a surprise to all. By contrast, persons engaged in mere surveying enlarge knowledge without being beset by problems or excited by dawning solutions, without experiencing triumph or causing surprise by completing their task. Surveying is dull because its performance is closely prescribed by rules, while science is and must be exciting, since it relies on largely unspecifiable clues which can be sensed, mobilized and integrated only by a passionate response to their hidden meaning. We have noted and analysed how perception is performed by straining our attention towards a problematic centre, while relying on hidden clues which are eventually embodied in the appearance of the object recognized by perception. This, I suggest, is also how the pursuit of science proceeds; this is the unaccountable element which enters into science at its source and vitally participates throughout even in its final result. In science this element has been called intuition. The purpose of this paper is to indicate that the structure of scientific intuition is the same as that of perception. Intuition, thus defined, is not more mysterious than perception—but not less mysterious either. Thus defined, it is as fallible as perception, and as surprisingly tending to be true. Intuition is a skill, rooted in our natural sensibility to hidden patterns and developed to effectiveness by a process of learning. Scientific intuition is one of the higher skills, like music, politics or boxing, all of which require special gifts, gifts in which a few exceptional people greatly exceed all others. Great powers of scientific intuition are called originality, for they discover things that are most surprising and make men see the world in a new way.

It is customary today to represent the process of scientific inquiry as the setting up of a hypothesis followed by its subsequent testing. I cannot accept these terms. All true scientific research starts with hitting on a deep and promising problem, and this is half the discovery. Is a problem a hypothesis? It is something much vaguer. Besides, supposing the discovery of a problem were replaced by the setting up of a hypothesis, such a hypothesis would have to be either one formulated at random or so chosen that it has a fair initial chance to be true. If the former, its chances of proving true would be negligible; if the latter, we are left with the question how it is arrived at. Why are exceptional scientific gifts required to find it? How do these operate? Such questions reveal instantly that the powers of intuition are indispensable, at all stages of establishing new scientific knowledge, and that any scheme which misses them out, or tacitly takes them for granted, or else includes them merely by the vagueness of its terms, is irrelevant to the subject of scientific inquiry and of the holding of scientific knowledge. Almost every paragraph of this paper presents an unsurmountable obstacle to any theory of knowledge which does not accord a decisive function to the intuitive powers of the mind as defined here.

But even the highest degree of intuitive originality can operate only by relying to a considerable extent on the hitherto accepted interpretative framework of science. This will supply the scientist with general clues for his inquiries, just as the experience stored at the back of our minds supplies us with general clues for the perception of novel objects. Such general clues are the premises of science and include the current methods of scientific inquiry. It is said that the Constitution of the United States is what the Supreme Court says it is. The premises of science are likewise what current discoveries prove them to be. Strictly speaking, the premises of science are today what the discoveries of tomorrow will reveal them to be.

Even so, these premises are rooted in the body of science as accepted today, and we must yet explain how the holding of our scientific knowledge today can guide scientists to discover further knowledge, unknown and indeed inconceivable today. This is recognized today by saying that the greatness of a discovery lies in its fruitfulness. But this description conceals what it would explain. It still leaves us with the paradox that we can know the presence of hidden knowledge, and can pursue its discovery guided by a sense of its growing proximity.

My own answer to this paradox is to restate an ancient metaphysical conception in new terms, guided by gestalt psychology. We make sense of experience by relying on clues of which we are often aware only as pointers to their hidden meaning; this meaning is an aspect of a reality which as such can yet reveal itself in an indeterminate range of future discoveries. This is, in fact, my definition of external reality: reality is something that attracts our attention by clues which harass and beguile our minds into getting ever closer to it, and which, since it owes this attractive power to its independent existence, can always manifest itself in still unexpected ways. If we have grasped a true and deep-seated aspect of reality, then its future manifestations will be unexpected confirmations of our present knowledge of it. It is because of our anticipation of such hidden truths that scientific knowledge is accepted, and it is their presence in the body of accepted science that keeps it alive and at work in our minds. This is how accepted science serves as the premise of all further pursuit of scientific inquiry.

The efforts of perception are induced by a craving to make out what it is that we are seeing before us. They respond to the conviction that we can make sense of experience, because it hangs together in itself. Scientific inquiry is motivated likewise by the craving to understand things. Such an endeavour can go on only if sustained by hope, the hope of making contact with the hidden pattern of things. By speaking of science as a reasonable and successful enterprise, I confirm and share this hope. This is about as much as I can say here in justification of a pursuit of knowledge based largely on hidden clues and arrived at and ultimately accredited on grounds of personal judgment. I believe that this commitment makes sense in view of man's position in the universe.

## EDITOR'S NOTE

The reader will find a more detailed listing of unspecifiabilities in scientific knowledge in Polanyi's 1967 address to the American Psychological Association, 'Logic and Psychology', *American Psychologist*, *23* (1968), 27–43. He has there embedded in his account of tacit knowing a specification of five indeterminacies: (1) the indeterminacy of empirical knowledge in its bearing on reality; (2) the unspecifiability of rules for establishing true, as distinct from illusory, coherence; (3) the indeterminacy of the grounds on which knowledge is held to be true; (4) the unspecifiability of the process of tacit integration by which knowledge is achieved; (5) the unspecifiability of the existential changes involved in modifying the grounds of scientific judgment.

# PART THREE

# Tacit Knowing

# 9
# Knowing and Being
## 1961

A few years ago a distinguished psychiatrist demonstrated to his students a patient who was having a mild fit of some kind. Later the class discussed the question whether this had been an epileptic or a hystero-epileptic seizure. The matter was finally decided by the psychiatrist: 'Gentlemen,' he said, 'you have seen a true epileptic seizure. I cannot tell you how to recognize it; you will learn this by more extensive experience.'

Clinical practitioners call the peculiar indescribable appearance of a pathological condition its *facies*; I shall call it a 'physiognomy', so as to relate it to the delicately varied expressions of the human face which we can likewise identify without being able to tell quite how we recognize them. We may describe as a physiognomy also the peculiar appearance of a species which can be recognized only 'aesthetically'[1] and further include among physiognomies the characteristics of wines and blends of tea which only experts can recognize.

Any effort to define a physiognomy more explicitly will aim: (1) at identifying its particulars and (2) at describing the relation between these particulars. I shall exemplify these two complementary efforts by reference to some comprehensive entities where the two can be observed separately.

(1) At the time when flying by aeroplane was first developed, around 1914–18, traces of prehistoric settlements were discovered from the air in fields over which many generations had walked without noticing them. Though the aerial photographs clearly revealed the outlines of the sites, the markings on the ground which constituted these outlines frequently remained unrecognizable. Such sites are comprehensive entities that are precisely traceable without mental effort from a distance, while the identification of their particulars at close quarters presents great difficulties.

The unspecifiability of particulars is here as complete as it was for a hystero-epileptic fit, but with the difference that the relation of the unspecifiable particulars is clearly definable, which it is not in case of a physiognomy.

Usually it is not impossible to identify some particulars of a comprehensive entity, for example, some symptoms of a clinically diagnosed disease. But in such cases another limitation of specifiability becomes apparent, as gestalt psychology has amply taught us. Specifiability remains incomplete in two ways. First, there is always a residue of particulars left unspecified; and second, even when particulars can be identified, isolation changes their appearance to some extent. Seen in isolation a jumping cat may appear to change its colour from white to dark grey, but when a window is included in the field of vision the cat is seen unchangingly the same white or grey. It has happened in Lancashire that a customer who ordered a shirting of green stripes on a white ground refused delivery, for he found the ground was purple. Since the colour of any patch of a surface varies with the context in which it is placed, coloured patterns are not specifiable in terms of their isolated particulars. The 'red patch' generally used as a paradigm of a primary sense datum can never be unambiguously identified as such.

(2) Now for the reverse effort which aims at specifying the relations of particulars within a comprehensive entity. It is conspicuous in the case of topographic anatomy. We can easily identify the several organs, including blood vessels and nerve tracts in the human body (which is the task of systematic anatomy), but their mutual relation inside the body can be grasped only by a sustained effort of the imagination, based on the partial aspects revealed by successive stages of dissection. Similar difficulties have to be overcome in achieving an understanding of a geological topography and of the spatial relation of the component parts of a complex machine. Even the regular structure of crystals may present such problems. In 1923 H. Mark and I established the atomic structure of white tin.[2] Shortly after that we had a visit by Professor van Arkel from Holland who claimed to have established an entirely different structure. Eventually, it transpired that this structure had the same arrangement of atoms as ours, but that he had described it along lines forming an angle of 45° to those along which we had seen it. This trivial difference

in viewing the atomic arrangement had rendered it mutually un-recognizable to both parties, simply because we lacked a sufficient understanding of the relationships involved in the atomic arrange-ment. To this extent any complex spatial arrangement of opaque objects is unspecifiable.

We can see then two complementary efforts aiming at the elucidation of a comprehensive entity. One proceeds from a recognition of a whole towards an identification of its particulars; the other, from the recognition of a group of presumed particulars towards the grasping of their relation in the whole.

I have called these two efforts complementary since they con-tribute jointly to the same final achievement, yet it is also true that each counteracts the other to some extent at every consecutive step. Every time we concentrate our attention on the particulars of a comprehensive entity, our sense of its coherent existence is temporarily weakened; and every time we move in the opposite direction towards a fuller awareness of the whole, the particulars tend to become submerged in the whole. The concerted advan-tage of the two processes arises from the fact that normally every dismemberment of a whole adds more to its understanding than is lost through the concurrent weakening of its comprehensive features, and again each new integration of the particulars adds more to our understanding of them than it damages our under-standing by somewhat effacing their identity. Thus an alteration of analysis and integration leads progressively to an ever deeper understanding of a comprehensive entity.

Medicine offers readily an illustration of what I have in mind here. A medical student deepens his knowledge of a disease by learning a list of its symptoms with all their variations, but only clinical practice can teach him to integrate the clues observed on an individual patient to form a correct diagnosis of his illness, rather than an erroneous diagnosis which is often more plausible.

There is a close analogy between the *elucidation of a compre-hensive object* and the mastering of a skill. A skill too is improved by alternate dismemberment and integration. Sportsmen like skaters, skiers, runners, swimmers; artists like dancers, pianists, or painters; skilled craftsmen and practitioners, all profit from motion-studies, followed by a skilful incorporation of the isolated motions into a complete performance.

Moreover, there are limits to the specifiability of skills, and these are analogous to those which apply to the specification of physiognomies and other comprehensive entities. The analysis of a skilful feat in terms of its constituent motions remains always incomplete. There are notorious cases, like the distinctive 'touch' of a pianist, in which the analysis of a skill has long been debated inconclusively; and common experience shows that no skill can be acquired by learning its constituent motions separately. Moreover, here too isolation modifies the particulars: their dynamic quality is lost. Indeed, the identification of the constituent motions of a skill tends to paralyse its performance. Only by turning our attention away from the particulars and towards their joint purpose, can we restore to the isolated motions the qualities required for achieving their purpose. Again, as in the case of knowing a physiognomy, this act of integration is itself unspecifiable. Imitation offers guidance to it, but in the last resort we must rely on discovering for ourselves the right feel of a skilful feat. We alone can catch the knack of it; no teacher can do this for us.

The structural kinship of the arts of knowing and doing is indeed such that they are rarely exercised in isolation; we usually meet a blend of the two. Medical diagnosis combines them about equally. To percuss a lung is as much a muscular feat as a delicate discrimination of the sounds thus elicited. The palpation of a spleen or a kidney combines a skilful kneading of the region with a trained sense for the peculiar feeling of the organ's resistance. It is apposite therefore to include skilful feats among comprehensive entities. Though we may prefer to speak of *understanding* a comprehensive object or situation and of *mastering* a skill, we do use the two words nearly as synonyms. Actually, we speak equally of *grasping* a subject or an art.

A peculiar combination of skilful doing and knowing is present in the working of our sense organs. I have mentioned before the interaction of all parts of the visual field in determining what we see. But it is our own active adjustment of our pupils and lenses and of the convergence of our eyes that fashion the two retinal images on which this picture is based; and the perceived picture depends on these actions once more as the messages received from the muscles adjusting the eyes are incorporated by us in the qualities of the perceived object. Nor is this all; our perception is effectively co-determined also by messages from the internal ear, from the muscles which keep our body and head in its position, as well as by an ample range of memories. These internal data both guide the reflexes of our eye-muscles in shaping our retinal images and control our evaluation in terms of perceptions of the sum total of relevant stimuli. There is also clear evidence to show that—as might be expected in the case of a skill—the capacity to see objects is acquired by training.

Visual perception does present, therefore, the main characteristics of a combined skilful doing and knowing. But there is also something new here, namely the fact that a major part of the particulars shaping the sight of an external object are *internal* actions and stimuli. Though our eye-muscles are subject to intentional control and we might even be dimly aware of a strain in them, such internal particulars are never clearly observable in themselves. And this unspecifiability is not of the same kind as found in the traces of a site which can only be seen jointly from the air; for the particulars of perception (other than smell and taste) have the distinctive peculiarity of being projected from the interior of the body into the space outside it.

A similar projection takes place in the use of tools and probes, and the process can be studied here more easily, since the stimuli that are projected here can be fairly well observed in themselves. The relevant facts are well known. The rower pulling an oar feels the resistance of the water; when using a paper-knife we feel the blade cutting the pages. The actual impact of the tool on our palm and fingers is unspecifiable in the same sense in which the muscular acts composing a skilful performance are unspecifiable; we are aware of them in terms of the tool's action on its object, that is, in the comprehensive entity into which we integrate them. But the impacts of a tool on our hands are integrated in a way similar to that by which internal stimuli are integrated to form our perceptions: the integrated stimuli are noticed at a distance removed outward from the point where they impinge on us. In this sense impacts of a tool on our hands function as internal stimuli, and a tool functions accordingly as an extension of our hands. The same is true of a probe used for exploring a cavity, or for a stick by which a blind man feels his way. The impact made by a probe or stick on our fingers is felt at the tip of the probe or stick, where it hits on objects outside, and in this sense the probe or stick is an extension of our fingers that grasp it.

The assimilation of a tool, a stick or a probe to our body is

K

achieved gradually, as its proper use is being learned and per-fected. The more fully we master the use of an instrument, the more precisely and discriminatingly will we localize at the farther end of it the stimuli impinging on our body while grasping and handling the instrument. This corresponds to the way we learn skilfully to use our eyes to see external objects.

We have now established analogous structures in several pro-cesses of knowing: namely, (1) the understanding of physiog-nomies, (2) the performance of skills, (3) the proper use of sen-sory organs, and (4) the mastery of tools and probes. In order to deal jointly with this whole family we need a general terminology for indicating the relation of a set of particulars to a compre-hensive entity. The essential feature throughout is the fact that *particulars can be noticed in two different ways.* We can be aware of them uncomprehendingly, i.e., in themselves, or understandingly, in their participation in a comprehensive entity. In the first case we focus our attention on the isolated particulars; in the second, our attention is directed beyond them to the entity to which they con-tribute. In the first case therefore we may say that we are aware of the particulars *focally*; in the second, that we notice them *sub-sidiarily in terms of their participation in a whole.*

These alternatives do not necessarily involve any change in the degree of attention given to the particulars. When, after having first looked uncomprehendingly at the symptoms of a patient, we hit on the diagnosis of his illness, his symptoms become meaning-ful without becoming less noticeable. Focal and subsidiary aware-ness are definitely *not two degrees* of attention but *two kinds* of atten-tion given to the *same* particulars. In the case of visual attention we may speak of *looking at* the particulars in themselves, as dis-tinct from *seeing them* while looking at the context of which they form part. But 'seeing' and 'looking at' cannot be generally used instead of subsidiary and focal noticing.

We can formulate this difference in terms of *meaning*. When we focus on a set of particulars uncomprehendingly, they are rela-tively meaningless, compared with their significance when noticed subsidiarily within the comprehensive entity to which they con-tribute. As a result we have two kinds of meaning: *one*, exem-plified by the particulars of a physiognomy, where the two things, namely (a) the isolated particulars and (b) what they jointly mean, are not clearly separated in space; and the *other*, exemplified by visual perception and the use of tools and probes, where the un-comprehended particulars are inside our body or at its surface, and what they mean extends into space outside. It may sometimes prove convenient to call the first kind of meaning *physiognostic* and the second *telegnostic*.

Our examples of unspecifiability can now be recapitulated in these terms. When a prehistoric site is discovered from the air we see the meaning of particulars which we cannot see in themselves. On the other hand, the study of topographic anatomy starts by seeing particulars in themselves uncomprehendingly, and then proceeds to realize their spatial relation, which represents their meaning, in the present sense of the term, e.g., to a surgeon. In the first case, unspecifiability *impedes the analysis of a given meaning*; in the second case, it *restricts the discovery of an unknown meaning*. In either case the alternation of analysis and integration progressively deepens both our insight into the meaning of a comprehensive entity in terms of its particulars and the meaning of these partic-ulars in terms of their joint significance. When applied to the performance of a skill, this alternation renders our muscular actions ever better adjusted to their joint purpose.

We possess a supremely important system of telegnostic mean-ing in the denotative meaning of words. A man's name, by itself a meaningless sound, acquires a meaning by being consistently used as a pointer to the person whom it designates, exactly as the knocking of objects by a stick acquires a meaning as we learn to use the stick skilfully for feeling our way in the dark. The use of *general* denotative terms involves the establishment of a physiog-nostic meaning, namely, the joint meaning of all the instances to which the general term is intended to refer. We meet meanings of analogous structure in the mastery of a skill, in the resourceful-ness with which a master handles every new and unprecedented situation.

General conceptions claim a kind of foreknowledge which, though never quite absent from the act of knowing, is more marked in this case than in any other surveyed so far. This offers a convenient transition to the process of discovery, in which fore-knowledge will be seen manifested even more effectively. I shall lead on to this fact by showing first that all manner of discovery proceeds by a see-saw of analysis and integration similar to that by which our understanding of a comprehensive entity is progressively deepened. The two complementary movements are here a search for the joint meaning of a set of particulars, alternating with a search for the specification of their hitherto uncomprehended meaning in terms of yet unknown particulars.

The process of empirical induction may appear to present only the first of these two movements, since it proceeds from the observation of particulars to the discovery of their relations fixed by universal laws. But actually both movements are involved, for advances towards generalization do alternate with verification. The process of inductive discovery is in fact an oscillation between movements of analysis and integration in which, on balance, integration predominates.

Physics is largely based on such integrative discoveries, but in the progress of biology it is mostly analysis that leads the way. Discoveries aiming at a better understanding of living beings accept for their starting point the existence of plants and animals as complex entities, and usually proceed to analyse these in terms of their organs and the functions of their organs, which are analysed in their turn in terms of physics and chemistry. In biology these particulars are specified as means to an end, and this applies also to the physical and chemical study of living beings. Physico-chemical processes may enable plants and animals to function well or else may disturb their functions, and they form the subject matter of biology only in so far as they have a bearing on life in one of these two ways.

But biological analysis alternates of course with integration, and this may even predominate. New comprehensive entities may be established in the manner in which Harvey discovered the circulation of the blood, partly by the observation of the valves in veins, or when the process of evolution was established partly from palaeozoic data.

We must remember also that great advances have been achieved in physics by pure deduction whenever surprising implications of accepted theories were discovered. Indeed, to an important degree all discovery is deductive. For no inquiry can succeed unless it starts from a true, or at least partly true, conception of the nature of things. Such foreknowledge is indispensable, and all discovery is but a step towards the verification of such foreknowledge.

The structural analogy between knowledge and skill allows us to expand our perspective from discovery to invention. Fore-knowledge which guides discovery has its counterpart in the purpose which guides the invention of a skill or of a new practical device. The most precious gift of the inventor is his capacity to conceive a practical purpose which might prove feasible. This is mostly the sole inventive function of a research director, who entrusts to his assistants the solution of the general problems set, or approved, by him. Agog with his problem, the inventor speculates on the possibilities offered by the field of experience, and by his sustained efforts to solve his problem brings about the emergence of its solution. Such is the heuristic power of a practicable problem. It has been beautifully described on an elementary level by Koehler for chimpanzees. He shows how a desire pondered upon by the animal evokes a re-organization of its field of vision, revealing to it both the instrument and the procedure for satisfying its desire. This is also how skills are acquired and perfected; this is how we learn to use tools or probes, and how we improve our powers of sensory perception. We may add that this is likewise the basic mechanism for solving a mathematical problem. The solution of a problem in mathematics is discovered by casting around with a view to filling the gaps left open in a situation which constitutes a solvable problem—exactly as a practical problem is solved by an invention.

We can lend greater precision now to what has been said earlier about the way induction is guided by our general conception of the nature of things. Successful induction can be conducted only in the light of a genuine problem. An inductive problem is an intimation of coherence among hitherto uncomprehended particulars, and the problem is genuine to the extent to which this intimation is true. Such a surmise vaguely anticipates the evidence which will support it and guides the mind engrossed by it to the discovery of this evidence. This usually proceeds stepwise, the original problem and surmise being modified and corrected by each new piece of evidence, a process which is repeated until eventually some generalization is accepted as final.

To hit upon a problem is the first step to any discovery and indeed to any creative act. To see a problem is to see something hidden that may yet be accessible. The knowledge of a problem is, therefore, like the knowing of unspecifiables, a knowing of more than you can tell. But our awareness of unspecifiable things, whether of particulars or of the coherence of particulars, is intensified here to an exciting intimation of their hidden presence. It is an engrossing possession of incipient knowledge which passionately strives to validate itself. Such is the heuristic power of a problem.

But we may yet say that what is usually called knowledge is structurally similar to the knowledge of a problem. Knowledge is an activity which would be better described as a process of knowing. Indeed, as the scientist goes on inquiring into yet uncomprehended experiences, so do those who accept his discoveries as established knowledge keep applying this to ever changing situations, developing it each time a step further. Research is an intensely dynamic inquiring, while knowledge is a more quiet research. Both are ever on the move, according to similar principles, towards a deeper understanding of what is already known.

A theory of knowledge must be applicable to both kinds of knowing. Its function must be to justify our reliance on our knowing (whether dynamic or quiet) in spite of its unspecifiable contents. I shall outline this matter by using as my example the recognition of a disease by its physiognomy, which will have also to stand for all the other cases of knowing already surveyed.

The knowing of a disease is doubly unspecifiable. (1) We cannot identify, let alone describe, a great number of the particulars which we are in fact noticing when we diagnose a case of the disease. (2) Though we can identify a case of the disease by its typical appearance, we cannot describe it adequately, and there are four closely related reasons for this. (a) We are ignorant (according to 1) of the unspecifiable particulars which would enter into the description. (b) The relation between the particulars —even if they could all be identified—could be described only in vague terms which the expert alone would understand. (c) Our identification of a disease in any one instance comprehends unspecifiably as its particulars the whole range of cases which, in spite of their individual differences, we have identified in the past, and (d) it relies on this comprehension for the future identification of an unlimited number of further cases which might differ from those known before in an infinite variety of unexpected ways. This is its heuristic function.

How can we justify such knowing? Clearly not in terms of its unspecifiable contents ranging over (1) and (2), (a), (b), (c), (d). Any justification of it must credit ourselves with unformalizable powers of the kind that Kant acknowledged, with reference to subsumptions of the type (2c) or (2d), by calling these powers 'an art hidden in the depth of the human soul'. We must accredit in particular our competence for comprehending unspecifiable entities, which will yet reveal themselves in the future in an unlimited number of unexpected ways.

This may seem absurd. To claim that we can know the unexpected may appear self-contradictory. It would indeed be self-contradictory if knowing included a capacity to specify completely what we know. But if all knowledge is fundamentally tacit, as it is if it rests on our subsidiary awareness of particulars in terms of a comprehensive entity, then our knowledge may include far more than we can tell. The true meaning of the heliocentric system was discovered only by Newton, but it was anticipated 140 years earlier by Copernicus.

We can account for this capacity of ours to know more than we can tell if we believe in the presence of an external reality with which we can establish contact. This I do. I declare myself committed to the belief in an external reality gradually accessible to knowing, and I regard all true understanding as an intimation of such a reality which, being real, may yet reveal itself to our deepened understanding in an indefinite range of unexpected manifestations. I accept the obligation to search for the truth through my own intimations of reality, knowing that there is, and can be, no strict rule by which my conclusions can be justified. My reference to reality legitimates my acts of unspecifiable knowing, even while it duly keeps the exercise of such acts within the bounds of a rational objectivity. For a claim to have made contact with reality necessarily legislates both for myself and others with universal intent.

I must admit that I can fulfil my obligation to serve the truth only to the extent of my natural abilities as developed by my education. No one can transcend his formative milieu very far, and beyond this area he must rely on it uncritically. I consider that this matrix of my thought determines my personal calling. It both offers me my opportunity for seeking the truth, and limits my responsibility for arriving at my own conclusions.

This conception of knowledge as personal knowing departs in

two closely related respects from the ideal of a strictly justifiable knowledge. It accredits man's capacity to acquire knowledge even though he cannot specify the grounds of his knowing, and it accepts the fact that his knowing is exercised within an accidentally given framework that is largely unspecifiable. These two acceptances are correlated within the effort of integration which achieves knowing. For this effort subsidiarily relies, on the one hand, on stimuli coming from outside, from all parts of our body and from tools or instruments assimilated to our body, and on the other hand, on a wide range of linguistic pointers which bring to bear our pre-conceptions—based on past experiences—on the interpretation of our subject matter. The structure of knowing, revealed by the limits of specifiability, thus fuses our subsidiary awareness of the particulars belonging to our subject matter with the cultural background of our knowing.

To this extent knowing is an indwelling: that is, a utilization of a framework for unfolding our understanding in accordance with the indications and standards imposed by the framework. But any particular indwelling is a particular form of mental existence. If an act of knowing affects our choice between alternative frameworks, or modifies the framework in which we dwell, it involves a change in our way of being. But since such existential choices are included in an act of knowing, they can be exercised competently, with universal intent. Nor do similar existential changes, undergone passively, impair the rationality of our personal judgment. They merely affect our calling. For while they modify our opportunities for seeking the truth, they still leave us free to reach our own conclusions within the limits granted by these opportunities. All thought is incarnate; it lives by the body and by the favour of society. But it is not *thought* unless it strives for truth, a striving which leaves it free to act on its own responsibility, with universal intent.

We have found that our subsidiary awareness of the particulars of a comprehensive entity is fused, in our knowing of the entity, with our subsidiary awareness of our own bodily and cultural being. Let me now attend to the effect exercised by the subsidiary character of these particulars on the kind of being that we ascribe to the entity known through them.

When we watch a man's face and try to fathom his thoughts, we do not examine his several features in isolation, but view them jointly as parts of his physiognomy. Thus we are aware of far more particulars, and relations between particulars, than we could specify. Moreover, even the particulars which we could identify would lose their meaning when seen in isolation and would get lost among the irrelevant details of their surroundings. It is generally impossible, therefore, to keep track of a man's mental manifestations, except by watching them as pointers to the mind from which they originate. This is analogously true of any aggregate of unspecifiable particulars forming a comprehensive entity. But it is more pronounced in the traces of a human mind than it is, say, in the traces of a prehistoric site, because a human mind is actively at work in its own traces.

To show this I must go back to glance at the lower levels of life. The moment we identify a plant or animal we attribute an achievement to it. For we recognize it by its typical shape, which it has achieved by growing up healthily. At the same time we will notice any imperfections of its shape. Thus even when we are considering merely their shapes, we can identify living beings only in terms that attribute success or failure to them as individuals. On this morphological level the centre of individuality is comparatively weak. But the manifestations of this centre become steadily more accentuated as we successively ascend, first, to the vegetative level of physiological functions, then to active, sentient and appetitive behaviour, thence to the level of intelligence and inventiveness, finally reaching the level of the responsible human person. Each time we identify the existence of an individual at one of these levels we thereby attribute to it a measure of success or failure. The moment we recognize a human being we attribute to him a measure of active, responsible intelligence. We know a normal human being as a person, and the particulars of his physiognomy gain a vivid significance by being known in terms of this person.

At whatever level we consider a living being, the centre of its individuality is real. For it is always something we ascertain by comprehending the coherence of largely unspecifiable particulars, and which we yet expect to reveal itself further by an indeterminate range of future manifestations. Thus the criteria of reality are fulfilled. The human mind in particular is real in this sense, and indeed more real than the lower centres of individuality. For an intelligent person's mind is expected to reveal itself over a far wider range of indeterminate manifestations than the lower centres which control his growth or appetitive action.

The progression from lower to higher levels of individuality involves a fundamental change in the relation between the observed individual and ourselves as observers. When comprehending the lower levels of life in an individual, we ascribe success or failure to it by standards which we deem appropriate to its kind. Throughout the usual compass of biology, we find this relation between the observer and his subject: he is always critical of it. But as our study, ascending to higher levels, reaches that of man, criticism becomes mutual; the subject of our study now criticizes us, just as we criticize it. Nor is this the end of the progression: our subject may ascend still further and become our master. We then become apprenticed to our subject and learn to accept its criticism of ourselves.

We arrive here at a process of education that, as such, is akin to the acceptance of our calling and which, indeed, forms part of it. For our cultural background is determined to a considerable extent by the influence of a limited number of men. Primitive cultures are transmitted orally by a few authoritative persons in each succeeding generation. Our modern, highly articulate culture flows largely from a small set of men whose works and deeds are revered and consulted for guidance. The knowing of these great men is an indwelling in the sense already defined. Our awareness of their works and deeds serves us (to repeat my definition) as a framework for unfolding our understanding in accordance with the indications and standards imposed by the framework.

This progressive transition is no mere sleight of hand; it is firmly grounded in the co-extension of knowing and being. We can see this by descending gradually from our educational dwelling in the works of great men to the biological study of plants and animals at lower levels. At no stage do we cease to participate in the life of the individual under observation. For we comprehend a living being at all levels by our subsidiary awareness of its particulars. These particulars are never observed in themselves; we *read* them as manifestations of an individual. We rely on them as pointers, as we rely on a probe or a written text, by making them parts of ourselves for reaching beyond them. Thus our understanding of living beings involves at all levels a measure of indwelling; our interest in life is always convivial. There is no break therefore in passing from biology to the acceptance of our cultural calling in which we share the life of a human society, including the life of its ancestors, the authors of our cultural heritage.

[1] 'Aesthetic recognition' is illustrated by C. F. A. PANTIN, 'The Recognition of Species', *Science Progress*, *42* (1954), pp. 587–98.
[2] See Essay 7 above.

# 10
# The Logic of Tacit Inference
## 1964

I propose to bring fresh evidence here for my theory of knowledge and expand it in new directions. We shall arrive most swiftly at the centre of the theory, by going back to the point from which I started about twenty years ago.[1] Upon examining the grounds on which science is pursued, I saw that its progress is determined at every stage by indefinable powers of thought. No rules can account for the way a good idea is found for starting an inquiry, and there are no firm rules either for the verification or the refutation of the proposed solution of a problem. Rules widely current may be plausible enough, but scientific inquiry often proceeds and triumphs by contradicting them. Moreover, the explicit content of a theory fails to account for the guidance it affords to future discoveries. To hold a natural law to be true is to believe that its presence may reveal itself in yet unknown and perhaps yet unthinkable consequences; it is to believe that natural laws are features of a reality which as such will continue to bear consequences inexhaustibly.

It appears then that scientific discovery cannot be achieved by explicit inference, nor can its true claims be explicitly stated. Discovery must be arrived at by the tacit powers of the mind, and its content, so far as it is indeterminate, can be only tacitly known.

But where to turn for a logic by which such tacit powers can achieve and uphold true conclusions? *We must turn to the example of perception.* This has been my basic assumption. I maintained that the capacity of scientists to perceive in nature the presence of lasting shapes differs from ordinary perception only by the fact that it can integrate shapes that ordinary perception cannot readily handle. *Scientific knowing consists in discerning gestalten that indicate a true coherence in nature.*

The study of perception by gestalt psychology has demonstrated the tacit operations that establish such coherence. When I move my hand before my eyes, it would keep changing its colour, its shape and its size, but for the fact that I take into account a host of rapidly changing clues, some in the field of vision, some in my eye muscles and some deeper still in my body, as in the labyrinth of the inner ear. My powers of perceiving coherence make me see these thousand varied and changing clues jointly as one single unchanging object, as an object moving about at different distances, seen from different angles, under variable illuminations. A successful integration of a thousand changing particulars into a single constant sight makes me recognize a real object in front of me.

Integration is almost effortlessly performed by adult eyes, but such powers of seeing things are acquired by early training in the infant child and are continuously developed by practice. Students of medicine struggle for weeks in learning to discern true shapes in the radiogram of a lung. Trained perception is basic to all descriptive sciences.

While the integration of clues to perceptions may be virtually effortless, the integration of clues to discoveries may require sustained efforts guided by exceptional gifts. But the difference is only one of range and degree: the transition from perception to discovery is unbroken. The logic of perceptual integration may serve therefore as a model for the logic of discovery.

Observe the way this integration works when we look at an object, for example a finger of our own, through a pinhole in a sheet of paper. If I do this and move my finger back and forth, I see it swelling as it approaches my eye. Psychologists have called this effect a 'de-realization'. The moving object has lost here some of its constancy, for it lacks confirmation from the periphery of the visual field; and with the loss of its constancy the object has lost some of its apparent reality.[2]

The remarkable thing here is the way the appearance of a thing at the centre of my attention depends on clues to which I am not directly attending. These clues are of two kinds. There are some that we cannot experience in themselves. The contraction of my eye muscles or the stirring inside of my labyrinth organ I cannot observe directly. These clues are *subliminal*. Other clues to the sight of my finger are the things covered up by the paper when I look at my finger through a pinhole. I normally see these things from the corner of my eye, and I *could* observe them directly, if I wanted to. We may call such clues *marginal*. To neither kind of clues do I attend directly, yet both kinds contribute to the apparent reality of the object on which my attention is focused. *We may say that my awareness of both kind of clues is subsidiary to my focal awareness of that object.*

These two kinds of awareness—the subsidiary and the focal— are fundamental to the tacit apprehension of coherence. Gestalt psychology has demonstrated that when we recognize a whole, we see its parts differently from the way we see them in isolation. It has shown that within a whole its parts have a *functional appearance* which they lack in isolation and that we can cause the merging of the parts in the whole by shifting our attention from the parts to the whole.

More than a century ago William Whewell described how the merging of hitherto isolated observations into elements of a scientific theory changes their appearance.

> To hit upon a right conception (he wrote) is a difficult step; and when this step is once made, the facts assume a different aspect from what they had before: that done, they are seen in a new point of view; and the catching this point of view, is a special mental operation, requiring special endowments and habits of thought.[3]

We may say that a scientific discovery reduces our focal awareness of observations into a subsidiary awareness of them, by shifting our attention from them to their theoretical coherence.

This act of integration, which we can identify both in the visual perception of objects and in the discovery of scientific theories is the tacit power we have been looking for. I shall call it *tacit knowing*.

It will facilitate my discussion of tacit knowing if I speak of the clues or parts that are subsidiarily known as the *proximal term* of tacit knowing and of that which is focally known as the *distal term* of tacit knowing. In the case of perception we are attending to an object separated from most of the clues which we integrate into its appearance; the proximal and the distal terms are then largely different objects, joined together by tacit knowing. This is not so when we know a whole by integrating its parts into their joint appearance, or when the discovery of a theory integrates observations into their theoretical appearance. In this case the proximal term consists of things seen in isolation, and the distal trem consists of the same things seen as a coherent entity.

But tacit knowing does exercise in both cases its characteristic powers of integration, merging the subsidiary into the focal, the proximal into the distal. We may say then that in tacit knowing we always attend *from* the proximal *to* the distal term.

In subordinating the subsidiary to the focal, tacit knowing *is directed from the first to the second*. I call this the *functional* aspect of tacit knowing. Since this functional relation is set up between two kinds of awareness, its directedness is necessarily conscious. Such directedness coincides then with the kind of intentionality which Franz Brentano has claimed to be a characteristic of all manner of consciousness.[4] This vectorial quality of tacit knowing will prove important.

We have seen that by attending from the proximal to the distal, we cause a transformation in the appearance of both: they acquire an integrated appearance. A perceived object acquires constant size, colour and shape; observations incorporated in a theory are reduced to mere instances of it; the parts of a whole merge their isolated appearance into the appearance of the whole. This is the *phenomenal* accompaniment of tacit knowing, which tells us that we have a real coherent entity before us. At the same time it embodies the *ontological claim* of tacit knowing. The act of tacit knowing thus implies the claim that its result is an aspect of reality which, as such, may yet reveal its truth in an inexhaustible range of unknown and perhaps still unthinkable ways.

My definition of reality, as that which may yet inexhaustibly manifest itself, implies the presence of an *indeterminate* range of *anticipations* in any knowledge bearing on reality. But besides this indeterminacy of its prospects, tacit knowing may contain also an *actual knowledge* that is indeterminate, in the sense that its content *cannot be explicitly stated*.

We can see this best in the way we possess a skill. If I know how to ride a bicycle or how to swim, this does not mean that I can tell how I manage to keep my balance on a bicycle or keep afloat when swimming. I may not have the slightest idea of how I do this or even an entirely wrong or grossly imperfect idea of it, and yet go on cycling or swimming merrily. Nor can it be said that I know how to bicycle or swim and yet do *not* know how to co-ordinate the complex pattern of muscular acts by which I do my cycling or swimming. I both know how to carry out these per-formances as a whole and also know how to carry out the elementary acts which constitute them, though I cannot tell what these acts are. This is due to the fact that I am only subsidiarily aware of these things, and our subsidiary awareness of a thing *may not suffice to make it identifiable*.

There are unspecifiable subsidiary elements present also in perception and in scientific discovery. We know a person's face and can recognize him among a thousand, indeed among a million. Yet we usually cannot tell how we recognize a face we know. There are many other instances of the recognition of a character-istic appearance—some commonplace, others more technical—which have the same structure as the identification of a person. University students are taught in practical classes to identify cases of diseases and specimens of rocks, plants and animals. This is the training of perception that underlies the descriptive sciences. The knowledge which such training transmits cannot be put into words, nor even conveyed by pictures; it must rely on the pupil's capacity to recognize the characteristic features of a physiognomy and their configuration in the physiognomy.

But does the successful teaching of skills and of the characteris-tic appearance of a physiognomy not prove that one *can* tell our knowledge of them? No, what the pupil must discover by an effort of his own is something we could not tell him. And he knows it then in his turn but cannot tell it.

This result actually takes me a step beyond the point I had aimed at. It exemplifies not only that the subsidiary elements of perception may be unspecifiable, but shows also that such tacit knowledge can be *discovered*, without our being able to identify what it is, what we have come to know. This holds equally for the learning of skills: we learn to ride a bicycle without being able to tell in the end how we do it.

Some fairly recent observations have demonstrated experi-mentally the process by which we acquire knowledge that we cannot tell. The experiment in question produces a fixed relation between two events, both of which we know but only one of which we can tell.

Lazarus and McCleary have shown this to take place when a person is presented for brief periods with several nonsense syllables and after certain of these syllables he is subjected to an electric shock.[5] Soon the person shows signs of anticipating the shock at the sight of the shock syllables; yet, on questioning, he fails to identify them. He has come to know when to expect a shock, but cannot tell what makes him expect it. He has acquired a knowledge similar to that which we have when we know a person by signs which we cannot tell, or perform a skill by co-ordinating elementary muscular motions according to principles that we cannot tell.

Lazarus has given the process he discovered the name of *subception*, and this has been widely adopted. The connection of subception with gestalt has, however, gone practically unnoticed. In the long-drawn controversy between Lazarus and C. W. Eriksen, which ended in 1960 by Eriksen's confirmation of subception, its connection with gestalt was not mentioned.

For my part, I regard subception as a striking confirmation of tacit knowing, as first revealed by gestalt psychology. I would indeed not rely so much on subception for demonstrating the structure of tacit knowing, had I not established this structure previously, from other, more richly documented evidence.

Psychologists have called subception a process of *learning without awareness*.[6] The description suits our present purpose. If there is learning without awareness, there must be also *discovery without awareness*, since discovery is but learning from nature. The way a novice discovers for himself the characteristic appearance of a specimen is but a minor replica of the act by which that appearance was first discovered by a scientist. Whewell's description of a discovery in mathematical physics (he had Kepler's discovery of elliptic paths in mind) has shown us a typical act of tacit integration at work. Discovery comes in stages, and at the beginning the scientist has but a vague and subtle intimation of its prospects. Yet these anticipations, which alert his solitary mind, are the precious gifts of his originality. They contain a deepened sense of the nature of things and an awareness of the facts that might serve as clues to a suspected coherence in nature. Such expectations are decisive for the inquiry, yet their content is elusive, and the process by which they are reached often cannot be specified. It is a typical feat of discovery without awareness.

Thus, in the structure of tacit knowing, we have found a mechanism which can produce discoveries by steps we cannot specify. This mechanism may then account for scientific intuition, for which no other explanation is known so far. Such intuition

L

is not the supreme immediate knowledge, called intuition by Leibniz or Spinoza or Husserl, but a work-a-day skill for scientific guessing with a chance of guessing right.

But are all these tacit operations not merely provisional? Are we to abandon the ideal of explicit inference, which alone can safeguard critical reason? My answer is that there is an important area in which explicit thought is ineffectual. No explicit direction can make us see a pair of stereoscopic photographs as one solid image; a person putting on right-left inverting spectacles will go about helplessly for days on end though he knows that he has merely to transpose the things he sees from right to left and from left to right. He will eventually learn to see with inverting spectacles without knowing how he does it. We cannot learn to keep our balance on a bicycle by taking to heart that in order to compensate for a given angle of imbalance $a$, we must take a curve on the side of the imbalance, of which the radius ($r$) should be proportionate to the square of the velocity ($v$) over the imbalance: $r \sim \dfrac{v^2}{a}$. Such knowledge is ineffectual, unless known tacitly.

We have seen *tacit knowledge* to comprise two kinds of awareness, *subsidiary awareness* and *focal awareness*. Now we see *tacit knowledge* opposed to *explicit knowledge*; but these two are not sharply divided. While tacit knowledge can be possessed by itself, explicit knowledge must rely on being tacitly understood and applied. Hence all knowledge is *either tacit* or *rooted in tacit knowledge*. A *wholly* explicit knowledge is unthinkable.

We can watch the process by which an explicit prescription becomes increasingly effective as it sinks deeper into a tacit matrix. Take a manual for driving a motor car and learn it by heart. Assuming that you have never seen a motor car, you will have to identify its parts from the illustrations of the manual. You can then sit down at the wheel and try to carry out the operations prescribed by the text. Thus you will start learning to drive and eventually establish the bearing of the manual on all the objects it indicates and the skills it teaches. The text of the manual is shifted to the back of the driver's mind, and is transposed almost entirely into the tacit operations of a skill.

The speed and complexity of tacit integration far exceeds in its own domain the operations of explicit inference. This is how intuitive insight may arrive at unaccountable conclusions in a flash. This has been pointed out by Konrad Lorenz.[7] While language expands human intelligence immensely beyond the purely tacit domain, the logic of language itself—the way language is used—remains tacit. Indeed, it is easy to see that the structure of tacit knowing contains a general theory of meaning which applies also to language.

When, in the experiment of Lazarus, certain syllables make the subject expect an electric shock, the approaching shock has become the meaning of these syllables to the subject. This view can be generalized, without straining the evidence, to all relations between a subsidiary and a focal term. The elementary motions that serve a cyclist to keep his balance are not meaningless: their meaning lies in the performance they jointly achieve. In this sense a characteristic physiognomy is the meaning of its features, which is in fact what we commonly say when a physiognomy expresses a particular mood. And finally, we may regard the appearance of a perceived object with constant properties as the joint meaning of the clues the integration of which produces that appearance. Such is the *semantic function* of tacit knowing.

A *set of sounds* is converted into the *name* of an object by an act of tacit knowing which integrates the sounds to the object to which we are attending. This is accompanied by a characteristic change in our impression of the sounds. When converted into a word they no longer sound as before; they have become, as it were, transparent: we attend *from* them (or through them) to the object to which they are integrated. Current theories which would explain meaning by the association of sounds with an object, leave unexplained this vectorial quality of meaning which is of its essence.[8]

There is a parallel to this transformation of sounds into words in the conversion of an object into a tool. Someone using a stick for the first time to feel his way in the dark, will at first feel its impact against his palm and fingers when the stick hits an object. But as he learns to use the stick effectively, a transformation of these jerks will take place into a feeling of the point of the stick touching an object; the user of the stick is no longer attending then *to* the meaningless jerks in his hand but attends *from* them to their meaning at the far end of the stick.

I have spoken of the subliminal clues of tacit knowing which cannot be experienced in themselves and of marginal clues which, though clearly visible, may not be identifiable. But we have now met a number of instances where tacit knowing integrates *clearly identifiable* elements and have observed the way the appearance of things changes when, instead of looking *at* them, we look *from* them to a distal term which is their meaning.

Once established, this *from-to* relation is durable. Yet it can be seriously impaired at will by switching our attention from the meaning to which it is directed, back to the things that have acquired this meaning. By concentrating attention on his fingers, a pianist can paralyse himself; the motions of his fingers no longer bear then on the music performed, they have lost their meaning.

We can identify then two alternative structures—omitting for the moment their necessary qualifications. So long as you look *at* X, you are *not* attending *from* X to something else, which would be its meaning. In order to attend *from* X to its meaning, you must cease to look *at* X, and *the moment you look at X you cease to see its meaning*. Admittedly, meaning is tenacious; once it is established, its destruction is not always feasible and is hardly ever complete, but it *would* be complete, if we could look at X again fully as an object.

In *Personal Knowledge*, I have described the destruction of the meaning of X when switching our attention back to X as due to the *logical unspecifiability of* X. But this does not show how the destructive powers of this shift of attention arise. What happens is that our attention, which is directed *from* (or through) a thing to its meaning, is distracted by looking *at* the thing. We shall presently see that to attend *from* a thing to its meaning is to *interiorize* it, and that to look instead *at* the thing is to *exteriorize* or *alienate* it. We shall then say *that we endow a thing with meaning by interiorizing it and destroy its meaning by alienating it*.

Consider once more the process of perception; how we attend *from* a large number of clues—some at the edge of our vision, others inside our body—*to* their meaning, which is what we perceive. This tranposition of bodily experiences into the perception of things outside then appears as an instance of the process by which we transpose meaningless experiences into their meaning at a distance from us, as we do when we use tools or probes.

It may be objected that many of the feelings transposed in the act of perception differ from those transposed in the use of tools and probes, by not being noticeable before their transposition. But Hefferline has shown that spontaneous muscular twitches, unfelt by the subject, can be as effective as the nonsense syllables of Lazarus in foreshadowing punishment.[9] And Russian observations, reported by Razran, have established the same fact for intestinal stimulations.[10] This exemplifies the way subliminal events inside our body are transposed by the act of perception into the sight of things outside.

It has been said that perception cannot be a projection, since we have no internal experiences to project into things perceived. But we have established that projection of this type does take place in various instances of tacit knowing, even when we do not orginally sense the internal processes in themselves. I would venture, therefore, to include in tacit knowing also the neural traces in the brain on the same footing as the subliminal stimuli inside our body. We may say then, quite generally, that wherever some process in our body gives rise to consciousness in us, tacit knowing will make sense of the event in terms of an experience to which we are attending.

This answers an old question. Imagine a physiologist to have mapped out completely all that takes place in the eyes and brain of a seeing man. Why do his observations not make him see that which the man sees? Because he looks *at* these happenings, while the subject attends *from* or through them *to* that which they mean to him. If the subject were to watch his own nervous system in a mirror, he would see there no more than the physiologist does. What we have here is a curtailment of meaning by *alienation*. The alienated view is not quite meaningless in this case, because the visual apparatus has a meaning as a mechanism of vision. To make the situation clear, imagine one person looking through a telescope and absorbed in admiring the moons of Jupiter, while another watched him using the telescope and observes the laws of geometrical optics. We are touching here on the problem which gives rise to Cartesian dualism.[11]

The way the body participates in the act of perception can be generalized further to include the bodily roots of all knowledge and thought. Our body is the only assembly of things known almost exclusively by relying on our awareness of them for attending to something else. Parts of our body serve as tools for observing objects outside and for manipulating them. Every time we make sense of the world, we rely on our tacit knowledge of impacts made by the world on our body and the complex responses of our body to these impacts. Such is the exceptional position of our body in the universe.

Phenomenology contrasts this feeling of our body with the view of the body seen as an object from outside.[12] The theory of tacit knowing regards this contrast as the difference between looking *at* something and attending *from* it at something else that is its meaning. Dwelling in our body clearly enables us to attend *from* it to things outside, while an external observer will tend to look *at* things happening in the body, seeing it as an object or as a machine. He will miss the meaning these events have for the person dwelling in the body and fail to share the experience the person has of his body. Again we have loss of meaning by alienation and another glimpse of the meaning of dualism.

I have shown how our subsidiary awareness of our body is extended to include a stick, when we feel our way by means of the stick. To use languge in speech, reading and writing, is to extend our bodily equipment and become intelligent human beings. We may say that when we learn to use language, or a probe, or a tool, and thus make ourselves aware of these things as we are of our body, we *interiorize* these things and *make ourselves dwell in them*. Such extensions of ourselves develop new faculties in us; our whole education operates in this way; as each of us interiorizes our cultural heritage, he grows into a person seeing the world and experiencing life in terms of this outlook.

Interiorization bestows meaning, alienation strips of meaning; when the two are applied alternately, they can *jointly develop* meaning—but this dialectic lies beyond my subject here.

The logical relation that links life in our body to our know-ledge of things outside us can be generalized to further instances in which we rely on our awareness of things for attending to another thing. When we attend from a set of particulars to the whole which they form, we establish a logical relation between the particulars and the whole, similar to that which exists between our body and the things outside it. In view of this, we may be prepared to consider the act of comprehending a whole *as an in-teriorization of its parts*, which makes us dwell in the parts. We may be said to live in the particulars which we comprehend, in the same sense as we live in the tools and probes which we use and in the culture in which we are brought up.

Such indwelling is not merely formal; it causes us to participate feelingly in that which we understand. Certain things can puzzle us; a situation may intrigue us—and when our understanding removes our perplexity, we feel relieved. Such intellectual success gives us a sense of mastery which enhances our existence. These feelings of comprehension go deep; we shall see them increasing in profundity all the way from the 'I–It' relation to the 'I–Thou' relation.

I shall start by taking up a loose end, left behind when analysing the meaning of a word as a name for a single object. We shall ask how a name can come to designate a *group of things*, like a species of plants or animals. This is the ancient problem of universals. It can be summed up in the question: What is a man like to whom the concept of 'man' refers? Can he be both fair and dark, both young and old, brown, black and yellow all at the same time? Or, if not, can he be a man without any of the properties of a man? The answer is that in speaking of man in general we are not attending to any kind of man, but relying on our subsidiary awareness of individual men, for attending to their joint meaning. This meaning is a comprehensive entity, and its knowledge is wiped out by attending to its particulars in themselves. This explains why the concept of man cannot be identified with any particular set of men, past or future. The concept represents all men—past, present and future—jointly, and the word 'man' applies to this comprehensive entity.[13]

The ontological claim of tacit knowing requires that this entity be real. This is confirmed by the fact that the members of a species are expected to have an indefinite range of yet undisclosed properties in common; this is the intension of the class formed by the species. Being real, the division of living beings into species is fundamental to biology. Moreover, the distinctive position of the human species underlies all social ties, all emotions between men, and between men and women, all conceptions of responsibility, indeed our whole life as men. Thus do we dwell in our conception of a species.[14]

Indwelling becomes deeper as we pass from the conception of a species to the knowledge of individual living beings. The main points of such knowledge were established long before the rise of science. Life and death were known before biology; sentience and insentience, the difference between intelligence and mindless stupidity, were all recognized before they were studied by science;

knowledge of plants and animals, of health and sickness, of birth, youth and old age, of mind and body, of organs and their functions, of food, digestion, elimination and many others, is immemorial. Such pre-scientific conceptions have formed the foundations of the biological sciences and still represent their major interests. Modern biology has vastly developed these ancient insights and thus confirmed their profundity.

Moreover, biologists still know these fundamentals by the same integrative powers by which they were first discovered before science, and they use similar powers for establishing their own novel biological conceptions. Morphology, physiology, animal psychology—they all deal with comprehensive entities. None of these entities can be mathematically defined, and the only way to know them is by comprehending the coherence of their parts.

To appreciate this achievement, remember once more how our eyes integrate a thousand rapidly changing clues into the appearance of an object of constant shape, size and colour, moving about before us. We have to multiply the complexity of this action a millionfold to approach the intricacy of the integrations performed in establishing our knowledge of life and of living shapes and functions.

This integration is guided by the active functions of the living being we are observing. A lion swooping down onto the back of a fleeing antelope co-ordinates its observations and actions in a highly complex and accurate way within a second. The naturalist watching the lion mentally integrates these co-ordinated elements into the conception of the lion hunting its prey. Some vital co-ordinations, like embryonic development, are much slower than this, but no less rich in co-ordinated details; the study of physiological functions fills many volumes; the co-ordinations performed by human intelligence are unlimited.

There are no mathematical expressions covering the shape of a lion and the way he pounces on an antelope, nor any that cover the many million characteristic shapes and co-ordinated actions of other living beings. None of these shapes and correlations are precisely definable.

I have said that we integrate these shapes and correlations by the tacit powers of perception. I may add that our perception of living beings consists largely in mentally duplicating the active co-ordinations performed by their functions. To this extent our knowledge of life is a sharing of life—a re-living, a very intimate kind of indwelling. Hence our knowledge of biotic phenomena contains a vast range of unspecifiable elements, and biology remains, in consequence, a descriptive science heavily relying on trained perception. It is immeasurably rich in things we know and cannot tell.

Such is life and such our knowledge of life; on such grounds are based the triumphs of biology. But this is repugnant to the modern biologist. Trained to measure the perfection of knowledge by the example of the exact sciences, he feels profoundly uneasy at finding his knowledge so inferior by this standard. The ideal of the exact sciences, derived from mechanics, aims at a mathematical theory connecting tangible, focally observed objects. Here everything is above-board, open to public scrutiny, wholly impersonal. The part of tacit knowing is reduced to the act of applying the theory to experience, and this act goes unnoticed. And the fact that tacit powers predominate in the very making of discoveries is set aside as forming no part of science.

The structure of biology is very different from this ideal. We know a living being by an informal integration of its coherent parts. Such knowledge combines two terms, one subsidiary, the other focal, which are known in different ways. The particulars of living beings are known as such by attending *from* them to their joint meaning which is the life of the organism. And this includes the sensorimotoric centre of the animal as well as the human mind as the bearer of intelligence and responsibility. Thus the *tangible focal objects* of exact science have been *split into two halves*. We have the tangible bodies of living beings, which are not viewed focally, while at the focus of our attention we have such intangible things as life and mind. Both of these halves are equally distasteful to the modern biologist, who finds their very duality unscientific and intolerable.

But tacit knowing is indispensable and must predominate in the study of living beings as organized to sustain life. The vagueness of something like the human mind is due to the vastness of its resources. Man can take in at a glance any one of $10^{40}$ different sentences. By my definition, this indeterminacy makes mind the more real, the more substantial. But such reality can be discerned only by a personal judgment: its knowledge is personal. The same is true of our subsidiary awareness of the organs and behaviour of a living being, by which we bring these to bear on its life or on its mind at the focus of our attention. All tacit knowing requires the continued participation of the knower, and a measure of personal participation is intrinsic therefore to all knowledge, but the continued participation of the knower becomes altogether predominant in a knowledge acquired and upheld by such deep indwelling.

An attempt to de-personalize our knowledge of living beings would result, if strictly pursued, in an alienation that would render all observations on living things meaningless. Taken to its theoretical limits, it would dissolve the very conception of life and make it impossible to identify living beings.

My argument will gain in sharpness by narrowing it to the knowledge of another mind. We know another person's mind by the same integrative process by which we know life. A novice trying to understand the skill of a master will seek *mentally* to combine his movements to the pattern to which the master combines them *practically*. By such exploratory indwelling the novice gets the feel of the master's skill. Chess players enter into a master's thought by repeating the games he played. *We experience a man's mind as the joint meaning of his actions* by dwelling in his actions from outside.

Behaviourism tries to make psychology into an exact science. It professes to observe—i.e., *look at* pieces of mental behaviour and to relate these pieces explicitly. But such pieces can be identified only within that tacit integration of behaviour which behaviourists reject as unscientific. Thus the behaviourist analysis is intelligible only because it paraphrases, however crudely, the tacit integration which it pretends to replace.

The claim of cybernetics to generate thought and feeling rests likewise on the assumption that mental processes consist in explicitly identifiable performances which, as such, would be reproducible by a computer. This assumption fails, because mental processes are recognized to a major extent tacitly, by dwelling in many particulars of behaviour that we cannot tell. But we would rightly refuse to ascribe thought and feeling to a machine, however perfectly it reproduced the outward actions of mental processes.[15] For the human mind works and dwells in a human body, and hence the mind can be known only as working and dwelling in a body. We can know it only by dwelling in that body from outside.

But could we not conceive of the body as a neurophysiological machinery performing the manifestations of the mind? The answer is that feeling, action and thought have mental qualities which we perceive by the same principles of tacit knowing by which we perceive the phenomenal qualities of external objects. All these qualities would vanish if we watched how parts of the human body carry out the performances of the mind. We had an example of this when we noted that looking at the neurophysiological mechanism of vision we do not see what the subject sees. We have now before us the full range of the dualism of which that case was a particular instance.

But I believe that for the case of organisms the dualism of looking *at* and *attending from* has a substantial foundation in the existence of distinct levels in the organism. The structure of tacit knowing has its counterpart in the way the principles determining the stability and power of an organism exercise their control over its parts. This is true also for machines; so to simplify matters, I shall deal first with machines. The result can then be generalized to the mechanical aspect of living beings, and from there to the entire organism.

Let me choose as an example of a machine the watch I wear on my wrist. My watch tells me the time. It is kept going by its mainspring, uncoiling under the control of the hair spring and balance wheel; this turns the hands which tell the time. Such are the operational principles of a watch, which define its construction and working. The principles cannot be defined by the laws of nature. No parts of a watch are formed by the natural equilibration of matter. They are artificially shaped and sagaciously connected to perform their function in telling the time. This is their meaning: to understand a watch is to understand what it is for and how it works. The laws of inanimate nature are indifferent to this purpose. They cannot determine the working of a watch, any more than the chemistry or physics of printers' ink can determine the contents of a book.

Viewed in themselves, the parts of a machine are meaningless; the machine is comprehended by attending *from* its parts to their joint function, which operates the machine. To this structure of knowing there correspond two levels controlled by different principles. The particulars viewed in themselves are controlled by the laws of inanimate nature; while viewed jointly, they are controlled by the operational principles of the machine. This dual control may seem puzzling. But the physical sciences expressly leave open certain variabilities of a system, described as its boundary conditions. The operational principles of a machine control these boundaries, and so they do not infringe the laws of physics and chemistry, which operate within these boundaries.

The same dualism holds for biology. Biologists will tell you that they are explaining living beings by the laws of inanimate nature, but what they actually do, and do triumphantly well, is to explain certain aspects of life *by machine-like principles*. This postulates a level of reality that operates on the boundaries left open by the laws of physics and chemistry.

This opens a perspective to a whole sequence of levels, all the way up to that of responsible humanity. This sequence would form a hierarchy of operations, each higher level controlling the margin left indeterminate by the one below it. We can illustrate such a structure by the production of a literary composition, for example, of a speech. It includes five levels. The first level, lowest of all, is the production of a voice; the second, the utterance of words; the third, the joining of words to sentences; the fourth, the working of sentences into a style; the fifth, and highest, the composition of the text.

The principles of each level operate under the control of the next higher level. The voice you produce is shaped into words by a vocabulary; a given vocabulary is shaped into sentences in accordance with grammar; and the sentences are fitted into a style, which in its turn is made to convey the ideas of the composition. Thus each level is subject to dual control; first, by the laws that apply to its elements in themselves and, second, by the laws that control the comprehensive entity formed by them.

Such multiple control is made possible by the fact that the principles governing the isolated particulars of a lower level, leave indeterminate their boundary conditions for the control by a higher principle. Voice-production leaves largely open the combination of sounds to words, which is controlled by a vocabulary. Next, a vocabulary leaves largely open the combination of words to form sentences, which is controlled by grammar; and so the sequence goes on.

Consequently, the operations of a higher level cannot be accounted for by the laws governing its particulars forming the next lower level. You cannot derive a vocabulary from phonetics; you cannot derive grammar from a vocabulary; a correct use of grammar does not account for good style; and a good style does not provide the content of a piece of prose.

A glance at the functions of living beings assures us that they have a broadly similar stratified structure. All living functions rely on the laws of inanimate nature in controlling the boundary conditions left open by these laws; the vegetative functions sustaining life at its lowest levels leave open, both in plants and animals, the possibilities of growth and also leave open in animals the possibilities of muscular action; the principles governing muscular action leave open their integration to innate patterns of behaviour; such patterns are open in their turn to be shaped by intelligence, and the working of intelligence can be made to serve the still higher principles of man's responsible choices.

Each pair of levels would present its own dualism, for it would be impossible to account for the operations of any higher level by the laws governing its isolated particulars. The dualism of mind and matter would be but one instance of the dualism prevailing between every pair of successive ontological levels.

*

I expect that the many points at which the views I have sketched out here diverge from those of current philosophic literature are obvious to you. I shall only try to show that, despite this divergence, they broadly respond to the development of modern philosophy.

Current writings on the history of science have confirmed the view I put forward years ago that the pursuit of science is determined at every stage by unspecifiable powers of thought, and I have shown here how this fact forms my starting point for developing a theory of non-explicit thought. You may call such a theory—using a term coined by Gilbert Ryle—an *informal logic* of science and of knowledge in general. Alternatively, you may call it a phenomenology of science and knowledge, by reference to Husserl and Merleau-Ponty. This would correctly relate my enterprise both to analytic philosophy and to phenomenology and existentialism.

Admittedly, my view that true knowledge bears on an essentially indeterminate reality and my theory of a stratified universe

are foreign to these schools of thought. And again, while knowledge by indwelling is clearly related to Dilthey and existentialism,
its extension to the natural sciences is contrary to these philosophies. Similarly, while Kant's categories, by which experience of
external objects is possible, reappear with me in the active knower
participating in all live knowledge, in this case such a knower,
responsibly legislating for himself with universal intent, is more
like the moral person of the Second Critique and the Metaphysics
of Morals.

The original intention of logical positivism was to establish all
knowledge in terms of explicit relations between sensory data.
In the course of the last twenty years this programme has been
gradually relaxed, by admitting more complex data and making
allowance for 'open textures' and 'flexibilities' of the framework.
The most recent development in this direction came to my notice
in Michael Scriven's assertion that problems of structural logic
in science can 'only be solved by reference to concepts previously
condemned by many logicians as "psychological not logical",
e.g. understanding, belief, and judgment'.[16]

I suggest that we transform this retreat into a triumph, by the
simple device of changing camp. Let us recognize that tacit
knowing is the fundamental power of the mind, which creates
explicit knowing, lends meaning to it and controls its uses.
Formalization of tacit knowing immensely expands the powers of
the mind, by creating a machinery of precise thought, but it also
opens up new paths to intuition; any attempt to gain complete
control of thought by explicit rules is self-contradictory, systematically misleading and culturally destructive. The pursuit of
formalization will find its true place in a tacit framework.

In this light, there is no justification for separate approaches to
scientific explanation, scientific discovery, learning and meaning.
They ultimately rest on the same tacit process of understanding.
The true *meaning* of Kepler's Third Law was *discovered* by
Newton, when he *explained* it as an outcome of general gravitation;
and *learning* by insight has the same three aspects on a minor
scale.

The claims of cybernetics represent a revival of logical positivism in its original insistence on strictly explicit operations of
the mind. Hence my rejection of a cybernetic interpretation of
thought and of behaviourism which are based likewise on the

assumption that the data and operations of mental processes are explicitly specifiable.

My analysis of machines and living beings entails the rejection of Ernest Nagel's claim to describe machines and living beings in non-teleological terms.[17] Nothing is a machine unless it serves a useful purpose, and living organs and functions are organs and functions only to the extent to which they sustain life. A theory of knowledge based on tacit knowing does not require that we purify science of references to mind or to the finalistic structure of living beings.

[1] See my *Science, Faith and Society*, Oxford: Oxford University Press, 1946; also my *Personal Knowledge*, London: Routledge & Kegan Paul and Chicago: University of Chicago Press, 1958.

[2] F. J. J. BUYTENDIJK, *Mensch und Tier*, Hamburg: Rowohts, 1958, p. 59.

[3] WILLIAM WHEWELL, *Philosophy of Discovery*, London: John W. Parker & Son, 1860, p. 254.

[4] FRANZ BRENTANO, *Psychologie Von Empirischen Standpunkt* (1874), quoted from the edition edited by Oskar Kraus, Leipzig: F. Meiner, 1924.

[5] R. S. LAZARUS and R. A. MCCLEARY, 'Autonomic Discrimination without Awareness: An Interim Report', *Journal of Personality*, *18* (1949), pp. 171–79 and 'Autonomic Discrimination without Awareness: A Study of Subception', *Psychological Review*, *58* (1951), pp. 113–22. These results were called in question by C. W. ERIKSEN, 'Subception: Fact or Artifact?', *Psychological Review*, *63* (1956), pp. 74–80 and defended by Lazarus, 'Subception: Fact or Artifact? A Reply to Eriksen', *Psychological Review*, *63* (1956), pp. 343–47. But in a later paper surveying the whole field ['Discrimination and Learning without Awareness: A Methodological Survey and Evaluation', *Psychological Review*, *67* (1960), pp. 279–300] Eriksen confirmed the experiments of Lazarus and McCleary and accepted them as evidence of subception.

[6] C. W. ERIKSEN, 'Discrimination and Learning . . .', *loc. cit.*

[7] KONRAD LORENZ in *General Systems*, VII, (1962), pp. 37–56.

[8] See, e.g., W. V. O. QUINE, *Word and Object*, Cambridge: Massachusetts Institute of Technology Press, 1960, p. 221. Rejects any reference to intentions as conceived by Brentano.

[9] F. HEFFERLINE, B. KEENAN, and A. R. HERFORD, 'Escape and Avoidance Conditioning in Human Subjects without Their Observation of the Responses', *Science*, *130* (1959), pp. 1338–39.

[10] G. RAZRAN, 'The Observable Unconscious and the Inferable Conscious in Current Soviet Psychology', *Psychological Review*, *68* (1961), pp. 81–147.

[11] See Essay 13 and the concluding section of 14.

[12] This distinction is most widely developed in M. MERLEAU-PONTY, *Phenomenology of Perception* (Colin Smith, trs.), London: Routledge, 1962, the English translation of *Phénoménologie de la Perception*, Paris: Gallimard, 1945.

[13] See Essay 11, pp. 165 ff; also Essay 12, pp. 190–91.

[14] This view was expressed, e.g., by PROFESSOR PAUL ZIFF, 'The Feelings of Robots' in *Minds and Machines* (A. R. ANDERSON, ed.), Englewood Cliffs, New Jersey: Prentice Hall, 1964. Other authors contested it. I regard my argument in its favour as decisive.

[15] See Essay 11.

[16] MICHAEL SCRIVEN, 'Explanations, Predictions, and Laws' in *Minnesota Studies in the Philosophy of Science*, III, Minneapolis: University of Minnesota Press, 1962, pp. 170–230, p. 172.
[17] ERNEST NAGEL, *The Structure of Science*, New York: Harcourt, Brace & World and London: Routledge, 1961, p. 417.

## *II*
# Tacit Knowing:
# Its Bearing on Some Problems
# of Philosophy
## 1962

In this paper I shall try to carry further, in outline, an inquiry that I have been pursuing for several years. For this purpose, it is necessary, first of all, to recapitulate some arguments which I have developed elsewhere. . . .*

To introduce the bearing of my analysis of tacit knowing on some problems of philosophy, I shall deal with a question raised fairly recently by Lord Brain. Having noted the curious fact that some patients feel part of their body to be an external object, the author raises the question as to how we normally distinguish our body from external objects. He suggests that 'dropableness' is the quality by which a small object differs from a part of one's own body.[1]

But we do distinguish our own body also from objects, whether small or large, that are not dropable. The distinction lies deeper. As I have said elsewhere, the special character of our body lies in the fact that it is the only collection of things which we know almost exclusively by relying on our awareness of them for attending to something else. Hence, the unique position of our body in the universe.

But hence also our capacity for assimilating to ourselves things outside, by relying on our awareness of them for attending to something else. When we use a tool or a probe and, above all, when we use language in speech, reading, or writing, we extend our bodily equipment and become more effective and more intelligent

* Editor's note: These arguments are stated in the two preceding essays.

M

beings. All human thought comes into existence by grasping the meaning and mastering the use of language. Little of our mind lives in our natural body; a truly human intellect dwells in us only when our lips shape words and our eyes read print.

Tacit knowing now appears as an act of *indwelling* by which we gain access to a new meaning. When exercising a skill we literally dwell in the innumerable muscular acts which contribute to its purpose, a purpose which constitutes their joint meaning. Therefore, since all understanding is tacit knowing, all understanding is achieved by indwelling. The idea developed by Dilthey and Lipps, that we can know human beings and works of art only by indwelling, can thus be justified.[2] But we see now also that these authors were mistaken in distinguishing indwelling from observation as practised in the natural sciences. The difference is only a matter of degree: indwelling is less deep when observing a star than when understanding men or works of art. The theory of tacit knowing establishes a continuous transition from the natural sciences to the study of the humanities. It bridges the gap between the 'I–It' and the I–Thou', by rooting them both in the subject's 'I–Me' awareness of his own body, which represents the highest degree of indwelling.

We can extend this perspective to include a more ancient philosophical problem. Galileo, Locke, and their successors have taught that external objects are merely masses in motion and that the sights, sounds, and smells which appear to belong to them, are not actually theirs but are generated in us by the impact of motions coming from them into our eyes, ears, and noses. Modern neurology has borne out the belief in the internal location of colours, sounds, and smells, by proving that they can be produced internally as after images, illusions, or hallucinations. Furthermore, it has gone beyond this by tracing the neural processes by which the external impact is conducted to the cerebral cortex and identifying the several cortical centres which produce our awareness of sights, sounds, and smells. Modern knowledge has thus added compulsive force to the philosophical problem: How do we come to know external objects, if our awareness of them is altogether internal?

The current remedy of analytic philosophy is to restrict the applicability of terms like 'seeing', 'hearing', 'smelling' to what is experienced by the speaker, disregarding the neural and cortical processes which underlie these experiences. This usage, however, is not acceptable for it would ban the language of sense physiology and thus ignore all its discoveries.

An earlier school of thought, originating with Lord Russell, assumes that the sights, sounds, etc., arise inside the brain where room is made for them by postulating a private perceptual space, as distinct from the physical space in which the brain itself is located. Lord Brain developed this idea further by assuming that these sensory qualities are experienced in the brain not in themselves, but as symbols by which we become aware of external objects with their corresponding qualities of colour, sound, smell, etc. Sensory experiences are compared to the pictures on a radar screen on which we can observe distant objects. But since the question is left open as to who interprets the symbols and by what means or who watches the radar screen and how he interprets its signs, Lord Brain's explanation brings us back to the original question, how we come to know external objects, of which we are originally aware internally.

Let us look at this question within the framework of tacit knowing. Remember the way we know skills and physiognomies, make tests, use tools and probes, utter words, and the way I have fitted visual perception into the structure that applies to all other instances of tacit knowing. These were all shown to be particular instances of the fundamental fact that we are able to make sense of clues or particulars to which we are not attending at the moment, by relying on our awareness of them for attending to something else—so that the appearance of that to which we are attending may be said to be the meaning of these clues or particulars. Once we had grasped this way of making sense, we also realized that the position at which the meaning of the clues appeared to be situated did not coincide with the position of the clues themselves and could lie in some cases nearer to, in others further away from them. We have seen that in the use of tools and probes the impact that their handle makes on our hands and fingers is not felt in itself at the place where it happens, but as an impact on our instrument where it hits its object. A similar process of integration rendered spoken words transparent, their meaning being found in the things they designate. Visual perception appears then as yet another instance of relying on a wide variety of clues, some inside, some outside our body, for attending to their joint meaning which in this case appears to us in terms of the shape, colour, size, position, and other visible features of an object.

Many of these clues, particularly those inside our body, cannot be experienced in themselves by those who use them. Their existence is revealed only by the physiological observation of the bodily processes affecting the way a subject sees things. But this does not distinguish visual perception from other instances of tacit knowing. I have quoted an experiment showing that we can actually be trained to control external events by minute muscular contractions which are too weak to be felt in themselves.* All the physiology of vision can thus be assimilated to previous instances of tacit knowing. The fact that the physiologist may be capable of tracing all the relevant clues to an act of visual perception without being able to rely on these clues for seeing what they mean to the subject, in the same way as he sees it, might be regarded as an instance of the destruction of meaning which takes place when we focus our attention on the isolated particulars bearing on a comprehensive entity. We may look upon this also as the difference between degrees of indwelling. The subject's awareness of his own neural processes has a much higher grade of indwelling than the physiological observation of them.[3]

One may distinguish, of course, between our awareness of subliminal impacts on, or in, our body and neural processes at cortical centres to which all stimuli are conducted; but this difference does not affect the issue. For we know that sensations which are primarily felt at some point of our body may come to be felt further out in space, for example at the tip of a probe, and that we can be conditioned to respond to impacts inside our body that are too weak to be felt at that point at all. Hence, if we were to assume that sensory experiences do occur in the first place in the cortex, we might still expect that a process of tacit knowing would make us sense them elsewhere; so that our assumption that they had occurred originally in a place where we do not feel them would not present a new problem.

This view of the localization of sights seen does not tell us how such sights, or any other states of consciousness, arise from (or in conjunction with) neural processes. *This problem is set aside in this paper.* We only assume that whenever we *have* conscious

* Editor's note: See preceding editor's note, especially footnote 9.

experiences, we also have the power of integrating them meaningfully. It is by this power then that we see things as we do, and the fact that the physiologist does not see these things when observing the visual processes in the cortex, can be ascribed to the fact that he attends to these neural processes in themselves. The rest of this paper will serve mainly to consolidate and elaborate this conclusion.

It is interesting to compare, with this in mind, the process of integration by which we arrive at tacit knowing with a formal process of inference by which we might arrive at the same conclusion. Optical illusions, such as the Ames skewed room experiment in which a boy appears taller than a man, offer a good example for such an inquiry.[4] In terms of tacit knowing we would say that we rely on our awareness of numberless rooms seen before, and of the other elements of the framework within which the two figures are presented to us, and integrate all these particulars in the way we see the boy and the man on whom our attention is focused.

Optical illusions cannot, as a rule, be dispelled by recognizing them to be illusory, and psychologists have refused to follow Helmholtz in describing as unconscious reasoning a process which compels our assent to what we know to be false. The question is whether we can substantially recast this discussion by classing an optical illusion as a case of mistaken tacit knowing.

I think we can, for the analysis of an optical illusion in terms of an unconscious inference corresponds to a process that fulfils an important function in respect of all manner of tacit knowing. It belongs to the same class as (1) the analysis of skills by motion studies, (2) the characterization of a physiognomy by listing its typical features, (3) the giving of detailed directions for carrying out a test or using a tool, (4) the analysis of speech by grammar, and (5) the physiological analysis of perception.

This may appear a bewilderingly disparate collection, remote from the interpretation of optical illusions as a process of unconscious reasoning. And this impression is hardened if we realize how vast are some of the areas I have set out here. Motion studies should be taken to include the practical teaching of every kind of artistic performance, of all skilled workmanship, and all manner of sports. The analysis of physiognomies covers an even richer field. It includes, along with the diagnostics of medicine and taxonomy, all criticism of art and literature, by which our understanding of paintings, architecture, music, poetry, drama, and fiction is educated, guided, and deepened. The analysis of speech includes, in addition to grammar, the study of voice production and phonetics, as well as lexicography, stylistics, and rhetoric. The field extends further to analytic philosophy, which studies language rules with a view to the clarification of philosophic problems. Finally, the theory of perception, which stands last on my list, is but an example of the whole range of sense physiology with its roots spread over anatomy, neurology, and psychology, with the selection of its particular subjects taken from the entire range of the animal kingdom.

Yet all these inquiries have it in common with each other and with the analysis of optical illusions that they attempt to understand acts of tacit knowing in which we attend to something by relying on our awareness of elements that we are not attending to in themselves at the time. These acts might be loosely called intuitive to distinguish them from processes of explicit reasoning, and the inquiries I have listed can then be said to be directed towards discovering explicit rules, the operations of which would be equivalent to these intuitive actions. These rules would have both to specify the particulars on the awareness of which intuition relies for attending to a comprehensive entity formed by them and to spell out the integrative relations by which the particulars form such entities.

If such formalization of tacit knowing were possible, it would convert all arts into mathematically prescribed operations, and thus destroy them as works of art. The analysis of art can be profoundly revealing, but only if it remains incomplete. It must limit itself to the discovery of maxims, the application of which is itself a work of art. However greatly it may profit from incorporating a skeleton of such maxims, the originally tacit act will still remain tacit, for it will rely on a subsidiary awareness of its maxims and keep their application under tacit control.

We can see also, accordingly, that in optical illusions, such as that which makes us see a boy taller than a grown man, 'unconscious reasoning' can serve only as the kind of rule which leaves open important alternatives to be decided by a tacit act of the subject. Instead of the premise 'all rooms are rectangular parallelepipeds', which leads to the conclusion that a young boy can be taller than a grown man, we could use the premise 'young boys are smaller than grown men', and reach the conclusion that a room can be skew-angled, which would dissolve the illusion and thus show that its formalization as unconscious reasoning does not explain why the eye prefers to see the illusion.

The reason for this preference lies in the fact that we irresistibly see the room as having a normal shape. Our subsidiary awareness of a great many normal rooms presents itself to us in terms of our seeing the room in this way. Most of these rooms cannot be identified. We cannot remember more than a few of the thousands of regular shaped rooms that we have seen in the past. Yet it is the joint weight of these memories at the back of our mind that is effective, as is shown by the fact that primitive people who have seen fewer normal rooms are less susceptible to this kind of illusion.[5] Moreover, an undefinable range of external clues can destroy the illusion. For example, if we are allowed to tap the wall of the room with a stick, at some point the cumulative effect of such clues will cause the skew room to emerge and the illusion to be destroyed.

This exemplifies the rival attraction of two alternative ways of seeing a system of clues. The one which preponderates over the other for any particular configuration may be said to be more readily integrated, or otherwise preferred, by the observer. Gestalt psychology has attempted to define the qualities of a figure which facilitate its integration, but my present paper will not go into this question. I merely accept, for example, that integration can be destroyed by focusing attention on the individual particulars and that this is favoured by certain ways of looking at the integrated whole, e.g., from very near. More about this later.

The process by which the conception of a normal room is formed here, and a particular object identified as an instance of it, bears on an ancient problem of philosophy, the elucidation of which will throw further light on the powers of tacit integration and the limit set to a formalization of these powers.

Plato was the first to be troubled by the fact that *in applying our conception of a class of things, we keep identifying objects that are different from each other in every particular*. If every man is clearly distinguishable from another and we yet recognize each of them as a man, what kind of man is this, as which all these men are recognized? Plato concluded that the general idea of man refers to a *perfect man* who has no particular properties, and of whom individual men are imperfect copies, corrupted by having such properties.

That something so utterly featureless as the concept of man should have such a perfectly characteristic nature presents great difficulties which have occupied philosophers ever since Roscelinus raised them close to 900 years ago. But his own view, that the word 'man' is but the name for a collection of individual men, leaves open the question how we can justify the labelling of a collection of different individuals by the same name—a question that is further accentuated by our expectation that we shall yet be able to subsume under this label future instances of men differing in every particular from any man thus labelled before. The difficulty is not eliminated by specifying the characteristic features of man, since in doing so we must again repeatedly use one name for instances of a feature that are different in every particular.

All these difficulties arise only because we are seeking *an explicit procedure* for forming collections of objects which can be justifiably designated by the same universal term. Let us watch instead the way in which perception identifies certain objects according to their nature. The illusion of seeing a skew room as normal should remind us of the fact that in thousands of other cases we have correctly seen normal rooms as such, however different each was from the other, and however different the angles were under which we saw any particular room at a particular moment. It also demonstrates that the identification of particular things goes on without naming them, which is confirmed by the fact that animals readily identify members of a class, though they have no language. What is at work here is a process, common to all manner of perception, in which we rely on our awareness of a great many clues to which we are not attending at the time, for seeing things in a particular way which is the meaning of these clues comprehended by us.

We must note here that the problem of how a universal concept is formed is part of the problem of empirical *induction*. All attempts to formulate strict rules for deriving general laws from individual experiences have failed. And one of the reasons is, again, that each instance of a law differs, strictly speaking, in every particular from every other instance of it. Such indeterminately variable experiences can indeed be subsumed under the same law only by relying on our awareness of them as clues to it. And just as for perception, many clues of empirical induction will be easily identified in themselves, while many will not be, and not all of them can be, identified. In other words, the scientist's 'hunches' may be based to a greater part on subception. And just as a keen eyesight enables one to discriminate objects that others cannot see, so does a gift of scientific discovery reveal natural laws in a scientific experience which signifies nothing to others not so gifted. Those who insist on finding a formal procedure of induction would reject the acknowledgment of such powers of discovery as mystery mongering. Yet these powers are not more mysterious than our powers of perception but of course not any less mysterious, either.

But am I not in fact disposing of an enigma by postulating a miracle? Not altogether. I am interpreting the formation of class concepts (along with the discovery of natural laws) as based ultimately on a process of tacit knowing, the operations of which I have exemplified in the learning of skills, the recognition of physiognomies, the mastery of tests, the use of tools, the uttering of speech, and the act of visual perception. The powers of integration which achieve these acts have the same structure throughout. And I believe that it can be shown, though this lies beyond the scope of this paper, that they are all variants of the same organismic process.

*Two points* concerning the formation of concepts require special attention. First, we are assuming here that our integrative powers can resolve the apparent contradiction involved in taking an aggregate of objects which differ in every particular to be nevertheless identical in some other way. Is there any evidence that tacit knowing can establish a uniform meaning for clues, which, regarded in themselves, have nothing that is the same in them? The answer is that tacit knowing can in fact integrate conflicting clues in various ways. In the Ames experiment the sight of a boy and a grown man contradicts the distance of their heads from the ceiling of the room, and perception integrates these contradictory clues by presenting the boy as taller than the man. This solution is admittedly illusory; but there is an important case when conflicting visual clues are integrated to a true sight. We fuse the two different pictures of an object cast on the retina of our eyes by forming its stereoscopic image. Here perception resolves a contradiction by revealing a *joint meaning* of conflicting clues in terms of a *new quality*. A similar synthesis is achieved when we hear a sound as coming from a definite direction by combining its impacts that reach first one ear and then the other. This is also what happens in the formation of a general conception.

But there is also an important difference which faces us as the *second point* to which we must attend. It lies in the curiously *unsubstantial character* of the joint meaning ascribed to a group of objects by a general term. Compared with optical illusions or stereoscopic images, general conceptions are abstract, featureless. The focus in terms of which we are aware of the members of a class appears vague and almost empty. We may ask whether there are other instances of tacit knowing of a similar structure. The question brings up yet another traditional problem of philosophy, the clarification of which will help to consolidate and elaborate further the conception of tacit knowing.

I have said that when we are attending to the joint appearance of the particulars composing a man's physiognomy, we are attending to his person, and that when we watch the mood expressed by his face, we are watching his mind at work in his face. Two things are apparent here. First, that tacit knowing may penetrate its object in stages. We may first recognize a man, then discover what he is doing, then again realize what his motives might be, and eventually reconsider our conception of his personality. An aspect apprehended by the integration of elementary particulars thus becomes, in its turn, a clue to a more comprehensive entity, and so on. I have also hinted that we thus gradually penetrate to things that are increasingly real, things which, being real, may yet manifest themselves on an indeterminate range of future occasions.

I can only deal briefly here with this analysis of the mind, which I have carried out at some length elsewhere. It should illustrate here the fact that, as we move to a deeper, more comprehensive, understanding of a human being, we tend to pass from more tangible particulars to increasingly intangible entities: to entities which are (partly for this reason) more real: more real, that is, in terms of my definition of reality, as likely to show up in a wider range of indefinite future manifestations.

The time sequence used for this description must not be taken literally. We usually take in all levels of a person to some extent straight away. We certainly recognize a human face at first sight and can say only from a subsequent analysis, and then rather inadequately, by what particulars we recognized it. If we could ever see the fragments of a face without realizing their coherence as parts of a face, we could not distinguish them from other things around them. This is actually true for any object and is more easily demonstrable for other objects than human faces. An object becomes invisible if its particulars cannot be picked out against a distinctive background, as, for example, when it is camouflaged. We then see the particulars of the object, but do not know which of them belong to the object that we do not see and may not even know about.

The position thus reached shows the impossibility of behaviourism. It follows from it that we can identify tangible manifestations of mental processes only by first recognizing the mind at work in them; that in fact a rational pattern of behaviour must be comprehended as a whole, before we can set out to analyse it; and finally that if we did succeed, *per impossibile*, in keeping track of the elements of mental behaviour without reference to mind, these particulars, observed in themselves, would remain meaningless, and experiments conducted with these meaningless fragments would also be meaningless. The actual practice of behaviourist experimental psychology is rescued from this fate, by tacitly relying on the mental interpretation of its observations, which are then translated into an objectivist language.

The present analysis also differs from that of Ryle by the distinction of two kinds of knowing.[6] If, as I suggest, we know the mind by relying on our awareness of its workings for attending to their joint meaning, then Ryle's conclusion that the workings of the mind *are* the mind, is like saying that the word 'table' *is* a table.

What I have said about the mind also bears on the theory of *phenomenalism*. This doctrine teaches us to look upon sense data as our ultimate information about the outside world, and to regard our knowledge of the objects to which sense data refer, as based on inference from these data. This gives rise to the insoluble problem of the manner in which such inference can be carried out.

The school of linguistic analysis disposed of this problem by affirming that we never perceive sense data as such, but are aware of them only as the qualities of objects, which are what we actually do perceive. This view, however, fails to account for the fact, demonstrated by the experiments on apes brought up in the dark, that learning to see needs considerable time and effort; a fact confirmed for human infants by observations on their eye movements. Before they learn to see objects, both apes and babies do in fact see sense data, that is, patches of light and colour. And this is the case also when normal adults observe the meaningless fragments of a puzzling sight and have to make an intelligent effort in order to see the objects of which these are the qualities.

Such an effort is a process of tacit integration by which the object is recognized as the meaning of the sense data which constitute its appearance. It is not a process of explicit inference, and hence the question of the ways in which such inference can be conducted does not arise. The same is true for the insoluble question of the way in which the existence of other minds is inferred. It does not arise; for we know other minds, not by explicit inference, but by a tacit process of integration. This solution of the problem of other minds differs from that proposed by Strawson, who shows by linguistic analysis that the doubting of the existence of other minds is self-contradictory.[7] This proves that modern usage implies belief in other minds. But in the language of Azande it is self-contradictory to doubt the efficacy of oracles, and this only proves that Zande language cannot be trusted in respect of oracles.[8]

The view of our knowledge of solid objects and of a person's mind as the meaning of their particulars restores the metaphysical notion of common sense, which speaks of things and a person's mind as distinct from the clues by which they happen to manifest themselves to the observer. And the same can be claimed then for universals: They are the joint meaning of things forming a class. This meaning is something real, for, to repeat my phrase, it is capable of yet manifesting itself indefinitely in the future.

It has, indeed, an heuristic power that is usually twofold. (1) A universal concept usually anticipates the occurrence of further instances of itself in the future, and if the concept is true, it will validly subsume these future instances in spite of the fact that they will unpredictably differ in every particular from all the instances subsumed in the past. (2) A true universal concept, designating a natural class, for example a species of animals, anticipates that the members of the class will yet be found to share an indefinite range of uncovenanted properties; i.e., that the class will be found to have a yet unrevealed range of intension.

This illustrates the most striking powers of tacit knowing, owing to which we can focus our attention on the joint meaning of particulars, even when the focus to which we are attending has no tangible centre. It represents our capacity to know a problem. A problem designates a gap within a constellation of clues pointing towards something unknown. If we hold a problem to be a good one, we also imply that this unknown can yet be discovered by our own efforts, and that this would be worth these efforts. To undertake the search for the solution of a problem is to claim the faculty of sensing the increasing proximity of its solution—since no inquiry can succeed without such guidance. In all these anticipations, essential to any scientific endeavour, we focus our attention on a centre that is necessarily empty.

This brings into sight once more the process of empirical *induction*. I have noted the heuristic powers of a true universal conception, and have now consolidated the idea of such powers by pointing out our capacity to recognize problems, to know good problems from bad ones, and to pursue these successfully, by feeling our steady approach to their solution. The work of the scientist consists in doing all these things. He notices clues that seem significant, and, if he is an experimenter, tries to turn up new clues that would give him further guidance. All the time his attention is fixed on the meaning of the clues he has collected so far, while he is feeling his way towards new ideas and new evidence, by following his sense of approaching discovery. This procedure does not essentially differ from that of perception, to which I have affiliated it. Any sustained effort to make out what confronts us in a confusing configuration of sights is an exercise of similar powers of searching for clues by sensing the nearness of a significant shape to which they might tend to crystallize.

I have said that the capacity to know a problem is the most striking instance of our powers to integrate the meaning of a set of particulars by fixing our attention on a gap behind which we anticipate the presence of yet hidden knowledge. Before developing this further, let me recall that we have already recognized these heuristic powers in a less dynamic form wherever we rely on our awareness of particulars for establishing the presence of a comprehensive entity. For this was always viewed as something real, which being real, might be expected yet to manifest itself at some future time in unexpected ways. I have shown how this confirmed in its own way the common sense metaphysical belief that solid objects were something beyond the aggregate of their observed properties and that the mind is something beyond its overt manifestations; I have also shown that this conception of meaning reveals the thing that is named by a universal term. But it is still the course of scientific inquiry in which the metaphysical conception of a reality beyond our tangible experience is written out most clearly, for all to see. From its very start, the inquiry assumes, and must assume, that there is something there to be discovered. The fascination, by which alone the inquiry can make progress, is fixed on discerning what it is that is there, and when discovery is achieved, it comes to us accredited by our conviction that its object was there all along, unrecognized. The rise, the path, the end, all point at the same reality and cannot but tell of it. Swearing by the existence of this reality, the scientist imposes on himself the discipline of his vocation. And his sense of approaching nearer to reality is not exhausted by the consummation of discovery. It persists in the belief that what he has discovered is real, and being real, will yet mark its presence by an unlimited range of unsuspected implications. Deemed to be an aspect of reality, the new knowledge is believed to be fruitful and is claimed to be universally valid.

Here we meet the conception of truth. Modern antimetaphysical philosophies, like pragmatism, operationalism, positivism, and logical positivism, have tried to spell out the implications of asserting a proposition to be true. But if the truth of a proposition lies in its bearing on reality, which makes its implications indeterminate, then such efforts are foredoomed. They have in fact failed, and must fail, for the indeterminate cannot be spelt out without making it determinate. It can be known in its indeterminate condition only tacitly, by those tacit powers by which we know more than we can tell.

The antimetaphysical analysis of science assumes that the logical foundation of empirical knowledge must be capable of definition by explicit rules. While the difficulties of this enterprise have not gone unnoticed, the reluctance to abandon it in principle still seems universal. My own attempts to acknowledge tacit powers of personal judgment as the decisive organon of discovery and the ultimate criterion of scientific truth, have been opposed by describing these agencies as psychological, not logical, in character. But this distinction is not explained by my critics. Is an act of perception which sees an object in a way that assimilates it to past instances of the same kind, a psychological process or a logical inference? We have seen that it can be mistaken and its results be false; and it certainly has a considerable likelihood of being true. To me this suggests that it is a logical process of inference even though it is not explicit. In any case, to perceive things rightly is certainly part of the process of scientific inquiry and to hold perceptions to be right underlies the holding of scientific propositions to be true. And, if, in consequence, we must accept the veridical powers of perception as the roots of empirical science, we cannot reasonably refuse to accept other tacit veridical processes having a similar structure. This is what I have been urging all along since I first wrote '. . . that the capacity of scientists to guess the presence of shapes as tokens of reality, differs from the capacity of our ordinary perception only by the fact that it can integrate shapes presented to it in terms which the perception of ordinary people cannot readily handle.' And this is what I have tried to elaborate also in my present paper.[9]

*

This concludes the philosophic survey set in motion by pondering the strange fact that the experience of our senses is somehow to be accounted for in terms of neural processes within our body. In conclusion, I shall deal now with the general context of the distinction between primary qualities representing the objective reality of all things and secondary qualities deemed to be subjective. Galileo's vision of a universe consisting ultimately of masses in motion ruled the minds of scientists and philosophers until the end of the nineteenth century, when it was first seriously modified within physics itself by the discovery of the electrical character of ultimate particles. Today we would have to regard as the primary qualities of the universe the parameters (statistical functions) determined by physics, and to ask how these give rise to the additional qualities of colours, sounds, tastes, and smells by means of a particular configuration of these parameters within the nervous system.

However, it will be simpler, and involve no loss of generality, if I set out the Laplacean vision in terms of its original model of primary qualities consisting of the masses, positions, velocities, and forces of ultimate particles. Laplace declared that the prediction of this configuration for the universe would supply us with a knowledge of 'all things to come'. It was always agreed that we were technically incapable of establishing the initial configuration on which to base such calculations and that we could not possibly carry out these calculations even if we knew the original configuration. But it has never been doubted that if we were presented with the complete atomic configuration of the universe at any moment, we would know about it everything that we might conceivably want to know. This is what I shall contest here.

The law of irreversibly increasing entropy governs the fundamental processes of equilibration in nature. But the entropy of a system cannot be computed from a knowledge of its atomic configuration, for it is measured by the extent to which this configuration is uncertain. This argument can be made more definite by assuming quantization. The entropy of a precisely known atomic configuration is, then, zero and remains zero throughout the future; equilibration by increasing entropy does not take place. We can have equilibration only if we introduce conceptions of probability, by assuming that the configuration of atoms is to a considerable extent uncertain.

We meet with the same kind of situation wherever we assess chances. If, in throwing dice, we know the exact physical particulars of our throws and hence could predict their outcome, the probability of any particular sides of the dice turning up would be inconceivable, and no actions based on such probabilities (e.g., betting) could be justified. Even so in physics, if all atomic particulars were specified, processes governed by probabilities, e.g., irreversible equilibrations, would be inconceivable and their actual occurrence could not be accounted for. We may regard, therefore, such processes as comprehensive features, which disappear when their particulars are specified in terms of a Laplacean topography.

This illustrates the logical deficiency of the Laplacean conception of universal knowledge at an elementary level. It faces us, more generally, in the fact that questions in which we are interested arise in the context of experiences which do not consist in atomic configurations, and which may not be derivable from the conceptual framework of atomic configurations.

Let me illustrate this further by the example of machines. Machines are solid structures made up of several parts, which have their several functions in the operation of the machine. Thus a machine can be described as a particular configuration of solids. The description would state the materials and shapes of the parts, and the boundary conditions by which they are joined together as a system. But this could describe only one particular specimen of one kind of machine. It could not characterize a class of machines of the same kind, which would include specimens of different sizes, often of different materials, and with an infinite range of other variations. Such a class would be truly characterized by the operational principles of the machine, including the principles of its structure. It is by these principles, when laid down in the claims of a patent, that all possible realizations of the same machine are legally covered; a class of machine is defined by its operational principles.

What conceptions, if any, are introduced here that cannot be derived from an atomic topography? Let us suppose, for the sake of simplifying the argument, that the difficulties of deriving the laws of physics and chemistry from a Laplacean knowledge of the world's atomic configuration could be overcome. We may observe then (1) that a particular specimen of a machine is characterized by the nature of its materials, by the shape of its parts and their mutual arrangement, which can be defined by the boundary conditions of the system,[10] and (2) that the laws of physics and chemistry are equally valid for all solids, whatever their materials and shapes, and the boundary conditions determining their arrangement. From which it follows that neither the materials nor the shapes of the solids forming part of a (particular) machine, nor their arrangement, can be derived from physics and chemistry. And that hence physics and chemistry cannot account for the existence of a machine, cannot even identify a machine as a machine, and still less identify its workings and account for these.

This limitation becomes clearer if we consider a *class* of one type of machine, for example, steam engines. Such a class could be effectively covered by a patent or be referred to in a trade agreement. The description of the principles on which steam engines are constructed and operated would enable a court of law to decide whether an object is a steam engine or not, and even to identify damaged engines that do not work. In order to account for the existence of such a class in terms of physics and chemistry, it would be necessary to derive from the laws of physics and chemistry a general relationship of materials and shapes of a group of solids, of their mutual arrangement, given by the boundary conditions of the system, and their purpose, which would jointly characterize all objects that are steam engines, even when broken down.

In order to envisage this task, we shall assume that an individual specimen of a certain type of machine has been fully described in terms of its physical and chemical topography. The task is then to identify and generalize such features of this topography as characterize a steam engine, including one that has broken down. The laws of thermodynamics will of course be referred to in any such generalization. But these laws do not define the steam engine: a steam engine is something that *relies* on these laws for its workings. To define a steam engine is to tell in what way it utilizes the laws of thermodynamics and other laws of physics and chemistry. That is why these principles are part of a distinctive science, the science of engineering. Engineering deals with principles of technical success, and hence can also identify technical failure, as in broken down steam engines.

It follows that even if physics and chemistry could be derived from predictions of atomic topography, the existence of the machines could not be stated, let alone accounted for, in these terms. And, accordingly, the knowledge of engineering (as defined above) and of all problems of engineering, as well as of inventions and arguments conducted in terms of engineering, would be absent in a knowledge of the physical and chemical topography of the universe, and, *a fortiori*, in its atomic topography.

The nature of this limitation is logical. Its reasons are of the same kind as those for which physics and chemistry cannot identify a printed page (even though printing relies on the laws of physics and chemistry), nor tell us what the print says.

I have argued this conclusion extensively, as much because of its general significance, as for its particular bearing on biology. Physiology is the study of the operational principles by which living things survive and propagate themselves. There is some difference of opinion today whether all living functions are machine-like; the *predominant view* is that they are all machine-like. I am not concerned here with the question whether or not this view is true; my argument bears on the *unanimous view*, held by both sides of the controversy, that the machine-like explanation of physiological functions is equivalent to their explanation in terms of physics and chemistry. My demonstration that machines cannot be accounted for in terms of physics and chemistry applies equally to the machine-like operations of animals. I must conclude, therefore, that to equate any machine-like explanation with an explanation in terms of physics and chemistry is a logical absurdity. This does *not* mean that these mechanisms could not have come into existence phylogenetically by processes of physics and chemistry. I myself do not think this is possible, but physiology is not a theory of evolution, and I do not include evolution in my conclusions here, any more than physiologists do, when saying that they are explaining physiological functions in terms of physics and chemistry.

Let me return then to my general argument. The Laplacean conception of universal knowledge, which is but a particular illustration of the theory of primary qualities on which science has been based since Galileo, has always been thought to require a super-human mind capable of collecting the initial data and then calculating future atomic constellations. But it has been consistently overlooked that at this point the universal mind meets with more fundamental difficulties. I believe that I have shown (1) that there is no evidence to suppose that the 'universal knowledge' conceived by Laplace would answer any questions that we are interested in; (2) that to find out the entropy, temperature, and pressure of a system from a Laplacean universal knowledge requires estimates of probability, a conception not derivable from an atomic topography; (3) that all engineering and technology comprising operational principles lies logically beyond the range of Laplacean knowledge; and (4) that the same is true for the operational principles established by physiology as the functions of living things.

The list could be extended indefinitely. An obvious case to be added would be the impossibility of accounting for sentience in terms of the primary qualities defined by physics. But enough has been said to substantiate a general conclusion in terms of the principles of tacit knowing explained in this paper. Atomic configurations are the ultimate particulars assumed to be underlying all the manifestations of more comprehensive entities in the universe. We have seen that the particulars of such entities lack the meaning which the entities possess. Consequently when we focus our attention on the ultimate particulars of the universe we are facing things which have the least possible meaning. A Laplacean mind that would compute from the present virtually meaningless atomic topography of the world its future similarly meaningless topography would not materially advance our knowledge of the world, let alone represent a universal knowledge of it.

The world could be known from such a topography only if we had the power to integrate it by an act of tacit knowing. But such powers are far from unlimited. The integration produced in the Ames experiment with the skew room is irretrievably lost by looking at the arrangement from a 'forbidden angle'. There is a well-known guessing game which makes use of the fact that photographs taken from an unusual angle make familiar objects unrecognizable. The full range of colours produced, according to Land, by super-imposing two monochromatic optical images, disappears when we look at the two components separately. All patterns vanish if we scan them through a sufficiently strong magnifying glass. (I repeat that these limits of our integrative powers are accepted in this paper as facts, without inquiring into their origin.)

This should suffice to explain the obvious fact that no human intelligence could apprehend, by looking at an atomic topography of a frog, that it *is* a frog, nor understand from the frog's computed future topographies, the physiology of a frog. And, of course, what is true for its atomic topography is equally true for a physical-chemical topography of the frog; we could perceive in it nothing of the frog. If we could rely on our awareness of the data forming such a topography for attending to their joint meaning, the topography would become transparent, in the same sense as a text is transparent when we read and understand it. But since this is not possible, it can only block our view by its meaningless body— even as a text does, when we concentrate our attention on its physical details.

When one reaches the conclusion that an assumption widely taken for granted during a long time is patently false, one asks oneself how such an error could have arisen and been perpetuated. The answer in this case is not far to seek. The Laplacean conception of universal knowledge, as well as its modern equivalents, are models of a completely formalized, or mathematical, representation of the universe. And ever since the middle of the eighteenth century, science has inflexibly set itself the ideal of casting all knowledge into mathematical form. Descriptive sciences were to be regarded as imperfect, immature branches of knowledge that would sometime be replaced by definitive mathematical formulations.

But this ideal is logically absurd. Imagine a set of mathematical formulas that would answer any questions that we might ask about matters of experience. The object of such experience must be other than the mathematical formulas which are to explain it, and hence these formulas are meaningless unless they bear on non-mathematical experiences. In other words, we can use our formulas only after we have made sense of the world to the point of asking questions about it and have established the bearing of the formulas on the experience that they are to explain. Mathematical reasoning about experience must include, besides the antecedent non-mathematical finding and shaping of experience, the equally non-mathematical relating of mathematics to such experience and the eventual, also non-mathematical, understanding of experience elucidated by mathematical theory. It must also include ourselves, carrying out and committing ourselves to these non-mathematical acts of knowing. Hence a mathematical theory of the universe claiming to include its own bearing on experience would be self contradictory in the same sense as the conception of a tool would be if the tool were described as including its own user and the things to which it was to be applied.

Knowing is a process in two stages, the subsidiary and the focal, and these two can be defined only within the tacit act which relies on the first for attending to the second. But again, why should this fact have been overlooked and a false ideal of science been perpetuated for centuries? Because the moment we admit that all knowing is rooted in an act of personal judgment, knowledge seems to lose all claim to objectivity. I have hinted at a

way out of this difficulty by my definition of reality, and a substantial treatment of it has been given elsewhere. But the answer
will yet have to be worked out fully in the future.

¹ LORD RUSSELL BRAIN, *Mind, Perception and Science*, Oxford: Oxford University
Press, 1951, pp. 18–19.
² Cf. e.g., W. DILTHEY, *Gesammelte Schriften*, Leipzig and Berlin: B. G. TEUBNER,
1914–37, VII, pp. 213–16. Trs. by H. A. Hodges, *Wilhelm Dilthey*, London: Routledge & Kegan Paul, 1944, pp. 121–24; and T. Lipps, *Ästhetik*, Hamburg, 1903.
³ This is not to accept the distinction of two kinds of experience, one from inside,
the other from outside. The physiologist's view of organs and their functions is an
internal comprehension of a living being, compared with a purely physical and
chemical topography of a living body which would contain no such understanding.
I am envisaging a continuous range in degrees of indwelling, not two aspects, one
from inside, the other from outside.
⁴ See Essay 8 above.
⁵ Cf. G. W. ALLPORT and T. F. PETIGREW, 'Cultural Influence on the Perception
of Movement: The Trapezoidal Illusion among Zulus', *Journal of Abnormal and
Social Psychology*, 55 (1957), pp. 104–13.
⁶ GILBERT RYLE, *The Concept of Mind*, New York: Barnes and Noble, 1950, and
London: Hutchinson, 1949.
⁷ P. F. STRAWSON, *Individuals*, London: Methuen, 1959, pp. 106 ff. The argument
is based here on the special character of 'P predicates', i.e., predicates referring to
persons. 'For just as there is not in general one . . . process of learning . . . an inner
private meaning of predicates of this class, then another process of learning to
apply such predicates to others on the strength of a correlation, noted in one's own
case, with certain forms of behaviour, so—and equally—there is not in general one
primary process of learning to apply such predicates to others on the strength of
behaviour criteria, and then another process of acquiring the secondary technique of
exhibiting a new form of behaviour, viz., first-person P-utterances' (pp. 107–8). The
author then goes on to warn that one must not couch one's rejection of this structure in the language of that structure.
⁸ E. E. EVANS-PRITCHARD, *Witchcraft, Oracles and Magic among the Azande*, Oxford:
Oxford University Press, 1937. 'Let the reader consider any argument that would
utterly demolish all Zande claims for the power of the oracle. If it were translated
into Zande modes of thought it would serve to support their entire structure of
belief' (p. 319–20). '. . . they reason excellently in the idioms of their beliefs but they
cannot reason outside, or against, their beliefs because they have no other idiom in
which to express their thoughts' (p. 338). Mr Strawson would rightly conclude that
belief in poison oracles is part of Zande metaphysics, which can be descriptively
studied in the logical structure of their language. But this would show only that
Azande would have to use a different language (or use Zande language with a new
meaning) if they wanted to repudiate their present metaphysical beliefs.
⁹ M. POLANYI, *Science, Faith and Society*, New York: Oxford University Press, 1946,
p. 10. I would emphasize at this point once more that the origin of the veridical
powers of tacit integration lies beyond the scope of this paper; I am concerned here
only with defining their structure and illustrating their range.
¹⁰ The purpose served by a device may also be decisive for its identification. Some
years ago Phillips (Eindhoven) and United Incandescent Lamps (Ujpest) were in
conflict about the question whether the newly invented sodium discharge lamps
were to be classed as 'neon lights' under an agreement to which both firms were
parties. An important point made for *not* classing them thus was that sodium lights
are used for *seeing by them* and neon lights for *being seen.*

# 12
# Sense-Giving
# and Sense-Reading
## 1967

I propose to inquire here into the way we endow our speech with meaning and into the way by which we make sense of speech that we hear spoken. I shall show that, notwithstanding their informal character, these acts possess a characteristic pattern, a pattern that I shall call the *structure of tacit knowing*; I shall show that to form such a structure is to *create meaning*. Both the way we endow our own utterances with meaning and our attribution of meaning to the utterances of others are acts of tacit knowing. They represent *sense-giving* and *sense-reading* within the structure of tacit knowing. My inquiry shall outline the total structure of language, comprising both its formal patterns successfully established by modern linguistics and its informal semantic structure, studied so far mainly by philosophy.

### 1  The Triad of Tacit Knowledge

Tacit knowing joins together three co-efficients. This triad is akin to the triad of Peirce: 'A stands for B to C'. But I shall prefer to write instead: A person A may make the word B mean the object C. Or else: The person A can integrate the word B into a bearing on C.

But to integrate a thing B into bearing on some C amounts to endowing B with a *meaning* that points at C. An obvious way to do this is to choose as B a finger pointing at C. Suppose a lecturer points his finger at an object, and tells the audience: 'Look at this!' The audience will *follow the pointing finger* and *look at the object*.

There is a fundamental difference between the way we attend to the pointing finger and its object. We attend to the finger by *following its direction* in order to look at the object. The object *is then at the focus of our attention*, whereas the finger *is not seen* focally, *but as a pointer* to the object. This directive, or vectorial way of attending to the pointing finger, I shall call our *subsidiary awareness of the finger*.

It is our subsidiary awareness of a thing that endows it with meaning: with a meaning that bears on an object of which we are focally aware. A meaningful relation of a subsidiary to a focal is formed by the action of a person who integrates one to the other, and the relation persists by the fact that the person keeps up this integration.

We may say, in slightly more general terms, that the triad of tacit knowing consists in subsidiary things (B) bearing on a focus (C) by virtue of an integration performed by a person (A); we may say also that in tacit knowing we attend *from* one or more subsidiaries *to* a focus on which the subsidiaries are brought to bear.

## 2   *Various Types of Tacit Knowing*

Consider now the range of different instances in which we meet this structure of meaning in tacit knowing. These are familiar examples, but I am here stressing their semantic aspect:

(a) In a skill we have a set of elementary motions, integrated in fulfilment of a joint performance. These elements are the subsidiaries of this focal act. They possess a joint meaning in being co-ordinated to this common purpose. We are attending *from* them *to* their integrated result.

(b) The same applies to the reading of a physiognomy. The several features which express the mood of a person are clues, or subsidiaries, bearing on the moody impression which they jointly compose. We attend *from* these features *to* the mood by integrating them to the appearance of the mood, and this physiognomy and the mood expressed by it are the meaning of these features.

(c) Our next example is the way we find our way blindfold by the use of a stick. We feel the impacts made on our palm and fingers as if they occurred where the stick hits an object. In other words, the impact made on our hand *means* the position of the object where it hits an object.

(d) We may take finally the case of a speculative skill. A chess player conducting a game sees the way the chess-men jointly bear on his chances of winning the game. This is the joint meaning of the chess-men to the player, as he decides from their position the choice of his next move.

### 3  Knowing our body: a paradigm of tacit knowing

In all our transactions with the world around us, we use our body as our instrument. Such uses are skilful. To fix our eyes on a moving object and to see rightly what it presents to us is to perform a watchful, intelligent operation. It jointly interprets dozens of clues in our eyes, in our memories, in muscles of every kind and in the labyrinth inside our skull.

And this applies to all the examples of tacit knowing that I have listed. The expert recognition of specimens, the use of probes and tools, the major skills of our body and mind are all based on a meaningful integration of our body and of the sensations felt by our body.

Throughout these exercises we are subsidiarily aware of the elements that we integrate inside our body and where our body touches things outside it. This is how we are usually aware of our body. Our internal parts are focally felt only when we are in pain; and the external appearance of our body is rarely observed by us; people having no large looking glasses know very little of their body externally. It is the subsidiary sensing of our body that makes us feel that it is *our* body. This is *the meaning our body normally has for us.*

Things like our clothes, spectacles, probes and tools, when in use, function like our body and resemble our body closely by the fact that we rarely know them focally. Indeed, whenever we experience an external object subsidiarily, we feel it in a way similar to that in which we feel our body. And hence we can say that in this sense all subsidiary elements are *interior to the body* in which we live. To this extent we dwell in all subsidiarily experienced things.

To sum up, meaning arises either by integrating clues in our own body or by integrating clues outside, and all meaning known outside is due to our subsidiary treatment of external things as we treat our body. We may be said to *interiorize these things or to pour ourselves into them.* It is by dwelling in them that we make them mean something on which we focus our attention.

This view presents us with two important features of *sense-giving.* Our body and the organs in our body are given to us as our own by birth, and there can be no question of embodying them in order to endow them with meaning. To enrich the meaning of our body, we have only to co-ordinate our motions and to integrate the sensory clues due to the impact of external events. The matter is different when we endow *external* things with meaning. The process of integration assimilates them to our body and to this extent *deprives them of their character as external objects.* We have, for example, two external stereo-images to start with, which we can look at as separate objects; when we interiorize them, these objects vanish into a single image of depth in space. There is also a change in the appearance of spoken or written words when their meaning is established and we attend *from* the words *to* that which they mean. A word focally observed—that is as a sequence of sounds or of marks on paper—appears to us as a meaningless external object; while its assimilation, which makes it a subsidiary thing, deprives it of the opaque externality of an object. The meaningful use of a word, which causes it to lose its bodily character, makes us *look through the word at its meaning.*

Yet another strange fact emerges from this context. When we co-ordinate parts of our body to achieve some external performance or make sense of impacts on our sentient organs, we include in our operations many hidden internal parts, commonly unknown to us. It is characteristic of our body that it submits to operations the particulars of which are virtually unknown to us and that these largely unspecifiable operations cannot be replaced effectively by any focally controlled operations. This offers us evidence of our capacity *to integrate and endow with meaning things of which we possess only a subsidiary awareness.*

This faculty is present also in sense-giving outside our body. In viewing a pair of stereo-pictures we integrate tiny differences of the two pictures, which we could hardly ever see in themselves, so that they form the spatial appearance of their joint image. The sense of a physiognomy and the characteristic appearance of a sickness or of a zoological or botanical specimen, are all largely based on features that are hardly identifiable in themselves. And we may add that scientific discovery is notoriously guided by many unidentifiable clues, and so is to an important extent our ultimate decision of accepting the claims of a scientific discovery as valid.

These facts are essential to the study of language. There could be no phonology if we could not control and use meaningfully a

complex pattern of vocal actions without any explicit knowledge
of what we are doing when relying on these grounds for our
utterance of words. Nor is the pattern of grammar on which we
rely for composing meaningful sentences commonly better known
to us. We can know them well only from linguistic studies. We
usually conduct these delicate and meaningful integrations without our being able to give more than the crudest account of such
subsidiary performances.

These unspecifiable powers of the mind will yet be clarified.
But in conclusion to the present section, I shall add that *sense-
giving* has its counterpart in the reverse process of *sense-deprivation*.
I have described the changes in the appearance of external things
when we endow them with meaning. They lose their bodily character and become as it were transparent. This is achieved by turning the focus of our attention away from the external object and
attending *from* it *to* something else which has become its meaning.
The reverse process works by switching the focus of our attention back on the object which is thereby rendered once more
external to us. And as it acquires the status of externality, the
object loses its meaning. It is well known how a word we speak
can be reduced to a meaningless utterance of sounds by repeating
it a number of times, attending closely to our lips and tongue and
the sounds they make. The fact that exteriorization kills meaning
confirms the sense-giving powers of indwelling.

### 4  *Communication: a triad of triads*

It may seem puzzling that so often the C on which we are focusing
our attention is even more meaningful than the B *from* which we
are attending to C. While the features of a face have their meaning
in a mood, the mood itself is even fuller of meaning than the
features are. And again, while the meaning of a string of words lies
in the sentence they form, the sentence is even more meaningful
than the words which form it.

Such consecutive levels of meaning are widespread, but it yet
seems reasonable to identify the several triads composing them.
Take the example of speech. Suppose we have a series of spoken
sounds that mean a word and a series of spoken words that form a
meaningful grammatical sentence, while a sequence of such sentences forms a meaningful piece of prose. A person A writing a
piece of prose performs a whole series of consecutive integrations

simultaneously. The sequence of triads that he controls can be described as a hierarchy of levels in which each lower level functions as subsidiary to the next higher level.

There is in fact another sequence of triads which throws a closer light on the main problem of sense-giving and sense-reading. Suppose we travel in a country we have not visited before. By the end of a morning we will be full of new experiences and may report them by letter to a friend so that he may read our message and try to understand our experiences. This is a sequence of three integrations. The *first* is an intelligent understanding of sights and events, the *second* the composing of a verbal account of this experience, and the *third* the interpretation of this verbal account with a view to reproducing the experience which is reported. The first two integrations are the work of one person, while the third is done by another person, the friend addressed by the first. We may note also some variation in the character of the three consecutive integrations. The first triad is mainly cognitive; it has the structure we met in the process of perception and, more strikingly perhaps, in the identification of a specimen by an expert. The second triad, which puts the result of the first into words, resembles more the performance of a practical skill, while the third returns once more to the cognitive type which integrates clues to a meaningful experience. The *first* triad is more a sense-*reading*, the *second* more a sense-*giving* and the *third*, once more, a sense-*reading*.

These two directions of using meaning can be illustrated by a small episode from my own experience.[1] My correspondence arrives at my breakfast table in various languages, but my son understands only English. Having just finished reading a letter I may wish to pass it on to him, but must check myself and look again to see in what language it was written. I am vividly aware of the meaning conveyed by the letter, yet know nothing of its words. If I look then and find that the letter is in a foreign language, I tell my son its content in English. These two phases clearly show that we can possess the meaning of a text without knowing the text itself, and can then put this inarticulate meaning into words. It illustrates the kind of inarticulate knowledge first acquired by the traveller by an act of sense-reading: the original meaning he then puts into words. It is the kind of understanding that we share with intelligent animals.

The fact that we can possess knowledge that is unspoken is of course a commonplace and so is the fact that we must know something yet unspoken before we can express it in words. It has been taken for granted in the philosophical analysis of language in earlier centuries, but modern positivism has tried to ignore it, on the grounds that tacit knowledge was not accessible to objective observation. The present theory of meaning assigns a firm place to the inarticulate meaning of experience and shows that it is the foundation of all explicit meaning. To this I shall yet return.

## 5 Sense-Reading

We shall see more fully what is involved in tacit semantic acts, and particularly in sense-reading, if we introduce a measure of difficulty that needs to be overcome by an effort. Take first two typical cases of sense-reading. First, noticing at night a strange outline in your garden you strain your eyes to make out what it is; second, from an inkling of a meaning suggested by a text, we strive for a fuller understanding of it. And thirdly, as a case of sense-giving, we may feel what we want to say, yet must grope desperately for words to say it.

These tacit efforts can perhaps be appreciated better if we note that each of them has a major form in which it manifests its powers more fully. Students of biology have for years past noticed the presence of certain microscopic structures which they called Golgi bodies. Most histologists accepted the claim that these shapes represented biological organs, but there were some who were sceptical, until the electron microscope proved that the Golgi bodies were real organs.[2] Take another similar case. Early in the nineteenth century the apparently integer value of atomic weights based on hydrogen induced William Prout to suggest that all elements were built of hydrogen. But sceptics rejected this claim on the grounds that the approximation to integer values was but crude. Their objections prevailed for nearly a century, until atomic physicists proved them wrong: matter was shown to be built of particles like hydrogen atoms.

We see here how heavily the course of scientific inquiry may rest on deciding whether certain regularities should be taken to be significant or be set aside as accidental. This is true also for juries drawing conclusions on the grounds of circumstantial evidence. They must decide whether certain suspicious circumstances do establish beyond reasonable doubt the guilt of the accused, or are to be set aside as pure coincidences.

Such decisions are open to argument, but yet remain substantially dependent on an informal judgment, which in the case of science may require exceptional powers of insight. It is to these powers that we owe our capacity for recognizing in our experience a meaning that can then be stated in words.

These instances of inarticulate sense-reading apply to the first of the consecutive integrations which make up the transmission of an experience to another person. Leaving aside for the moment the process of verbalization, which is a sense-giving, I pass on to the third integration—that is, the reception of a message—which is another act of sense-reading. When a message reaches the person to whom it is addressed, he will try to make sense jointly of its text and of the experience described by the text. For the understanding of a verbal communication of a meaningful experience, we can usually rely on our previous understanding of familiar experiences. But we often have to understand language for which this does not hold. Our education is largely based on absorbing communications about experiences that are novel to us and are recorded in a language we don't understand.

Some time ago I described the arduous process by which a medical student learns to interpret radiograms of pulmonary diseases.[3] He begins by watching in a darkened room the shadowy traces on a fluorescent screen placed against a patient's chest, and hears the radiologist commenting to his assistants, in technical language, on the significant features of these shadows. The student is completely puzzled, for he can see in the X-ray picture of a chest only the shadows of the heart and the ribs, with a few spidery blotches between them. The experts seem to be romancing; he can see nothing that they are talking about. But as he goes on listening for a few weeks, looking carefully at the pictures of different cases, gradually a rich panorama of significant details will be revealed to him: of physiological variations and pathological changes, of scars, of chronic infections and signs of acute disease. He has entered a new world. He still sees only a fraction of what the experts can see, but the pictures are definitely making sense now and so do most of the comments made on them. Thus, at the very moment when he has learned the language of pulmonary radiology, the student will also have learned to understand pulmonary radiograms.

An unintelligible text referring to an unintelligible matter presents us with a dual problem. Both halves of such a problem jointly guide our minds towards solving them and will in fact be solved jointly by the understanding of the objects referred to and the words referring to it. The meaning of the things and of the terms designating them is discovered at the same time. I have said that this dual act of sense-reading is the paradigm of the educational expansion of our mind; it also bears on the process by which a child learns to understand speech, which is a basic problem of linguistic theory. I shall lead up to this as I go on.

## 6  *Experience and Report*

Let me return then to the scene when I received a letter, took in its content and remembered it, though I had forgotten in what language the letter was written. The knowledge I thus retained was the meaning of the letter as I understood it. Suppose the letter described a scene its writer was witnessing at the time he wrote to me. He had an understanding of the scene, and this was its meaning to him; we may ask then how the meaning of the scene that I gained from this letter compares with the meaning it had for him who wrote it.

We may say that the observed meaning of an experience differs structurally from one conveyed in a letter. They are the focus of two very different triads. The first triad is formed by the integration of perceived objects impinging on our senses, while the second triad integrates the meaning of written words. In the first case we experience sensory qualities that cannot be gained by reading a letter. We may say that the first meaning is *immediately experienced*, while the second is *only present in thought*.

We find similar differences between various semantic triads. When I point my finger at an object I mean that object, and so this object is the meaning of my pointing finger. This relation can also be expressed verbally by naming the object at which I am pointing. But the appearance of the object is never quite the end point of our attention, for even when we look at a real, clearly circumscribed object, we know that it could be observed also in many other ways. In other cases the range of our attention can be altogether intangible. A stereoscopic picture is intangible and so is the strategy pursued by a chess player. In such cases our attention is not focused on an object before us, but is fixed instead on distant matters towards which our proximal experience is pointing. The less tangible the focus, the more purely mental is its object: from a meaning that consists in an object we pass to a meaning consisting in a conception.

Thus the conflict between the view that denotative language bears on objects and the classical view, which holds that language bears on conceptions, is resolved here by admitting both possibilities and establishing a continuous transition between the two.

But to speak of conceptions evokes an ancient logical problem. The traveller who admires a landscape sees a particular image of trees, fields, rivers and peaks, and nearer to his position he hears church-bells ringing and sees villagers walking to attend service. His experience is composed of particular instances of the classes denoted by the terms 'tree', 'river', 'peak', 'church-bell', 'villagers', 'walking' and 'religious service', etc., but when he *reports* the scene he is admiring, his experience will be represented in these general terms, which will not transmit the particular instances that his senses are witnessing. While these experiences will remain his private recollections, his report will convey to its reader merely a conception of the writer's experience. The question is how such a conception can apply to a multitude of disparate instances of it so that the mention of the conception can tell that an instance of it has been observed. The ancient problem, how one general word can cover a multitude of disparate things, comes back here as a problem of verbal communication.

We meet this problem in the reverse direction in the way a writer selects words for reporting his experience. Let us now study this action. I have described the tacit process of understanding experience and that of understanding a report on an experience as two acts of *sense-reading*. In the process by which a writer picks his words for describing his experience, we meet an act of *sense-giving*. And in view of the use he makes of universal terms, we may say that this sense-giving is an act of *conceptual subsumption*, while we may call the intelligent reading of a description an act of *conceptual exemplification*.

To understand verbal communication requires therefore that we resolve the problem of universals: we must explain how a single word can apply to an aggregate of objects that differ in every particular. An attempt made by F. Waismann in 1945 to answer this question has gained wide attention. He pointed out that general terms have an 'open texture', which admits differences in the instances to which it applies. But this merely shifts the question. For to ascribe 'open texture' to a word is merely to imply that among an indefinitely extending series of different objects the word properly applies to some objects and not to the rest. The question how this is done remains open, exactly as before.

Kant wrote of the process of subsuming particular instances under a general term that it was 'a skill so deeply hidden in the human soul that we shall hardly guess the secret that Nature here employs'. The secret was indeed inaccessible so long as one looked for an *explicit procedure* to account for the subsumption of particulars under a general term, but the secret can be found in a tacit operation of the mind. Take as our paradigm the viewing of stereoscopic pictures. There is a slight but decisive difference between each pair of corresponding particulars in the two pictures and, viewing these jointly, these disparities are fused to a single image possessing a novel quality. No explicit procedure can produce this integration. This is our key to the problem of general terms. Our conception of a tree, for example, is formed in a similar way. It arises by the tacit integration of countless experiences of different trees and pictures and reports of still others: deciduous and evergreen, straight and crooked, bare and leafy. All these encounters are included in forming the conception of a tree; they are all used subsidiarily with a bearing on the conception of a tree, which is what we mean by the word 'tree'.

When groping for words to describe an experience, we are using this very path. We use the particulars we have seen and heard as clues to conceptions covering them, and we then designate these particulars by the names of these conceptions.

Conversely, a general term can be readily used as a guide to its instances. When reading about meadows, church-bells and village folk we can readily think of possible examples of them. In a description composed of a number of general terms these will mutually restrict the range of their possible instances, and this is what a description conveys to the reader.

o

## 7   Nature of Meaning

We have now explained an important example of sense-giving and a corresponding sense-reading by the powers of tacit integration. But we must yet deal with the more elementary fact that a word can mean anything at all, for example, a single object. The brilliant advances of modern linguistics in phonology and generative grammar have cast no new light on the strange fact that language means something. This failure is due to the same reason which rendered the function of universals inexplicable. The relation of a word to that which it denotes is established by a tacit integration in which we rely on a subsidiary awareness of the word for directing our attention to its meaning.

We have seen how this integration deprives the word of its existence as an observed body and makes it in a way transparent. And we have seen also that the interiorization of the word and the meaning acquired through its interiorization can be wiped out by switching the focus of our attention back on the word and turning it thus once more into an opaque meaningless object.

This is in fact what happens if we try to interpret meaning by an explicit procedure. Listen to the following formulation of this attempt by Charles Morris: 'The sign vehicle itself is simply one object, and its denotation of other objects resides solely in the fact that there are rules of usage which correlate the two sets of objects.'[4] This is to convert words into mere sounds and then to subject them to the operation of rules corresponding to the meaning they possessed before. But this does not work. Any rules that will operate on meaningless sounds endowing them with such powers as they would possess if they had a meaning will be found to include actions—like pointing at something—which introduce the very kind of meaningful integration which the operation was to eliminate.

The explanation of meaning by a habitual association of sounds and objects, which has recently been renewed by W. V. O. Quine, fails likewise to account for the actually observed function of words to mean something.[5] For to observe the frequent coincidence of certain sounds with a particular sight keeps the sound and the sight equally in the focus of our attention, and this necessarily keeps the sound opaque and meaningless.

The kind of meaning that the sound of a word actually conveys is destructible by switching our attention from the thing meant to that which means it; to explain such meaning we must explain its destructibility, as I have done. A positivistic analysis of meaning would evade the necessity of explaining the actual meaningfulness by offering an explicit substitute for this meaning. But this is pointless; it would be pointless even if such substitutes were feasible, which they are not.

Some writers have noticed the inequality in the status between language and the things meant by language and ascribed to this inequality the functions of meaning. Erwin Straus writes:

> That which is to function as a sign must not only be lowered in rank and value, it must be closer and more accessible to me than the designate.... The sign and the designated, therefore, cannot exchange their roles within a single semiotic relationship. The semiotic role belongs to a three-cornered relation if one may put it so. Only because in this world one thing is to us less important, closer, and more accessible than another, can it function for us a sign of the other. Its only purpose is to point beyond itself towards something else, to be in its own nullity a sign of *the other*. This opens up in detail a wide range of subjective interpretation. The semiotic reference is inseparable from our egocentricity, from the bodily subjection of our existence.[6]

Earlier still, Susanne K. Langer had observed the relative worthlessness of signs: '. . . little noises (she writes) are ideal conveyors of concepts, for they give us nothing but their meaning. This is the source of "transparency" of language on which several scholars have remarked.'[7]

However, words would not lose their meaning, even if cast in gold while referring to mere flies, and the content of a priceless medieval bible is the same as that of the shabbiest copy of the same text. Our capacity to endow language with meaning must be recognized as a particular instance of our sense-giving powers. We must realize that to use language is a performance of the same kind as our integration of visual clues for perceiving an object, or as the viewing of a stereo picture, or our integration of muscular contractions in walking or driving a motor car, or as the conducting of a game of chess—all of which are performed by relying on our subsidiary awareness of some things for the purpose of attending focally to a matter on which they bear. These are exercises of an integrative power which can comprehend a triad in which the person A sees a B as bearing on a C, or else uses a B for the purpose C, and these integrations can be seen to be essentially tacit.

## 8  *Inference: tacit and explicit*

Let me insert here a *caveat*. I have spoken of the two kinds of awareness comprised by tacit knowing as a lower and a higher level. But it would be a mistake to identify subsidiary awareness with subconscious or pre-conscious awareness or with the fringe of consciousness described by William James. When writing a letter I am fully aware of the pen and paper I am using. The fact that I am focusing my attention on these particulars, but attending *from* them *to* that which they mean, reduces them to a subsidiary status, but does not render my knowledge of them subconscious or pre-conscious, or such as one has of an indefinable Jamesian fringe. The clues of tacit knowing and the elements of tacit performing are usually difficult to identify and sometimes they are quite unspecifiable. Again, tacit integration may often take place effortlessly unnoticed by ourselves. But all this does not make a subsidiary state an unconscious one.

Conversely, when an integration meets with difficulties, and this evokes a deliberate effort in us, this does not make the integration any less tacit. The sailor straining his eyes to make out what he sees on the horizon, or the athlete concentrating every fibre of his body while approaching the barrier for a high jump, does not proceed by calculations. And even in the highest mathematical sciences the pursuit of discovery is essentially a tacit operation.

It is the *function* of a subsidiary item that counts in classing it as subsidiary. We may call it its *logical function*. When I see visual clues as a coherent object, the relation between any awareness of the clues to the knowledge derived from them is similar to that between premises and conclusions derived from them: it is a logical relationship. The clues enter here into a procedure of *tacit inference*, with integration replacing deduction. The performance of a skill can also be regarded as a logical operation by regarding a skilful co-ordination of several moves as a process of construction, like the construction of a triangle from three elements. Integration takes here the place of operations by ruler and compass.

But if these claims of tacit knowing are accepted, what is left of explicit knowledge arrived at by explicit inference? If the meaning of language is the work of tacit integration, surely the same holds of mathematical formulae, and thus tacit knowledge seems to swallow up all discursive thought.

The answer is not far to seek. In my paradigm of the traveller, we have met a purely tacit knowledge of an experience; both its subsidiary and its focal awareness were tacit. At the next stage, this focal awareness of an experience was introduced subsidiarily into a communication which was a piece of explicit knowledge, the meaning of which was tacit. *All knowledge falls into one of these two classes: it is either tacit or rooted in tacit knowledge.*

The ideal of a strictly explicit knowledge is indeed self-contradictory; deprived of their tacit coefficients, all spoken words, all formulae, all maps and graphs, are strictly meaningless. An exact mathematical theory means nothing unless we recognize an inexact non-mathematical knowledge on which it bears and a person whose judgment upholds this bearing.[8]

The false ideal of a strictly explicit knowledge was pursued with the greatest zeal in the twentieth century by modern positivism. The attempt of Charles Morris to identify the meaning of language in operational terms, as well as Skinner's behaviourist representation of language leading up to Quine's associationist definition of meaning, all flow from a compelling desire to eliminate any reference to a tacit structure of meaning, which is necessarily mental. The most important achievements of modern linguistics were due to turning attention to the sound of language, as best suited to an exact, objective investigation and going beyond this only in the study of formal relations underlying the grammatical structure of language. The fact that language is nothing unless it has conscious meaning was set aside as a temporary difficulty for modern, strictly empirical linguistics.

However, a distinct tendency to break with strict empiricism and to revive the classical conception of language, which recognizes the mental character of meaning, has been expressed recently by Noam Chomsky,[9] and my present study supports this by showing that speech has the fundamental structure of all meaningful uses of consciousness in animals and men.

## 9   *The Dynamics of Tacit Knowing*
I shall now turn to two problems of linguistics defined by Chomsky, who regards them as crucial.

(1) 'It seems plain [writes Chomsky] that language acquisition is based on the child's discovery of what from a formal point of view is a deep and abstract theory—a generative grammar of his language—many of the concepts and principles of which are only remotely related to experience by long and intricate chains of unconscious quasi-inferential steps.'[10] The question is how the child can possibly discover the highly sophisticated generative grammar of his language.

(2) Another great problem is . . . the fundamental fact about the normal use of language, namely the speaker's ability to produce and understand instantly new sentences that are not similar to those previously heard in any physically-defined sense . . . nor obtainable from them by any sort of "generalization" known to psychology or philosophy'.[11]

Of the grounds on which language is learned, Chomsky writes: 'The language-acquisition device is only one component of the total system of intellectual structures that can be applied to problem solving and concept formation; in other words, the *faculté de langage* is only one of the faculties of the mind'.[12] But he goes no further in defining these faculties. My view is that the use of language is a tacit performance; the meaning of language arises, as many other kinds of meaning do, in tacitly integrating hitherto meaningless acts into a bearing on a focus that thereby becomes their meaning. I would try to trace back the roots of this faculty to primordial achievements of living things. All animals are capable of tacitly integrating their bodily actions; indeed, meaningful integration can be found in the very process of coherent growth. But I shall refer here only to the intelligent forms of this power, as exercised by the higher animals.

Lashley has demonstrated in a famous experiment the powers of 'latent' learning in animals. When a rat, trained to run a maze, was severely mutilated, including blinding its eyes, the animal still succeeded in finding its way—however clumsily—through the maze. Mutilated rats performing this feat invoked unhesitatingly muscles and senses not used before in learning to run the maze and thus improvised a totally unprecedented integration of their bodies. Such instantaneous practical integrations are matched in the conceptual powers of animals by which they recognize disparate individuals of a species. They instantly identify very different specimens of a class, e.g. different human beings.

We can see here in the behaviour of animals the sources of man's power to utter or understand promptly unprecedented sentences. This relationship was observed a number of years ago by G. H. Humphrey, who already aligned the capacity to express knowledge in an unlimited variety of spoken terms with the capacity of a rat to manifest its knowledge of a maze in an unlimited number of different actions.[13]

But the mere kinship of man's linguistic performances with a rat's varied expressions of its understanding of a maze cannot satisfy us here. We must acknowledge the fact that speech is the application of complex rules of phonetics and grammar and must show how the theory of tacit knowing accounts for the acquisition and practice of such rules.

Our knowledge of linguistic rules and our application of them in speech is commonly called an unconscious knowledge applied unconsciously. I shall call it a subsidiary knowledge and call its application a tacit integration. The difference is essential. To say that we are subsidiarily aware of a thing or action is to attribute to it a particular function, namely a bearing on its meaning, which is at the focus of our attention. The level of consciousness at which we are aware of a subsidiary particular may vary over the whole range of possible levels. Some subsidiary things, like the processes in our inner ear, of which we are aware in feeling the position of our head, are profoundly unconscious, strictly subliminal. But we are not unconscious of a pointing finger the direction of which we are following, nor of the features of a face that we are seeking to recognize, nor of the paper and pen used with a bearing on the content of a written message we are composing. A pianist who, having improved his touch on the keys by a spell of finger practice, integrates this skill to his musical performances, has rendered his awareness of it subsidiary, but still feels the working of his fingers. He has not lost consciousness of them.

I have said that to switch our attention to a subsidiary particular deprives it of its meaning. Such action admittedly does make us more fully conscious of such a particular, but its loss of meaning is due not to this but to the accompanying loss of its subsidiary functions. This is how the generative grammar appears to us when set out in formal, explicit terms. To look at these formulae does not make them work as they do when we rely on their guidance for putting something into words. Our task is now to discover how such rules are developed within our subsidiary awareness and how they perform their functions from this subsidiary condition in controlling the behaviour on which they bear.

I shall take as my first example a skill by which a person does no more than carry out a purpose of utmost simplicity, and yet cannot do so, except by the use of a skill implemented by subsidiary operations.[14] If you put on spectacles which make you see things upside-down—or inverted between right and left—you feel completely lost. You are unable to use your hands or to walk about the room. Yet you seem to have a perfect solution to your problem. It is obvious that what you see above you through upside-down spectacles is really below you—while what you see below you is in fact above you; and with horizontally inverting spectacles, what you see on your right is at your left and *vice versa*. But this prescription, which appears to be all you have to know, is useless: it does not prevent you from responding to what you falsely see.

By contrast, a persistent effort to find one's way while wearing inverted spectacles will correct the inversion. Stratton first discovered this fact in 1896, and after eight days overcame the upside-down glasses he was wearing.[15] Other observers have confirmed this result; but for half a century and more it was almost universally misinterpreted as the reversal of the visual image. Even today it is little known that the observations of Snyder and Pronko (1952) and of Kottenhoff (1956) have proved that the position of the visual image remains inverted when the subject has learnt to move around with inverting spectacles. Kottenhoff has shown that the subject gets to find his way around because he has acquired *a new way of seeing things*, which appropriately co-ordinates his inverted vision with his muscular feelings, his sense of balance and his hearing.[16] This re-integration of sense impressions produces a novel sensory quality to which the usual terms of 'upside-down or right-way-up', 'or right to left' do not apply. A subject wearing right-left inverting glasses will say that 'depending on whether I attend more to my hand or to the rest of the visual field, I would ascribe to it the quality of rightness or leftness'.[17] Kottenhoff writes that at this stage 'the question whether something is to the right or to the left was felt to be rather annoying'.[18] Snyder and Pronko observed the same tendency to confusion as follows.[19] The subject, wearing upside-down inverting spectacles, 'was observing the scene from a tall building. Suddenly someone asked, "Well, how do things look to you? Are they upside-down?" The subject replied "I wish you hadn't asked me. Now, when I recall how they *did* look *before* I put on these lenses, I must answer that they look upside-down *now*. But until the moment that you asked me I was absolutely unaware of it and hadn't given a thought to the question whether things were right-side-up or upside-down.'

Thus, not only was the obvious explicit interpretation of the inverted images useless, but it was disturbing to remember it. The reason being, as Kottenhoff observes, that these corrections use the words 'right', 'left', 'up', and 'down', which refer to the normal integration of sensory data and thus confirmed this integration just when it had to be discarded and replaced by a novel integration.

Explicit directions for correcting the vision presented by inverting spectacles are ineffectual then for two reasons. First, they do not tell us that we have to re-integrate our senses, on the contrary they confirm their normal integration and hinder their re-integration; second, even if some rule did tell us what we have to do, this would be useless, since we cannot directly control the integration of our senses.

What is it then that brings about the solution? What causes a process of re-integration to take place, of which we have no focal knowledge, and which we could not carry out in response to such knowledge even if we had it? The process does not take place spontaneously: it is the result of a protracted, sometimes strenuous, effort. We try to see rightly, and it is established by all observers that only sustained practical efforts to find one's way about will lead to success. Kottenhoff analyses this effort into two parts. (1) The attempt to revise the meaning of the inverted image in the sense of our tacit experiences. (2) The attempt to extend this re-interpretation to the surroundings of the field of vision. For we must comprehensively revise our *visual ideas* in the sense of our re-integrated vision, if the revision is to be stable.

We must conclude then that it is the effort of our imagination, seeking to re-interpret our vision in a way that will control the scene before us, which produces the right way of seeing inverted images. This is *the dynamics of tacit knowing: the questing imagination vaguely anticipating experiences not yet grounded in subsidiary particulars evokes these subsidiaries and thus implements the experience the imagination has sought to achieve.*

This principle has already been touched upon in Section 3 when I spoke of the way we integrate the muscles moving our limbs, without any focal knowledge of this muscular performance. This was first described by William James as the structure of all voluntary motion, and he observed also that it was set in motion by the imagination striving to anticipate the result of the action. It would seem that we can move our body only indirectly by thrusting forward our imagination, which then evokes subsidiarily the means of its own implementation.

This is again the way we keep our balance when riding a bicycle. We can see here clearly the work of the imagination by which a practical knowledge of focally ineffectual rules is acquired. The learner's imagination is fixed on the aim of keeping his balance, and this effort of the imagination implements its aim by subsidiarily evoking an observance of the rules that secure the cyclist's equilibrium: rules which would be useless to him if explicitly formulated.[20]

This broadly answers the first problem of linguistics I quoted from Chomsky. To the question how a child can learn to perform a vast set of complex rules, intelligible only to a handful of experts, we can reply that the striving imagination has the power to implement its aim by the subsidiary practice of ingenious rules of which the subject remains focally ignorant.

This kind of rule can be acquired tacitly and *only* tacitly, and it can also be practised *only* tacitly. The elaborate systems of grammar discovered by linguists in the speech of 'the idealized native speaker' belong to this class of rules.

The second fundamental question of linguistics, how we can instantly understand and produce totally novel sentences, can also be readily answered now. For in riding a bicycle we do something quite similar. We keep our balance at each moment by solving, in effect, the equilibrium equation for ever new sets of values taken on by its variables. The cyclist's striving imagination, which had discovered within a few weeks a whole tacit system of balancing, may well be credited with the performance of instantly re-applying this system to new conditions. The *faculté de langage*, which can discover a whole system of tacit grammar, might be credited likewise with evaluating it instantly for meeting any new case for its application.

## 10   *Heuristics and Language Acquisition*

My scheme of tacit dynamics is obviously incomplete; the self-implementation of the imagination of which I have spoken must have limits. My white hair will not turn black however assiduously I strain my imagination to accomplish this. There must be some principle which excludes mere fancies and selects feasible, or at least possibly feasible, tasks for the imagination to strive for.

We meet this principle of reasonable endeavour in the scientist's choice of a problem. But I shall approach this matter indirectly by looking first at the way a bright idea emerges to solve a scientific problem. Discovery takes place in two more or less separate stages, an arduous straining of the imagination is followed by a virtually spontaneous appearance of the solution. In his classic study of heuristics, Poincaré has described cases in which these two phases were sharply separated: the effort of the imagination had ceased for several hours, when the bright idea turned up. Poincaré thinks that first a strenuous search loosens possible bits of a solution and that discovery is then achieved by an effortless integration of these bits. He calls this integration an illumination; I shall name it intuition.

Intuition, as I understand it, ranges widely. It stands for integrative acts taking place at any stage of a scientific inquiry, from start to finish. The scientist's intuitive powers consist firstly in the faculty for surmising with a fair degree of probability the presence of a hidden coherence in nature. It is this faculty that espies a problem, the pursuit of which the scientist may accept as his task. The inquiry goes ahead then, guided by a series of surmises, which also have a reasonable chance of being right. Thus a discovery is reached—or may be reached—which solves the problem.

Poincaré emphasizes that illumination does not come without the previous work of the imagination. This applies also to what I call intuition. A problem fit for inquiry comes to the scientist in response to his roaming vision of yet undiscovered possibilities. Having chosen a problem, he thrusts his imagination forward in search of clues and the material he thus digs up—whether by speculation or experiment—is integrated by intuition into new surmises, and so the inquiry goes on to the end.

But the kind of intuition which starts off a successful inquiry, and then serves to guide it, differs somewhat from the final integration of the solution which Poincaré has called illumination. To start on an inquiry that may take years of effort and consume all his current resources—and to repeat such enterprises throughout his professional life—the scientist must be sure that a problem on which he enters has a fair chance of being well founded. A good problem must not only tell him the probable presence of something hidden in a certain direction in nature, but also assess the chances of reaching this hidden truth and anticipate with a reasonable degree of reliability whether the result will be worth the time, effort and money that will be needed for finding it. This requirement is conspicuous in the pursuit of technical inventions, for practical advantage is central here, but it is important also for the pursuit of natural science.

One might try to recognize the kind of clues that will lead to a hidden coherence in nature. Many successful scientific inquiries have started from an unexplained regularity in nature, but others, on the contrary, from an unexplained deviation from regularity or from any strange unexplained phenomenon. Others again have started from an apparent conflict between two established principles, and some, on the contrary, from the apparent chance of deriving one principle from another. In any case, such clues can merely offer a possible occasion for discovery: they do not tell us how to make a discovery. For this one must either discover a problem that no one has yet sighted, or hit upon new ways for solving a known problem. The scientist who achieves this is usually not better placed than others, but he is more gifted. He possesses to an exceptional degree the faculty for integrating signs of potentialities, a faculty that we may call the power of *anticipatory intuition*.

Compare this with the *final intuition* that Poincaré called illumination. A final intuition is a claim to discovery and is thus at the point of being proved true or mistaken, while a problem—a a feat of anticipatory intuition—can usually be justified only after a long and uncertain pursuit. Both a problem and a suggested solution are in the nature of surmises, but they differ in their degrees of explicitness. A suggested solution can usually be clearly communicated and its convincing power be transmitted to others, for its grounds are largely tangible. By contrast, a problem—or any other surmise arising in the course of an inquiry—is difficult to explain to others, let alone make convincing to others, for its grounds are mainly unspecifiable.

From the inception of an inquiry to its successful conclusion intuitive judgments become progressively more concrete, more fully grounded in focally observed evidence, but this should not obscure the essential kinship of heuristics and verification. For if this be lost sight of, we can understand neither the logic of scientific inquiry nor the grounds on which a discovery is accepted.

We have arrived now at the mechanism by which the imagination implements its aims, as purified and guided by intuition. Intuition thus fills the gap I left open in my previous section on the dynamics of tacit knowing. After this it is easy to fill the part of intuition also in such sensorimotoric feats as the mastering of inverted vision or learning to ride a bicycle; we need not pursue this here.

But let me introduce a further feature of tacit dynamics that comes out most clearly in sensorimotoric achievements. To learn a skill or to invent one, whether a skill of the senses or of the muscles, is an essentially coherent task. It sets out to solve a coherent problem, and any progress towards its mastery will but fill in the body of this anticipatory outline. Random trial and error unguided by such a perspective will never add up to a skilful performance.

This applies also to the progress of a scientific or technical inquiry. A steady unity of purpose, sustained from start to finish, is perhaps more marked in practical research, the aim of which is set from the start and is rarely modified in the course of its pursuit. But any initial clues of a purely scientific inquiry—of which I have listed examples in my list of possible problems—usually determine the framework of the enterprise from beginning to end. We shall find a similar persistence of basic ideas prevailing in the course of language achievement.

Let me start by applying this mechanism of imagination-*cum*-intuition to the production of a single sentence. In his contribution to the *Hixon Symposium* of 1948, K. S. Lashley shows that associative chain theories fail to explain the production of a spoken sentence. He describes what actually happens.[21] Prior to the internal or overt enunciation of the sentence, an aggregate of word units is partially activated or readied. This shows in the fact that words, destined for a sentence, may be found scrambled in a hasty utterance of it. I regard this as the period described by Poincaré in which the imagination loosens potential elements for solving a problem. Given sufficient time for intuitive reorganization, this would lead to a solution in the form of a correct sentence, but in a premature utterance the words will come out in disorder.

This mechanism explains in general the formation of a time sequence, each item of which is related to all the others, by their joint meaning. This was in fact the general problem raised and left open by Lashley in his contribution to the *Hixon Symposium*.

We can at last approach the question how language is acquired by the child. Rejecting current attempts to explain language acquisition by the assumption of behavioural psychology, Noam Chomsky writes:

> The real problem is that of developing a hypothesis about initial structure that is sufficiently rich to account for acquisition of language yet not so rich as to be inconsistent with the known diversity of language.[22]

The dynamics of tacit knowing has made this problem more manageable. We are no longer faced with the question how people who learn to speak a language can identify, remember and apply a set of complex rules known only to linguists. They do not identify these rules, let alone memorize and explicitly apply them, and do not need to do so. According to the dynamics of tacit knowing, the rules are acquired subsidiarily, without focal knowledge of them.

But this dynamics must be kept moving by the combination of intuition and imagination. We have met this combination of imagination-*cum*-intuition at work in the utterance of a single sentence, and we may add now that such utterances, as well as the intelligent listening to a spoken sentence, can make a contribution to the development of language.

A sentence spoken during childhood and adolescence will not infrequently include a word never used before and thus expand the speaker's vocabulary. The same happens when taking in the meaning of a sentence—be it heard or read—if it contains words not met before. Moreover, with this growth of the vocabulary, the clarity of understanding and the precision in using language will continue to improve. The moment more than a minimum of words is used, some rules of grammar emerge and increase in range and complexity as the speaker's vocabulary expands further, while the observance of grammatical rules will become ever more precise.[23]

This type of language acquisition can of course only proceed from one stage of language to the next. But even so, its range is immense. It extends from the first babbled morpheme used as a word-sentence, and from the child's response to similar sounds used by adults, to the eventual mastery of literary language and culture. From its very start, it takes up the problem which will guide its quest throughout—the task of improving communication. The growth of vocabulary and the acquisition of ever more complex and subtle grammatical rules are both actuated by the imaginative search for further enrichment and greater precision of communication. Semantic sense-giving and sense-reading are striven for ever further, as the twin powers of intuition and imagination work towards this from start to finish.

The manifest parallelism of this conception to the heuristics of science and technology is clear. To apply it more closely, we may note that pure science discovering meaning in Nature is a pursuit of *sense-reading*, while technical invention which makes things into instruments for a set purpose is a *sense-giving*. Thus a language achievement that develops a rudimentary beginning of language to its fullness bears analogies to the pursuit of scientific discovery combined with technical inventions.

But I would liken language achievement rather to *a sequence of advances* in a basic problem of science or technology. Think of the consecutive discoveries of classical mechanics extending over more than two centuries from Galileo to Hamilton, or of the successive inventions which improved the airplane from the first model of the Wright brothers to the giant supersonic machine about to be constructed today—these consistent creative developments of a single idea may offer a paradigm of the way a mature language is formed from its rudimentary beginnings by successive stages of a growing intelligence.

But we must yet take a look at the previous development of the infant which leads from empty babbling to rudimentary speech.

The child's discovery of semantic sense-giving and sense-reading arises within a multitude of parallel achievements. His imagination is at work from the start exploring the nature of the things he is encountering. The conception of enduring objects is formed, along with the knowledge of persons. New skills of crawling, standing, walking and the use of objects for various purposes are mastered. Within such ceaseless action of sense-reading and sense-giving, the child may well come to feel puzzled by the talking of adults and also sense the possibility of making itself better understood by imitating them. This should set his heuristic powers at work.

This rough sketch of the way language may arise in the midst of the earliest growth of human intelligence must suffice here. But there is an ancient question to which I must yet respond. If language is rooted in primitive faculties which we share with the higher animals, why can animals neither invent language nor learn to speak? An ape can learn to ride a bicycle, tacitly discovering ingenious operations that might well rival in complexity those used by small children when they speak. Why can the ape be so clever at one thing and not at another?

Note firstly that the tacit acquisition of an ingenious operation is no mark of high intelligence; the proper standard is the degree of abstraction presented by a problem. The cycling ape has his problem of keeping his balance right in front of him, and he has the clues to solve the problem too within his immediate experience. Not so the child. His problem, both to discover what adults mean by talking and to learn to address them in similar terms, is a highly speculative enterprise, that transcends by far the child's immediate experience. Animals cannot master such abstract problems, and this explains why animals have not invented language as man has, nor can even learn to speak, as children do.

When language is understood as tacit knowing, and the acquisition of language is accordingly explained by the dynamics of tacit knowing, man's unique linguistic powers appear to be due simply to his higher general intelligence.

1 Described in my *Personal Knowledge*, London: Routledge & Kegan Paul and Chicago: University of Chicago Press, 1958, p. 57. The ideas on language developed in the present paper were largely anticipated in this book, particularly in Chapter 4 on 'Skills', pp. 49–65 and in Chapter 5 on 'Articulation', pp. 69–131.
2 See J. R. BAKER, 'New Developments in the Golgi Controversy', *Journal of the Royal Microscopical Society of London*, *82* (1963), pp. 145–57.

[3] POLANYI, *op. cit.*, p. 101.

[4] CHARLES MORRIS, *Foundations of the Theory of Signs* in the *International Encyclopedia of Unified Science, I* (1938), Chicago: University of Chicago Press, 1938, p. 24.

[5] W. V. O. QUINE, *Word and Object*, Cambridge: Massachusetts Institute of Technology Press, 1960.

[6] ERWIN STRAUS, *The Primary World of the Senses*, Pt. II., Ch. B, Sec. 3, p. 149, first published in German as *Vom Sinn der Sinne*, Berlin: Springer, 1956, and trs. by Jacob Needleman, London: The Free Press of Glencoe, 1963.

[7] S. K. LANGER, *Philosophy in a New Key*, New York: Mentor, 1941, p. 61.

[8] M. POLANYI, *The Tacit Dimension*, London: Routledge, 1967, and Garden City: Doubleday, 1966, p. 21.

[9] Of his own 'generative grammar' Chomsky writes that 'its roots are firmly in traditional linguistics'. Noam Chomsky, *Current Issues in Linguistic Theory*, The Hague: Mouton & Co., 1964, p. 20.

[10] NOAM CHOMSKY, *Aspects of the Theory of Syntax*, Cambridge: Massachusetts Institute of Technology Press, 1965, p. 58.

[11] *Ibid.*, pp. 57–58.

[12] *Ibid.*, p. 56.

[13] G. H. HUMPHREY, *Thinking*, London: Methuen & Co., 1951, pp. 261–62.

[14] A similar, somewhat briefer, account of the following illustration was given by M. POLANYI, 'The Creative Imagination', *Chemical and Engineering News, 44:3* (1966), pp. 85–93

[15] G. M. STRATTON, 'Vision without Inversion of the Retinal Image', *Psychological Review, 4* (1897), pp. 341–60 and 463–81.

[16] F. W. SNYDER and N. H. PRONKO, *Vision Without Spatial Inversion*, Wichita, Kansas: University of Wichita Press, 1952, and H. Kottenhoff, 'Was ist Richtiges Sehen mit Umkehrbrillen und in welchem Sinne stellt sich das Sehen um?', *Psychologia Universalis, 5* (1961). Kottenhoff's inquiry was carried out as a doctoral dissertation in the Institute of Experimental Psychology of the University of Innsbruck under Professor T. Erisman. It was completed in 1956.

Nor did Stratton claim that the right way of seeing with inverting spectacles (achieved after eight days) consists in the turning back of the visual image. He identifies the result with 'upright vision', for, he says, 'the real meaning of upright vision' is a 'harmony between touch and sight.'

[17] KOTTENHOFF, *op. cit.*, p. 78.

[18] *Ibid.*, p. 80, also p. 64 and *passim*.

[19] SNYDER and PRONKO, *op. cit.*, p. 113.

[20] See Essay 10 above, p. 144.

[21] K. S. LASHLEY, 'The Problem of Serial Behavior', in *Cerebral Mechanisms in Behavior, The Hixon Symposium, 1948* (L. A. JEFFRESS, ed.) London: Chapman and Hall, and New York: John Wiley and Sons, 1951, pp. 112–36, p. 119.

[22] CHOMSKY, *Aspects of the Theory of Syntax, op. cit.*, p. 58.

[23] This is true in general for the discovery or learning of skills. New principles make their appearances first in mere tendencies which are then sharpened and eventually consolidated.

# PART FOUR

# Life and Mind

# *13*
# The Structure
# of Consciousness
## 1965

Sir Francis Walshe, in whose honour this essay was first published,[1] has often spoken of the inadequacy of anatomic structures to account for the full range of mental actions; he insisted on the presence of integrative mental powers not explicable in these terms. Toward the end of this paper I shall give reasons supporting this view.

1  *Two Kinds of Awareness*
I shall start with an analysis of perception and shall arrive by successive generalizations of the result to a stratified structure of living things, which will include the structure of consciousness in higher animals.

Take a pair of stereoscopic photographs, viewed in the proper way, one eye looking at one, the other eye at the other. The objects appear then distributed in depth, more rounded and real, harder and more tangible. This result is due to slight differences between the two pictures, taken from two points a few inches apart. All the information to be revealed by the stereoscopic viewing is contained in these scarcely perceptible disparities. It should be possible to compute from them the spatial dimensions of the objects and their distribution in depth, and I could imagine cases in which the result of such processing may be of interest. But this would not tell us what the things photographed look like. If you want to remember a family party or identify a criminal, you must integrate the stereo-pictures by looking at them simultaneously with one eye on each.

When looking at the stereo-image, we do see the separate pictures too; for we see the stereo-image only because we have a precise impression of the two pictures which contribute to it. But we must distinguish between the two kinds of seeing: we are *focusing our attention on the stereo-image*, while we *see the two pictures only as they bear on the stereo-image*. We don't look at these two in themselves, but see them as clues to their joint appearance in the stereo-image. It is their function to serve as clues.

We may describe the situation by saying that we are *focally aware* of the stereo-image, by being *subsidiarily aware* of the two separate pictures. And we may add that the characteristic feature of subsidiary awareness is to have a *function*, the function of bearing on something at the focus of our attention. Next we may observe that the focal image, into which the two subsidiary pictures are fused, *brings out their joint meaning*; and thirdly, that this fusion *brings about a quality* not present in the appearance of the subsidiaries. We may recognize then these three features as parts of a process of knowing a focal object by attending subsidiarily to the clues that bear on it. We meet here the structure of *tacit knowing*, with its characteristic *functional*, *semantic*, and *phenomenal* aspects.

I have developed this analysis of tacit knowing many times before and have now chosen the example of stereoscopic viewing in order to prevent a recurrent misconception.[2] It is a mistake to identify subsidiary awareness with subconscious or preconscious awareness, or with the fringe of consciousness described by William James. The relation of clues to that which they indicate is a *logical relation* similar to that which a premise has to the inferences drawn from it, but with the important difference that tacit inferences drawn from clues are not explicit. They are informal, tacit.

Remember that Helmholtz tried to interpret perception as a process of inference, but that this was rejected, because optical illusions are not destroyed by demonstrating their falsity. Tacit inference is like this. The fusion of the two stereoscopic pictures to a single spatial image is not the outcome of an argument; and if its result is illusory, as it can well be, it will not be shaken by argument. The fusion of the clues to the image on which they bear is *not a deduction* but an *integration*.

Jean Piaget has drawn a striking distinction between a sensorimotor act and an explicit inference. Explicit inference is reversible: we can go back to its premises and go forward again to its conclusions, rehearse the whole process as often as we like. This is not true for the sensorimotor act: for example, once we have seen through a puzzle, we cannot return to an ignorance of its solution.

The seeing of two stereo-pictures as one spatial image is, indeed, irreversible in two senses. Firstly, it is difficult to find our way back to the clues in the two pictures, because they are hardly visible. And there are many other clues to seeing something, like memories and the feeling inside our eye muscles, which we either cannot trace or cannot experience in themselves at all; they are *largely submerged, unspecifiable.*

Secondly—and this is more important for us—to go back to the premises of a tacit inference brings about its reversal. It is not to retrace our steps, but to efface them. Suppose we take out the stereo-pictures from the viewer and look at them with both eyes. All the effects of the integration are cancelled; the two pictures no longer function as clues, their joint meaning has vanished. What has happened here may be regarded as the inverse of tacit inference; a process of *logical disintegration has reduced a comprehensive entity to its relatively meaningless fragments.*

The best-known example of this is the way a spoken word loses its meaning if we repeat it a number of times, while carefully attending to the movement of our lips and tongue and to the sound we are making. All these elements are meaningful, so long as we attend through them to that on which they bear, but lose their meaning when we attend to them in themselves, focally. The famous tight-rope walker, Blondin, says in his memoirs that he would instantly lose his balance if he thought directly of keeping it; he must force himself to think only of the way he would eventually descend from the rope.[3]

*The purpose of this paper is to show that the relation between body and mind has the same logical structure as the relation between clues and the image to which the clues are pointing.* I believe that the paradoxes of the body-mind relation can be traced to this logical structure and their solution be found in the light of this interpretation.

The example of stereo-vision stands of course for a wide range of similar intellectual and practical feats of knowing. We know a comprehensive whole, for example a dog, by relying on our awareness of its parts for attending focally to the whole. When we perform a skill, we attend focally to its outcome, while being aware subsidiarily of the several moves we co-ordinate to this effect. I have carried out this analysis often elsewhere and shall take it for granted here.[4] But there is a further step which I must restate once more. I shall say that we observe external objects by being subsidiarily aware of the impact they make on our body and of the responses our body makes to them. All our conscious transactions with the world involve our subsidiary use of our body. And our body is the only aggregate of things of which we are aware almost exclusively in such a subsidiary manner.

I am speaking here of *active* consciousness, which excludes incoherent dreams or pathological bursts of temper. Active consciousness achieves coherence by integrating clues to the things on which they bear or integrating parts to the wholes they form. This brings forth *the two levels of awareness*: the lower one for the clues, the parts or other subsidiary elements and the higher one for the focally apprehended comprehensive entity to which these elements point. A deliberate act of consciousness has therefore not only an identifiable object as its focal point, but also a set of subsidiary roots which function as clues to its object or as parts of it.

This is the point at which our body is related to our mind. As our sense organs, our nerves and brain, our muscles and memories, serve to implement our conscious intention, our awareness of them enters subsidiarily into the comprehensive entity which forms the focus of our attention. A suitable term is needed to speak of this relation briefly. I shall say that we attend *from* the subsidiary particulars *to* their joint focus. Acts of consciousness are then not only conscious *of* something, but also conscious *from* certain things which include our body. When we examine a human body engaged in conscious action, we meet no traces of consciousness in its organs; and this can be understood now in the sense that subsidiary elements, like the bodily organs engaged in conscious action, lose their functional appearance when we cease to look *from* them at the focus on which they bear, and look instead *at* them, in themselves.

The way we know a comprehensive entity by relying on our awareness of its parts for attending to its whole is the way we are aware of our body for attending to an external event. We may say therefore that we know a comprehensive entity by *interiorizing* its parts or by making ourselves *dwell in them*; and the opposite process of switching attention to the parts can be described as turning the parts into *external objects* without functional meaning; it is to *externalize* them.

This formulation of tacit knowing is particularly suited for describing the way we know another person's mind. We know a chess player's mind by dwelling in the stratagems of his games and know another man's pain by dwelling in his face distorted by suffering. And we may conclude that the opposite process, namely of insisting on looking at the parts of an observed behaviour as several objects, must make us lose sight of the mind in control of a person's behaviour.

But what should we think then of current schools of psychology which claim that they replace the study of mental processes, by observing the several particulars of behaviour as objects and by establishing experimentally the laws of their occurrence? We may doubt that the identification of the particulars is feasible, since they will include many unspecifiable clues; but the feasibility of the programme will not only be uncertain, it will be logically impossible. To objectivize the parts of conscious behaviour must make us lose sight of the mind and dissolve the very image of a coherent behaviour.

Admittedly, behaviourist studies do not reach this logical consequence of their programme. This is due to the fact that we cannot wholly shift our attention to the fragments of conscious behaviour. When we quote a subject's report on a mental experience in place of referring to this experience, this leaves our knowledge of that experience untouched; the report has in fact no meaning, except by bearing on this experience. An experimenter may speak of an electric shock as an objective fact, but he administers it only because he knows its painful effect. Afterwards he observes changes in the conductivity of the subject's skin which in themselves would be meaningless, for they actually signify the expectation of an electric shock—the skin response is in fact but a variant of goose flesh.

Thus a behaviourist analysis merely paraphrases mentalist descriptions in terms known to be symptoms of mental states and its meaning consists in its mentalist connotations. The practice of such paraphrasing might be harmless and sometimes even appropriate, but a preference for tangible terms of description will often be restrictive and misleading. The behaviourist analysis of learning, for example, has banned the physiognomies of surprise, puzzlement, and concentrated attention, by which Koehler described the mental efforts of his chimpanzees. It avoids the complex, delicately graded situations which evoke these mental states. The study of learning is thus cut down to its crudest form known as conditioning. And this oversimple paradigm of learning may then be misdescribed as it was by Pavlov, when he identified *eating* with an *expectation to be fed*, because both of these induce the secretion of saliva. Wherever we define mental processes by objectivist circumlocutions, we are apt to stumble into such absurdities.

The actual working of behaviourism therefore confirms my conclusion that strictly isolated pieces of behaviour are meaningless fragments, not identifiable as parts of behaviour. Behaviourist psychology depends on covertly alluding to the mental states which it sets out to eliminate.

### 2 *Principles of Boundary Control*

But is not the material substance of all higher entities governed throughout by the laws of inanimate matter? Does it not follow then that it must be possible to represent all their workings in terms of these laws? Yes, this would follow. If I claim that these higher entities are irreducible, I must show that they are governed in part by principles beyond the scope of physics and chemistry. I shall do so. I shall show first that a number of different principles can control a comprehensive entity at different levels. I have repeatedly presented this theory in more particular terms.[5] It will be developed here on general lines.

There exist principles that apply to a variety of circumstances. They can be laws of nature, like the laws of mechanics, or be principles of operation, like those of physiology, as for example those controlling muscular contraction and co-ordination; or they can be principles laid down for the use of artifacts, like the vocabulary of the English language or the rules of chess. Not all important principles have such wide scope; but I need not go into this, for it is enough to have pointed out that some principles exist that do.

We can go on to note then that such a principle is necessarily compatible with any restriction we may choose to impose on the situation to which it is to apply; it leaves wide open the conditions under which it can be made to operate. Consequently, these conditions lie beyond the control of our principle and may be said to form its boundaries, or more precisely its *boundary conditions*. The term 'boundary conditions'—borrowed from physics—will be used here in this sense.

Next we recognize that in certain cases the boundary conditions of a principle are in fact subject to control by other principles. These I will call higher principles. Thus the boundary conditions of the laws of mechanics may be controlled by the operational principles which define a machine; the boundary conditions of muscular action may be controlled by a pattern of purposive be-haviour, like that of going for a walk; the boundary of conditions of a vocabulary are usually controlled by the rules of grammar, and the conditions left open by the rules of chess are controlled by the stratagems of the players. And so we find that machines, purposive actions, grammatical sentences, and games of chess, are all entities subject to *dual control*.

Such is the stratified structure of comprehensive entities. They embody a combination of two principles, a higher and a lower. Smash up a machine, utter words at random, or make chess moves without a purpose, and the corresponding higher principle—that which constitutes the machine, that which makes words into sen-tences, and that which makes moves of chess into a game—will all vanish and the comprehensive entity which they controlled will cease to exist.

But the lower principles, the boundary conditions of which the now effaced higher principles had controlled, remain in opera-tion. The laws of mechanics, the vocabulary sanctioned by the dictionary, the rules of chess, they will all continue to apply as before. Hence no description of a comprehensive entity in the light of its lower principles can ever reveal the operation of its higher principles. *The higher principles which characterize a compre-hensive entity cannot be defined in terms of the laws that apply to its parts in themselves.*

On the other hand, a machine does rely for its working on the laws of mechanics; a purposive motoric action, like going for a walk, relies on the operations of the muscular system which it directs, and so on. The operations of higher principles rely quite generally on the action of the laws governing lower levels.

Yet, since the laws of the lower level will go on operating, whether the higher principles continue to be in working order or not, the action of the lower laws may well disrupt the working of the higher principles and destroy the comprehensive entity controlled by them.

Such is the mechanism of a two-levelled comprehensive entity. Let me show now that the two-levelled logic of tacit knowing performs exactly what is needed for understanding this mechanism.

Tacit knowing integrates the particulars of a comprehensive entity and makes us see them forming the entity. This integration recognizes the higher principle at work on the boundary conditions left open by the lower principle, by mentally performing the workings of the higher principle. It thus materializes the *functional structure* of tacit knowing. It also makes it clear to us how the comprehensive entity works by revealing the meaning of its parts. We have here the *semantic aspect* of tacit knowing. And since a comprehensive entity is controlled as a whole by a higher principle than the one which controls its isolated parts, the entity will look different than an aggregate of its parts. Its higher principle will endow it with a stability and power appearing in its shape and motions and usually produce also additional novel features. We have here the *phenomenal aspect* of tacit knowing.

And finally, we are presented also with an ontological counterpart of the *logical disintegration* caused by switching our attention from the integrating centre of a comprehensive entity to its particulars. To turn our attention from the actions of the higher principle, which defines the two-levelled entity, and direct it to the lower principle controlling the isolated parts of the entity is to lose sight of the higher principle and indeed of the whole entity controlled by it. This mirrors the destruction of a comprehensive entity when it is pulled to pieces. The logical structure of tacit knowing thus covers in every detail the ontological structure of a combined pair of levels.

3   *Application of these Principles to Mind and Body*

The next question is whether the functioning of living beings and of their consciousness is in fact stratified. Is it subjected to the joint control of different principles working at consecutive levels?

The laws of physics and chemistry do not ascribe consciousness to any process controlled by them; the presence of consciousness proves, therefore, that other principles than those of inanimate matter participate in the conscious operations of living things.

There are two other fundamental principles of biology which

are beyond the scope of physics and chemistry. The structure and functioning of an organism is determined, like that of a machine, by constructional and operational principles which control boundary conditions left open by physics and chemistry. We may call this a *structural principle*, lying beyond the realm of physics and chemistry. I have explained this a number of times before and will not argue it here again.[6]

Other functions of the organism not covered by physics and chemistry are exemplified by the working of the morphogenic field. Its principles are expressed most clearly by C. H. Waddington's 'epigenetic landscapes'. These show that the development of the embryo is controlled by the gradient of potential shapes, in the way the motion of a heavy body is controlled by the gradient of potential energy.[7] We may call this principle an *organizing field* or speak of it as an *organismic principle*.

Most biologists would declare that both the principles of structure and of organizing fields will be reduced one day to the laws of physics and chemistry. But I am unable to discover the grounds —or even understand the meaning—of such assurances, and hence I will disregard them and recognize these two principles as actually used in biology today.

Living beings consist in a hierarchy of levels, each level having its own structural and organismic principles. On the mental level, explicit inferences represent the operations of fixed mental structures, while in tacit knowing we meet the integrating powers of the mind. In all our conscious thoughts these two modes mutually rely on each other, and it is plausible to assume that explicit mental operations are based on fixed neural networks, while tacit integrations are grounded mainly in organizing fields. I shall assume also that these two principles are interwoven in the body, as their counterparts are in thought.

The purpose of this paper is to explain the relation between body and mind as an instance of the relation between the subsidiary and the focal in tacit knowledge. The fact that any subsidiary element loses its meaning when we focus our attention on it explains the fact that, when examining the body in conscious action, we meet no traces of consciousness in its organs. We lose the meaning of the subsidiaries in their role of pointing to the focal. Using this principle, we are now ready to complete our project.

We have seen that we can know another person's mind by

dwelling in his physiognomy and behaviour; we lose sight of his mind only when we focus our attention on these bodily workings and thus convert them into mere objects. But a neurophysiologist, observing the events that take place in the eyes and brain of a seeing man, would invariably fail to see in these neural events what the man himself sees by them. We must ask why the neurologist cannot dwell in these bodily events, as he could in the subject's physiognomy or intelligent behaviour.

We may notice that the latter kind of indwelling, for which we appear to be equipped by nature, enables us to read only *tacit* thoughts of another mind: thoughts and feelings of the kind that we may suitably ascribe to organismic processes in the nervous system. We can get to know the *explicit* thoughts of a person— which may correspond to anatomically fixed functions of the nervous system—only from the person's verbal utterances. The meaning of such utterances is artificial; though ultimately based on demonstrations pointing at tacit experiences, such utterances have no direct appeal to the native mind. The facility for indwelling can be seen to vary also when prehistoric sites, unperceived from the ground, are discerned from the air. Our incapacity for experiencing the neural processes of another person in the manner he experiences them himself may be aligned with these gradual variations of indwelling.

*We arrive thus at the following outline.* Our capacity for conducting and experiencing the conscious operations of our body, including that of our nervous system, lies in the fact that we dwell fully in them. No one but ourselves can dwell in our body directly and know fully all its conscious operations; but our consciousness can be experienced also by others to the extent to which they can dwell in the external workings of our mind from outside. They can do this fairly effectively for many tacit workings of our mind by dwelling in our physiognomy and behaviour; such powers of indwelling are fundamentally innate in us. By contrast, our explicit thoughts can be known to others only by dwelling in our pronouncements, the making and understanding of which is founded on artificial conventions. Objectivization, whether of another person's gestures or of his utterances, cancels our dwelling in them, destroys their meaning and cuts off communication through them. The nervous system, as observed by the neurophysiologist, is always objectivized and can convey its meaning to the observer only indirectly, by pointing at a behaviour or at reports that we understand by indwelling.

The logic of tacit knowing and the ontological principles of stratified entities were derived here independently of each other, and we found that our tacit logic enables us to understand stratified entities. It shows us then that the higher principle of a stratified entity can be apprehended only by our dwelling in the boundary conditions of a lower principle on which the higher principle operates. Such indwelling is logically incompatible with fixing our attention on the laws governing the lower level. Applied to mind and body, as to two strata in which the higher principles of the mind rely for their operations on the lower principles of physiology, we arrive at three conclusions.

(1) No observations of physiology can make us apprehend the operations of the mind. Both the mechanisms and organismic processes of physiology, when observed as such, will always be found to work insentiently.

(2) At the same time, the operations of the mind will never be found to interfere with the principles of physiology, nor with the even lower principles of physics and chemistry on which they rely.

(3) But as the operations of the mind rely on the services of lower bodily principles, the mind can be disturbed by adverse changes in the body, or be offered new opportunities by favourable changes of its bodily basis.

The way integration functions in tacit knowing, as well as the presence of irreducible organismic principles in living beings, are both consonant with the arguments presented by Sir Francis Walshe for the presence of integrative mental powers, not accounted for by the fixed anatomic structures of the central nervous system.[8]

## 4 Retrospect

Many philosophic efforts of our century can be seen to have pointed towards such conclusions. A systematic attempt to safeguard the content of unsophisticated experience against the effects of a destructive analysis was made by Edmund Husserl during the first three decades of this century with far-reaching influence on Continental philosophy. But its bearing on the body-mind problem was derived mainly later by Merleau-Ponty in his *Phenoménologie de la Perception* (1945). He gives a vivid and elaborate description of the way we experience our body. The body is 'known to us', he writes, 'through its functional value'; its parts engaged in the performance of our actions 'are available to us in virtue of their common meaning';[9] our body expresses meaning but 'language does not express thought, it *is* the subject's taking up of a position in the world of his meanings'.[10] 'If a being is conscious it must be nothing but a network of intentions;'[11] 'I do not understand the gestures of others by an act of intellectual interpretation. . . . The act by which I lend myself to the spectacles must be recognized as irreducible to anything else;'[12] our experience of our body is an existential act, not based either on observation nor on explicit thought. These remarks foreshadow my analysis, but I find among them neither the logic of tacit knowing nor the theory of ontological stratification, which I regard as indispensable for the understanding of the phenomena described by Merleau-Ponty.

Another follower of Husserl, Dr F. S. Rothschild, arrived even earlier at the conclusion that the mind is the meaning of the body.[13] He developed this idea widely in neurophysiology and psychiatry, where I am not competent to follow him.

The mainstream of contemporary English and American philosophy ignores the inquiries of phenomenologists. But it shares their rejection of Cartesian dualism, and the kinship of the two movements goes beyond this. Deprive my quotations from the *Phenomenology of Perception* of their existentialist perspective, and they can be equated with observations of Ryle in the *Concept of Mind* (1949).[14] But such a transition brings out the theoretical inadequacy of these observations and results in drawing false conclusions from them. Take a simple example. Merleau-Ponty says 'I do not understand the gestures of others by an act of intellectual interpretation', and Ryle says the same: 'I am not inferring to the workings of your mind, I am following them;'[15] but Merleau-Ponty finds an alternative to 'intellectual interpretation' in existential experience, while Ryle has none and affirms, therefore, that 'most intelligent performances are not clues to the mind; they are those workings',[16] which is absurd. Many vivid and often subtle phenomenological descriptions are used by Ryle to demonstrate that the mind does not explicitly operate on the body, and from this result he concludes that body and mind are 'not two things',[17] 'not tandem operations',[18] containing no 'occult causes',[19] 'no occult antecedents',[20] no 'ghost in the machine',[21] in other words, no Cartesian duality. But what actually follows from the fact that mind and body do not interact explicitly is that they interact according to the logic of tacit knowing. And it is this logic that disposes of the Cartesian dilemma by acknowledging two mutually exclusive ways of being aware of our body.

As Ryle's powerful argument leads him to fallacious conclusions, it offers a compelling demonstration of the troubles arising from the absence of the cognitive and ontological principles outlined in the present paper; that is why I selected his work for representing anti-Cartesian thought in contemporary British and American literature.

[1] *Brain, 88* (1965), pp. 799-810.

[2] Recent publications of the author on which this paper draws: 'Clues to an Understanding of Mind and Body', *The Scientist Speculates* (I. J. GOOD, ed.), London: Heinemann, 1962, p. 67; 'Tacit Knowing and Its Bearing on Some Problems of Philosophy', *Reviews of Modern Physics, 34* (1962), pp. 601-16 (Essay 11 above); 'Science and Man's Place in the Universe', in *Science as a Cultural Force* (H. WOOLF, ed.), Baltimore: Johns Hopkins Press, 1964, Oxford University Press, 1965; 'On the Modern Mind', *Encounter* (May, 1965); 'The Logic of Tacit Inference', *Philosophy* (Jan. 1966) pp. 1-18 (Essay 10 above); 'The Creative Imagination', *Chemical and Engineering News, 44* (1966), pp. 85-93; *The Tacit Dimension*, Garden City: Doubleday, 1966.

[3] Referred to in F. J. J. BUYTENDIJK, *Traité de Psychologie Animale*, Paris: Presses Universitaires de France, 1952, p. 126.

[4] See 2 above.

[5] *Ibid.* See also Essay 14 below.

[6] *Ibid.* See also Essay 14 below.

[7] Cf. e.g., C. H. WADDINGTON, *The Strategy of the Genes*, London: Allen & Unwin, 1957; particularly the explanation of genetic assimilation, p. 167.

[8] F. WALSHE, *Critical Studies in Neurology* and *Further Critical Studies in Neurology with other Essays and Addresses*, Edinburgh: Livingstone and Co., 1948 and 1965, respectively.

[9] M. MERLEAU-PONTY, *Phenomenology of Perception*, London: Routledge, 1962, p. 149.

[10] *Ibid.*, p. 193.

[11] *Ibid.*, p. 121.

[12] *Ibid.*, p. 185.

[13] See Rothschild's earlier writings, which extend back to 1930. A fairly recent summary of them is given in the monograph: F. S. ROTHSCHILD, *Das Zentralnervensystem als Symbol des Erlebens*, Basel and New York: S. Karger, 1958, VII, pp. 1-134. In this monograph, Dr Rothschild points out on pp. 10-11 that the meaning of the CNS manifested in consciousness is lost by examining the CNS as an object—just as the denotative meaning of a word is lost by such an examination. This anticipates part of my theory of body and mind. For a briefer summary in

English, of Dr Rothschild's work, see F. S. ROTHSCHILD, 'Laws of Symbolic Mediation in the Dynamics of Self and Personality', *Annals of the New York Academy of Sciences, 96* (1962), pp. 774-84.

[14] G. RYLE, *Concept of Mind*, London: Hutchinson, 1949.

[15] *Ibid.*, p. 61.

[16] *Ibid.*, p. 58.

[17] *Ibid.*, p. 74.

[18] *Ibid.*, p. 46.

[19] *Ibid.*, p. 50.

[20] *Ibid.*, p. 115.

[21] *Ibid.*, pp. 15-16.

# *14*
# Life's Irreducible Structure¹
## 1968

---

1   *Boundaries Harness the Laws of Inanimate Nature*

If all men were exterminated, this would not affect the laws of inanimate nature. But the production of machines would stop, and not until men arose again, could machines be formed once more. Some animals can produce tools, but only men can construct machines; machines are human artifacts, made of inanimate material.

The Oxford dictionary describes a machine as 'an apparatus for applying mechanical power, consisting of a number of inter-related parts, each with a definite function'. It might be, for example, a machine for sewing or printing. Let us assume that the power driving the machine is built in and disregard the fact that it has to be renewed from time to time. We can say, then, that the manufacture of a machine consists in cutting suitably shaped parts and fitting them together so that their joint mechanical action should serve a possible human purpose.

The structure of machines and the working of their structure are thus shaped by man, even while their material and the forces that operate them obey the laws of inanimate nature. In constructing a machine and supplying it with power, we harness the laws of nature at work in its material and in its driving force and make them serve our purpose.

This harness is not unbreakable; the structure of the machine and with it its working can break down. But this will not affect the forces of inanimate nature on which the operation of the machine relied; it merely releases them from the restriction the machine imposed on them before it broke down.

So the machine as a whole works under the control of two distinct principles. The higher one is the principle of the machine's design, and this harnesses the lower one, which consists in the physical chemical processes on which the machine relies. We commonly form such a two-levelled structure in conducting an experiment; but there is a difference between constructing a machine and rigging up an experiment. The experimenter imposes restrictions on nature in order to observe its behaviour under these restrictions, while the construction of a machine restricts nature in order to harness its workings. But we may borrow a term from physics and describe both these useful restrictions of nature as the imposing of *boundary conditions* on the laws of physics and chemistry.

Let me enlarge on this. I have exemplified two types of boundaries. In the machine our principal interest lay in the effects of the boundary conditions, while in an experimental setting we are interested in the natural processes controlled by the boundaries. There are many common examples of both types of boundaries. When a saucepan bounds a soup that we are cooking, we are interested in the soup; and, likewise, when we observe a reaction in a test-tube, we are studying the reaction, not the test-tube. The reverse is true for a game of chess. The strategy of the player imposes boundaries on the several moves, which follow the laws of chess, but our interest lies in the boundaries—that is, in the strategy, not in the several moves as exemplifications of the laws. And similarly, when a sculptor shapes a stone or a painter composes a painting, our interest lies in the boundaries imposed on a material and not in the material itself.

We can distinguish these two types of boundaries by saying that the first represents a test-tube type of boundary whereas the second is of the machine type. By shifting our attention, we may sometimes change a boundary from one type into the other.

All communications form a machine type of boundary, and these boundaries form a whole hierarchy of consecutive levels of action. A vocabulary sets boundary conditions on the utterance of the spoken voice; a grammar harnesses words to form sentences; and the sentences are shaped into a text which conveys a communication. At all these stages we are interested in the boundaries imposed by a comprehensive restrictive power, rather than in the principles harnessed by them.

2   *Living Mechanisms are Classed with Machines*

From machines we pass to living beings, by remembering that animals move about mechanically and that they have internal organs which perform functions as parts of a machine do—functions which sustain the life of the organism much as machines serve the interests of their users. For centuries past the workings of life have been likened to the working of machines, and physiology has been seeking to interpret the organism as a complex network of mechanisms. Organs are accordingly defined by their life preserving functions.

Any coherent part of the organism is indeed puzzling to physiology, and also meaningless to pathology, until the way it benefits the organism is discovered. And I may add that any description of such a system in terms of its physical chemical topography is meaningless except for the fact that the description may covertly recall the system's physiological interpretation—much as the topography of a machine is meaningless until we guess how the device works, and for what purpose.

In this light the organism is shown to be, like a machine, a system which works according to two different principles: its structure serves as a boundary condition harnessing the physical chemical processes by which its organs perform their functions. Thus, this system may be called a system under dual control. Morphogenesis, the process by which the structure of living beings develops, can then be likened to the shaping of a machine which will act as a boundary for the laws of inanimate nature. For just as these laws serve the machine, so they serve also the developed organism.

A boundary condition is always extraneous to the process which it delimits. In Galileo's experiments on balls rolling down a slope, the angle of the slope was not derived from the laws of mechanics, but was chosen by Galileo. And as this choice of slopes was extraneous to the laws of mechanics, so are the shape and manufacture of test-tubes extraneous to the laws of chemistry. The same thing holds for machine-like boundaries; their structure cannot be defined in terms of the laws which they harness. Nor can a vocabulary determine the content of a text, and so on. Therefore, if the structure of living things is a set of boundary conditions, this structure is extraneous to the laws of physics and chemistry, which the organism is harnessing. Thus the morphology of living things transcends the laws of physics and chemistry.

### 3   DNA Information Generates Mechanisms

But the analogy between machine components and live functioning organs is weakened by the fact that the organs are not shaped artificially as the parts of a machine are. It is an advantage, therefore, to find that the morphogenetic process is explained in principle by the transmission of information stored in DNA, as interpreted in this sense by Watson and Crick.

A DNA molecule is said to represent a code—that is, a linear sequence of items, the arrangement of which is the information conveyed by the code. In the case of DNA, each item of the series consists of one out of four alternative organic bases (more precisely: four alternatives consisting in two positions of two different compound organic bases). Such a code will convey the maximum amount of information if the four organic bases have equal probability of forming any particular item of the series. Any difference in the binding of the four alternative bases, whether at the same point of the series or between two points of the series, will cause the information conveyed by the series to fall below the ideal maximum. The information content of DNA is in fact known to be somewhat reduced by such redundancy, but I accept here the assumption of Watson and Crick that this redundancy does not prevent DNA from effectively functioning as a code. I shall accordingly disregard for brevity the redundancy in the DNA code and talk of it as if it were functioning optimally, with all of its alternative basic bindings having the same probability of occurrence.

Let us be clear what would happen in the opposite case. Suppose that the actual structure of a DNA molecule were due to the fact that the bindings of its bases were much stronger than the bindings would be for any other distribution of bases, then such a DNA molecule would have no information content. Its codelike character would be effaced by an overwhelming redundancy.

We may note that this is actually the case for an ordinary chemical molecule. Since its orderly structure is due to a maximum of stability, corresponding to a minimum of potential energy, its orderliness lacks the capacity to function as a code. The pattern of atoms forming a crystal is another instance of complex order without appreciable information content.

There is a kind of stability which often opposes the stabilizing force of a potential energy. When a liquid evaporates, this can be understood as the increase of entropy accompanying the dispersion of its particles. One takes dispersive tendency into account by adding its powers to those of potential energy, but the correction is negligible for cases of deep drops in potential energy or for low temperatures, or for both. We can disregard it, to simplify matters, and say that chemical structures established by the stabilizing powers of chemical bonding have no appreciable information content.

In the light of the current theory of evolution, the code-like structure of DNA must be assumed to have come about by a sequence of chance variations established by natural selection. But this evolutionary aspect is irrelevant here; whatever may be the origin of a DNA configuration, it can function as a code only if its order is not due to the forces of potential energy. It must be as physically indeterminate as the sequence of words is on a printed page. As the arrangement of a printed page is extraneous to the chemistry of the printed page, so is the base sequence in a DNA molecule extraneous to the chemical forces at work in the DNA molecule. It is this physical indeterminacy of the sequence that produces the improbability of occurrence of any particular sequence and thereby enables it to have a meaning—a meaning that has a mathematically determinate information content equal to the numerical improbability of the arrangement.

### 4    DNA Acts as a Blueprint

But there remains a fundamental point to be considered. A printed page may be a mere jumble of words and it then has no information content. So the improbability count gives the *possible*, rather than the *actual*, information content of a page. And this applies also to the information content attributed to a DNA molecule; the sequence of the bases is deemed meaningful only because we assume with Watson and Crick that this arrangement generates the structures of the offspring by endowing it with its own information content.

This brings us at last to the point that I aimed at when I undertook to analyse the information content of DNA: can the control of morphogenesis by DNA be likened to the designing and shaping of a machine by the engineer? We have seen that physiology interprets the organism as a complex network of mechanisms, and that an organism is—like a machine—a system under dual control. Its structure is that of a boundary condition harnessing the physical chemical substances within the organism in the service of physiological functions. Thus, in generating an organism, DNA initiates and controls the growth of a mechanism that will work as a boundary condition within a system under dual control. And we may add that DNA itself is such a system, since every system conveying information is under dual control, for every such system restricts and orders, in the service of conveying its information, extensive resources of particulars that would otherwise be left at random, and thereby acts as a boundary condition. In the case of DNA this boundary condition is a blueprint of the growing organism.[2]

We can conclude that in each embryonic cell there is present the duplicate of a DNA molecule having a linear arrangement of its bases—an arrangement which, being independent of the chemical forces within the DNA molecules, conveys a rich amount of meaningful information. And we see that when this information is shaping the growing embryo, it produces in it boundary conditions which, themselves being independent of the physical chemical forces in which they are rooted, control the mechanism of life in the developed organism.

To elucidate this transmission is a major task of biologists today, to which I shall yet return.

### 5  *Some Accessory Problems Arise Here*

We have seen boundary conditions introducing principles not capable of formulation in terms of physics or chemistry into inanimate artifacts and living things; we have seen them as necessary to information content in a printed page or in DNA, and as introducing mechanical principles into machines as well as into the mechanisms of life.

Let me add now that boundary conditions of inanimate systems established by the history of the universe are found in the domains of geology, geography and astronomy, but that these do not form systems of dual control. They resemble in this respect the test-tube type of boundaries of which I spoke above. Hence the existence of dual control in machines and living mechanisms represents *a discontinuity between machines and living things on the one hand and inanimate nature on the other hand,* so that both machines and living mechanisms are irreducible to the laws of physics and chemistry.

Irreducibility must not be identified with the mere fact that the joining of parts may produce features which are not observed in the separate parts. The sun is a sphere and its parts are not spheres, nor does the law of gravitation speak of spheres; but mutual gravitational interaction causes the parts of the sun to form a sphere. Such cases of holism are common in physics and chemistry. They are often said to represent a transition to living things, but this is not the case, for they are reducible to the laws of inanimate matter, while living things are not.

But there does exist a rather different continuity between life and inanimate nature. For the beginnings of life do not sharply differ from their purely physical chemical antecedents. One can reconcile this continuity with the irreducibility of living things by recalling the analogous case of inanimate artifacts. Take the irreducibility of machines; no animal can produce a machine, but some animals can make primitive tools, and their use of these tools may be hardly distinguishable from the mere use of the animal's limbs. Or take a set of sounds conveying information; the set of sounds can be so obscured by noise that its presence is no longer clearly identifiable. We can say then that the control exercised by the boundary conditions of a system can be reduced gradually to a vanishing point. The fact that the effect of a higher principle over a system under dual control can have any value down to zero may allow us also to conceive of the continuous emergence of irreducible principles within the origin of life.

6 *We Can Now Recognize Additional Irreducible Principles*
The irreducibility of machines and printed communications teaches us also that the control of a system by irreducible boundary conditions does not interfere with the laws of physics and chemistry. A system under dual control relies in fact for the operations of its higher principle on the working of principles of a lower level, such as the laws of physics and chemistry. Irreducible higher principles are *additional* to the laws of physics and chemistry. The principles of mechanical engineering and of communication of information, and the equivalent biological principles, are all additional to the laws of physics and chemistry.

But to assign the rise of such additional controlling principles to a selective process of evolution leaves serious difficulties. The production of boundary conditions in the growing fetus by transmission to it of the information contained in DNA presents a problem. Growth of a blueprint into the complex machinery that it describes seems to require a system of causes not specifiable in

R

terms of physics and chemistry, such causes being additional both to the boundary conditions of DNA and to the morphological structure brought about by DNA.

The missing principle which builds a bodily structure on the lines of an instruction given by DNA may be exemplified by the far-reaching regenerative powers of the embryonic sea urchin, discovered by Driesch, and by Paul Weiss's discovery that completely dispersed embryonic cells will grow, when lumped together, into a fragment of the organ from which they were isolated.[3] We see an integrative power at work here, characterized by Spemann and by Paul Weiss as a 'field', which guides the growth of embryonic fragments to the forming of the morphological features to which they embryologically belong.[4] These guides of morphogenesis are given a formal expression in Waddington's 'epigenetic landscapes'.[5] They show graphically that the growth of the embryo is controlled by the gradient of potential shapes, much as the motion of a heavy body is controlled by the gradient of potential energy.

Remember how Driesch and his supporters fought for recognition that life transcends physics and chemistry, by arguing that the powers of regeneration in the sea urchin embryo were not explicable by a machine-like structure, and how the controversy has continued, along similar lines, by those who insisted that regulative ('equipotential' or 'organismic') integration was irreducible to any machine-like mechanism and was therefore irreducible also to the laws of inanimate nature. Now if, as I claim, machines and mechanical processes in living beings are themselves irreducible to physics and chemistry, the situation is changed. If mechanistic and organismic explanations are both equally irreducible to physics and chemistry, the recognition of organismic processes no longer bears the burden of standing alone as evidence for the irreducibility of living things. Once the field-like powers guiding regeneration and morphogenesis can be recognized without involving this major issue, I think the evidence for them will be found to be convincing.

There is evidence of irreducible principles, additional to those of morphological mechanisms, in the sentience that we ourselves experience and that we observe indirectly in higher animals. Most biologists set aside these facts as unprofitable considerations. But again, once it is recognized, on other grounds, that life transcends physics and chemistry, there is no reason for suspending recognition of the obvious fact that consciousness is a principle that fundamentally transcends not only physics and chemistry but also the mechanistic principles of living beings.

7   *Biological Hierarchies Consist in a Series of Boundary Conditions*
The theory of boundary conditions recognizes the higher levels of life as forming a hierarchy, each level of which relies for its workings on the principles of the levels below it, even while it itself is irreducible to these lower principles. I shall illustrate the structure of such a hierarchy by showing the way five levels make up a spoken literary composition.

The lowest level is the production of a voice; the second, the utterance of words; the third, the joining of words to make sentences; the fourth, the working of sentences into a style; the fifth, and highest, the composition of the text.

The principles of each level operate under the control of the next higher level. The voice you produce is shaped into words by a vocabulary; a given vocabulary is shaped into sentences in accordance with a grammar; and the sentences are fitted into a style, which in its turn is made to convey the ideas of the composition. Thus each level is subject to dual control: (i) control in accordance with the laws that apply to its elements in themselves, and (ii) control in accordance with the laws of the powers that control the comprehensive entity formed by these elements.

Such multiple control is made possible by the fact that the principles governing the isolated particulars of a lower level leave indeterminate conditions to be controlled by a higher principle. Voice production leaves largely open the combination of sounds into words, which is controlled by a vocabulary. Next, a vocabulary leaves largely open the combination of words to form sentences, which is controlled by grammar, and so on. Consequently, the operations of a higher level cannot be accounted for by the laws governing its particulars on the next lower level. You cannot derive a vocabulary from phonetics; you cannot derive grammar from a vocabulary; a correct use of grammar does not account for good style; and a good style does not supply the content of a piece of prose.

Living beings comprise a whole sequence of levels forming such a hierarchy. Processes at the lowest level are caused by the

forces of inanimate nature, and the higher levels control throughout the boundary conditions left open by the laws of inanimate
nature. The lowest functions of life are those called vegetative;
these vegetative functions, sustaining life at its lowest level, leave
open—both in plants and in animals—the higher functions of
growth and in animals also leave open the operations of muscular
actions; next in turn, the principles governing muscular actions in
animals leave open the integration of such actions to innate patterns of behaviour; and, again, such patterns are open in their
turn to be shaped by intelligence, while the working of intelligence itself can be made to serve in man the still higher principles
of a responsible choice.

Each level relies for its operations on all the levels below it.
Each reduces the scope of the one immediately below it by imposing on it a boundary that harnesses it to the service of the
next higher level, and this control is transmitted stage by stage
down to the basic inanimate level.

The principles additional to the domain of inanimate nature are
the product of an evolution, the most primitive stages of which
show only vegetative functions. This evolutionary progression is
usually described as an increasing complexity and an increasing
capacity for keeping the state of the body independent of its surroundings. But if we accept, as I do, the view that living beings
form a hierarchy in which each higher level represents a distinctive principle that harnesses the level below it (while being itself
irreducible to its lower principles), then the evolutionary sequence
gains a new and deeper significance. *We can recognize then a strictly
defined progression, rising from the inanimate level to ever higher additional principles of life.*

This is not to say that the higher levels of life are altogether
absent in earlier stages of evolution. They may be present in
traces long before they become prominent. Evolution may be
seen then as a progressive intensification of the higher principles
of life. This *is* what we witness in the development of the embryo
and of the growing child, processes akin to evolution.

But this hierarchy of principles raises once more a serious
difficulty. It seems impossible to imagine the sequence of higher
principles, transcending further at each stage the laws of inanimate nature, incipiently present in DNA and ready to be transmitted by it to the offspring. The conception of a blueprint fails

to account for the transmission of faculties, like consciousness, which no mechanical device can possess. It is as if the faculty of vision were to be made intelligible to a person born blind by a chapter on sense physiology. It appears, then, that DNA *evokes* the ontogenesis of higher levels, rather than *determining* these levels. And it would follow that the emergence of the kind of hierarchy I have defined here can only be evoked, but not determined, by atomic or molecular accidents. However, this question cannot be argued here.

### 8    *Understanding a Hierarchy Needs 'From-at' Conceptions*[6]

I have said before that the transcendence of atomism by mechanism is reflected in the fact that the presence of a mechanism is not revealed by its physical chemical topography. We can say the same thing of all higher levels: their description in terms of any lower level does not tell us of their presence. We can generally descend to the components of a lower level by analysing a higher level, but the opposite process involves an integration of the principles of the lower level, and this integration may be beyond our powers.

In practice this difficulty may be avoided by an important qualification. To take a common example, suppose that we have repeated a particular word, closely attending to the sound we are making, until these sounds have lost their meaning for us; we can recover this meaning promptly by evoking the context in which the word is commonly used. Consecutive acts of analysing and integrating are in fact generally used for deepening our understanding of complex entities comprising two or more levels.

Yet the strictly logical difference between two consecutive levels remains. You can look at a text in a language you do not understand and see the letters that form it without being aware of their meaning, but you cannot read a text without seeing the letters that convey its meaning. This shows us two different and mutually exclusive ways of being aware of the text. When we look at words without understanding them, we are focusing our attention on them, whereas, when we read the words, our attention is directed to their meaning, as part of a language. We are aware then of the words only subsidiarily, as we attend to their meaning. So in the first case we are looking at the words, while in the second, we are looking *from them at their meaning*; the reader of a text has a *from-at* knowledge of the words' meaning while he has only a *from* awareness of the words he is reading; should he be able to shift his attention *fully* towards the words, these would lose their linguistic meaning for him.

Thus a boundary condition which harnesses the principles of a lower level in the service of a new, higher level, establishes a semantic relation between the two levels. The higher comprehends the workings of the lower and thus forms the meaning of the lower. And as we ascend a hierarchy of boundaries, we reach to ever higher levels of meaning. Our understanding of the whole hierarchic edifice keeps deepening as we move upwards from stage to stage.

9   *The Sequence of Boundaries Bears on our Scientific Outlook*
The recognition of a whole sequence of irreducible principles transforms the logical steps for understanding the universe of living beings. The idea, which comes to us from Galileo and Gassendi, that all manner of things must ultimately be understood in terms of matter in motion is refuted. The spectacle of physical matter forming the basic tangible ground of the universe is found to be almost empty of meaning. The universal topography of atomic particles (with their velocities and forces) which, according to Laplace, offers us a universal knowledge of all things is seen to contain hardly any knowledge that is of interest. The claims made, following the discovery of DNA, that all study of life could be reduced eventually to molecular biology have shown once more that the Laplacean idea of universal knowledge is still the theoretical ideal of the natural sciences; current opposition to these declarations has often confirmed this ideal, by defending the study of the whole organism as being only a temporary approach. But the analysis of the hierarchy of living things shows that to reduce this hierarchy to ultimate particulars is to wipe out our very sight of it. Such analysis proves this ideal to be both false and destructive.

Each separate level of existence is of course interesting in itself and can be studied in itself. Phenomenology has taught this by showing how to save higher, less tangible levels of experience by not trying to interpret them in terms of the more tangible things in which their existence is rooted. This method was intended to prevent the reduction of man's mental existence to mechanical structures. The results of the method were abundant and are still flowing, but phenomenology left the ideal of exact science untouched and thus failed to secure the exclusion of its claims. Thus phenomenological studies remained suspended over an abyss of reductionism. Moreover, the relation of the higher principles to the workings of the lower levels in which they are rooted was lost from sight altogether.

I have mentioned how a hierarchy controlled by a series of boundary principles must be studied. When examining any higher level, we must remain subsidiarily aware of its grounds in lower levels and, turning our attention to the latter, we must continue to see them as bearing on the levels above them. Such alternation of detailing and integrating admittedly leaves open many dangers. Detailing may lead to pedantic excesses, while too broad integrations may present us with a meandering impressionism. But the principle of stratified relations does offer at least a rational framework for an inquiry into living things and the products of human thought.

I have said that the analytic descent from higher levels to their subsidiaries is usually feasible to some degree, while the integration of items of a lower level so as to predict their possible meaning in a higher context may be beyond the range of our integrative powers. I may add now that the same things may be seen to have a joint meaning when viewed from one point but to be lacking this connection when seen from another point. From an aeroplane we can see the traces of prehistoric sites which, over the centuries, have gone unnoticed by people walking over them; indeed, once he has landed, the pilot himself may no longer see these traces.

The relation of mind to body has a similar structure. The mind-body problem arises from the disparity between the experience of a person observing an external object, e.g., a cat, and a neurophysiologist observing the bodily mechanism by use of which the person sees the cat. The difference arises from the fact that a person placed inside his body has a *from*-knowledge of the bodily responses evoked by the light in his sensory organs, and this from-knowledge integrates the joint meaning of these responses to form the sight of the cat; whereas the neurophysiologist looking at these responses from outside has but an *at*-knowledge of them which, as such, is not integrated to the sight of the cat. This is the same duality that exists between the airman and the pedestrian in interpreting the same traces; and also the same that exists between a person who, when reading a written sentence, sees its meaning and another person who, being ignorant of the language, sees only the writing. Mind is the meaning of certain bodily mechanisms; it is lost from view when we look *at* them focally.

Awareness of mind and body confronts us, therefore, with two different things. Owing to the existence of two kinds of awareness—the focal and the subsidiary—we can distinguish sharply between the mind as a from-to experience and the subsidiaries of this experience, when seen focally, as a bodily mechanism. We can see then that, though rooted in the body, the mind is free in its actions—exactly as our common sense knows it to be free. The mind harnesses neurophysiological mechanisms; though it depends on them, it is not determined by them.

Moreover, the mind itself includes an ascending sequence of principles. Its appetitive and intellectual workings are transcended by principles of responsibility. Thus the growth of man to his highest levels is seen to take place along a sequence of rising principles. And we see this evolutionary hierarchy built as a sequence of boundaries, each aiming at higher achievements by harnessing the strata below them, to which they themselves are not reducible. These boundaries control a rising series of relations which we can understand only by being aware of their constituent parts subsidiarily, as bearing on the upper level which they serve.

The recognition of certain basic impossibilities has laid the foundations of some major principles of physics and chemistry; similarly, recognition of the impossibility of understanding living things in terms of physics and chemistry, far from setting limits to our understanding of life, will guide it in the right direction. And even if the demonstration of this impossibility should prove of no great advantage to the pursuit of discovery, it would help to draw a truer image of life and man than the present basic conceptions of biology present.

*Summary*
Mechanisms, whether man-made or morphological, are boundary conditions harnessing the laws of inanimate nature, being themselves irreducible to those laws. The pattern of organic bases in

DNA which functions as a genetic code is a boundary condition irreducible to physics and chemistry. Further controlling principles of life may be represented as a hierarchy of boundary conditions extending, in the case of man, to consciousness and responsibility.

[1] Expanded contribution to the Symposium of the American Association of the Advancement of Science on December 30, 1967: 'Do Life's Processes Transcend Physics and Chemistry?'. The first half of this article was anticipated in my paper 'Life Transcending Physics and Chemistry', *Chemical and Engineering News*, *45* (1967), pp. 54–66.

[2] The blueprint carried by the DNA molecule of a particular zygote also prescribes individual features of this organism, which will contribute to the sources of selective evaluation; but we shall set these features aside here.

[3] See PAUL WEISS, 'The Compounding of Complex Macromolecular and Cellular Units into Tissue Fabrics', *Proceedings of the National Academy of Science*, *42* (1956), pp. 819–30.

[4] The field concept was first used by Spemann (1921) in describing the organizer; Paul Weiss (1923) introduced it for the study of regeneration and extended it (1926) to include ontogeny. Cf. PAUL WEISS, *Principles of Development*, New York: Henry Holt, 1939, p. 290.

[5] Cf., e.g., C. H. WADDINGTON, *The Strategy of the Genes*, London: Allen & Unwin, 1957, particularly the graphic explanation of 'genetic assimilation' on p. 167.

[6] Cf., e.g., M. POLANYI, 'Logic and Psychology', *American Psychologist*, *23* (1968), pp. 27–43.

# Index